reckoning with ourselves. This book is an excavation of the deepest and most complex corridors of the heart."

—David L. Ulin, author of *The Lost Art of Reading*

"Urgent, subversive, and brave, *Blow Your House Down* is a path-breaking feminist manifesto, impossible to put down or dismiss. Gina Frangello tells the morally complex story of her adulterous relationship with a lover and her shortcomings as a mother, and in doing so, highlights the forces that shaped, silenced, and shamed her: everyday misogyny, puritanical expectations regarding female sexuality and maternal sacrifice, and male oppression. It's a story that is not hers alone—though many will prefer to think so—and one that I will not soon forget."

—Adrienne Brodeur, author of *Wild Game*

"Gina Frangello can always make me think and laugh; she's also one of the very few authors who's made me cry. *Blow Your House Down* is searing, honest, heartbreaking, heart-mending, and a hell of a wild ride. Frangello says things women aren't allowed to say, even to ourselves."   —Rebecca Makkai, author of *The Great Believers*

"Gina Frangello's *Blow Your House Down* blazes open a radical new portrait of a woman's life with dazzling honesty and breathtaking beauty. Threading through the terrors of breast cancer and caretaking a dying father, navigating the end of a long-term marriage and the burst of new love, *Blow Your House Down* reveals the epic journey of one woman's life and body. This book is a heart beating, not beaten. This book is a mighty heartsong."

—Lidia Yuknavitch, author of *Verge* and *The Chronology of Water*

Blow Your House Down

ALSO BY GINA FRANGELLO

Every Kind of Wanting
A Life in Men
Slut Lullabies
My Sister's Continent

Blow
Your House
Down

A Story of Family, Feminism, and Treason

————————

GINA FRANGELLO

Counterpoint
Berkeley, California

The following sections have been published in different forms: "Death's Monkeysphere" (as "The Lion and the Mouse") on *The Nervous Breakdown*; "Embers" in *Flashed: Sudden Stories in Comics and Prose*; "What Women Do" (as "This Is Happiness") on *The Nervous Breakdown*; "Big Blonde" (as "Did My Best Friend Really Know Me?") on *Dame*; "The Summer of Light and Dark" on *The Rumpus*

Library of Congress Cataloging-in-Publication Data
Names: Frangello, Gina, author.
Title: Blow your house down : a story of family, feminism, and treason / Gina Frangello.
Description: Berkeley, California : Counterpoint Press, 2021.
Identifiers: LCCN 2020015730 | ISBN 9781640093164 (hardcover) | ISBN 9781640093171 (ebook)
Subjects: LCSH: Frangello, Gina. | Authors, American—21st century— Biography. | Authors, American—21st century—Family relationships. | Marriage—United States. | Adultery—United States. | Cancer—Patients—United States.
Classification: LCC PS3606.R3757 Z46 2021 | DDC 813/.6—dc23
LC record available at https://lccn.loc.gov/2020015730

Jacket design by Sarah Brody
Book design by Wah-Ming Chang

COUNTERPOINT
2560 Ninth Street, Suite 318
Berkeley, CA 94710
www.counterpointpress.com

Printed in the United States of America

1 3 5 7 9 10 8 6 4 2

Author's Note

This is a work of creative nonfiction. In it, I describe experiences that had a profound emotional impact on me. The events in this book are true to the best of my recollection. For readability, in some cases I altered the order of or compressed sequences of events. I do not pretend that I am capable of remembering everything that took place exactly or offering everyone's perspective. This is my story and I write about what struck me personally. To protect the privacy of real individuals, I have changed or left out many names and identifying details, or used composite characters, and in some cases omitted people from the story.

To "John LaSalle"—liar, madman, Anglophile, storyteller, and the world's kindest accidental father—for his rare and unwavering gentleness in a brutal world.

And to Alice Merry Frangello, who saw light in every shadowy place and heard music in every person. Mom, your unconditional love and support allowed me to imagine another kind of future and continues to inspire me to become a better version of myself.

I want to be with those who know secret things
or else alone.
I want to be a mirror for your whole body,
and I never want to be blind, or to be too old
to hold up your heavy and swaying picture.
I want to unfold.
I don't want to stay folded anywhere,
because where I am folded, there I am a lie.
and I want my grasp of things to be
true before you.

—Rainer Maria Rilke

Contents

Aperture

The Story of A

The lie which elates us is dearer than a thousand sober truths.

—Anton Chekhov (misquoting Pushkin)

A is for Adulteress
But you knew that. There is virtually no history of literature without the Adulteress. Anna Karenina, Emma Bovary, Edna Pontellier, Hester Prynne, Daisy Buchanan, Molly Bloom. The adulteress throws herself in front of a train, runs over her husband's lover with a car, walks into the ocean intent on dying without a care for her children. A is for Adulteress, Agent of Ruin. Woman.

A is for Accused
Researchers at Cardiff Metropolitan University revealed that when there has been infidelity in a marriage, most wives tend to blame the other woman, whereas most husbands see their cheating wife as the guilty party.

Basically, whoever dropped dead in the broom closet: the Adulteress did it.

A is for Author
Allow me to reveal the A on my breast. For the sake of this narrative, my name might as well be A. Once a woman becomes an Adulteress, her other identities—mother, daughter, friend, editor, writer, teacher—become largely invisible to others, as irrelevant as the clothing she (whorishly, treasonously) shed.

A is for Asshole?
There is no slur for men to match the equivalent of "mistress," or even "other woman." "Philanderer" doesn't have the same punch and is sex-nonspecific. "Cuckold" denotes a man who is being cheated *on*. A "player," or even a "dog," can be single or married. An "asshole" can be the guy who took your parking space at Trader Joe's as well as the man who fucked your wife.

There are no names specifically for men who break their promises to women.

A is for Age
For the first time in documented human history, among adults ages eighteen to twenty-nine who have ever been married, a General Social Survey reports that women are marginally more likely than men to be unfaithful. The survey also found that infidelity rates increase in middle age for both men and women, and that, contrary to both social and literary stereotypes, women reach their highest levels of infidelity in their sixties.

A is for Analysis
While wives initiate almost 70 percent of divorces, the researcher Michael Rosenfeld recently made the surprising discovery that no similar gap between the sexes—or any gap at all—exists between the percentage of breakups initiated by women and men living together without marriage. Rosenfeld also found that, although married

women have long reported lower levels of satisfaction with relationship quality than married men, those in nonmarital relationships reported equal levels of quality. These results, Rosenfeld says, "support the feminist assertion that some women experience heterosexual marriage as oppressive or uncomfortable."

A is for Adultery

In the United States, adultery remains illegal across seventeen states, while sodomy remains illegal across fourteen. In Illinois, where A first kissed her lover, the wronged spouse can even sue the cheater's lover for "alienation of affection." In Massachusetts, where A and her lover reinstigated their Affair 2.0 after having been "broken up" for nearly nine months—and where her lover once screamed, "Don't move, don't you dare move!" while he came in her ass—adultery is a felony, theoretically punishable by up to life in prison.

~~A is for Old~~
~~A is for Hag~~
~~A is for Crone~~
A is for Ancient

Various recent studies using extensive data from online dating sites have revealed that women's perceived attractiveness by men hits its highest point at the age of eighteen and declines steadily thereafter (Elizabeth Burch), and that the peak age of women's attractiveness is somewhere around twenty-two or twenty-three (Christian Rudder). According to Rudder, co-founder of OkCupid, "Younger is better and youngest is best of all." For men, by contrast, attractiveness seems to increase steadily with age, peaking somewhere between forty-six and fifty.

Given these "facts," one might wonder what irrational force could possibly have prompted A to believe that she still matters enough for all this fuss to begin with—for all this inconveniencing of other, upstanding people who had expectations of and plans involving her? Just look at the way she's carrying on, as though she honestly doesn't realize she is statistically Unfuckable anyway.

A is for the Audacity of her

A is for Animal Testing

In Esther Perel's *The State of Affairs*, the author indicates that while rates of infidelity are on the incline, public compassion for adulterers is not. According to a 2017 Gallup poll, Americans have become more relaxed about most things sexual, from premarital to teen to gay sex, but adultery remains condemned at higher rates than "abortion, animal testing, or euthanasia."

A is for Audience

Recently A attended a party celebrating a novel about a married professor who gets a terrifying medical diagnosis and goes out and begins fucking her student. The novel's author began her reading that night by stating that if her middle-aged protagonist had been a man, there likely would be no book, because nothing out of the ordinary would have happened. After the reading, all the audience really wanted to talk about was how "immoral," "inexcusable," and "wrong" the novel's protagonist was, pressing the author to concur with their judgments and thereby transforming her narrative of disruption into a narrative of reassurance. The author, trained as all women are to be agreeable in crowds, demurred that she did not recommend anyone trying her protagonist's behavior at home, but suggested that might not be the point. One audience member asserted that the very outrageousness of the protagonist's behavior qualified the novel as Satire, even though everyone present, including the men, seemed to agree with the author that, had the protagonist been a man, there would be no book at all.

A is for Alice
A's mother, Alice, was once told by A's father that she should "take a lover" because A's father was no longer interested in sex (at least with his wife) and could not satisfy her. Although she had two opportunities that A knows of, **Altruistic** Alice nonetheless remained faithful to her **Asexual** husband even past his death.

A is for Antiheroine
Um. This is not that kind of book.

A is for Antecedent
In 1997, the year A first encountered her future lover by accepting one of his stories over-the-transom for the magazine she was newly editing, **Adultery** laws were used to charge a Harvey, Illinois, woman for the same crime A would—fifteen years later—commit.

A is for Anthology
For the anthology *Homewrecker*, in which A had a story years before becoming an Adulteress herself, the editor, Daphne Gottlieb, wrote: "I am a few years older now and I know this: There are tastes of mouths I could not have lived without; there are times I've pretended it was just about the sex because I couldn't stand the way my heart was about to burst with happiness and awe and I couldn't be that vulnerable . . . That waiting to have someone's stolen seconds can burn you alive. That the shittiest thing you can do in the world is lie to someone you love; also that there are certain times you have no other choice—not honoring this fascination, this car crash of desire, is also a lie. That there is power in having someone risk everything for you. That there is nothing more frightening than being willing to take this freefall. That it is not as simple as we were always promised. Love—at least the pair-bonded, prescribed love—does not conquer all."

A is for Aphorism
Esther Perel: "Infidelity has a tenacity that marriage can only envy."

A is for Animosity
In the state of Connecticut, where A's lover was born and raised, six people were charged under adultery laws between 1985 and 1990, the year A met her husband. Although a New Haven attorney referred to the law as "a dinosaur," Connecticut authorities claimed they had "no choice but to enforce it." A misdemeanor carrying a $1,000 fine, the law also carried the possibility of imprisonment for up to a year. Single people cannot be charged, which may be the only aspect of such outdated morality laws that actually break from misogynistic tradition by making it possible to prosecute a cheating husband but not his so-called mistress unless she, too, is married.

One can presume that, although there are only six arrests on record during this time period, more than six human beings did commit adultery in the state of Connecticut between 1985 and 1990. So in other words, the real requirement for being arrested for adultery is the presence of a spouse who is angry enough at your deception that they would like to see you in prison for it.

A is for Artifice
It seems the real reason the Harvey, Illinois, Police Department charged that woman and the auto mechanic she was fucking with adultery, in goddamn 1997, may have been that they were afraid that her husband, who had come home to find them in bed, would become violent and kill them, hence they carted all three off to the police department and pressed charges against the wife and mechanic, to hold them there. Cook County prosecutors later decided not to pursue the case.

A is for Abstract

Babis Dermitzakis posits in his article "Some Observations about the Suicide of the Adulteress in the Modern Novel" that in three major male-authored European novels—*Madame Bovary, Anna Karenina,* and *Thérèse Raquin*—the protagonists are wives who commit adultery ending in suicide. In contrast, texts by women authors of the period show no similar description and perception of adultery by women. Dermitzakis suspects that the male writers did not simply fictionalize a specific social behavior or condition; rather, they likely imported their own prejudices about women's adultery—and more generally about women's sexuality—into their writing. Biographical evidence of the three authors appears to support such a hypothesis.

A is for Aphrodisiac

"I tried to keep myself away from him by using con words like 'fidelity' and 'adultery,' by telling myself that he would interfere with my work, that if I had him I'd be too happy to write. I tried to tell myself I was hurting [him], hurting myself, making a spectacle of myself. I was. But nothing helped. I was possessed. The minute he walked into a room and smiled at me, I was a goner."

—Erica Jong, *Fear of Flying*

A is for Atonement

A's lover, when she mentioned wanting to write an **Amends** letter to his wife: "She doesn't want to hear from you and that's never going to change."

A's husband on the matter: "Letters are for cowards."

When A thinks of the word "Atonement," she usually thinks, almost accidentally, *Alonement.*

A is for Arithmetic

No matter how ashamed of herself a narrator may be, the mathematics of **Accountability** nonetheless dictate clearly that A+A+A+A can never equal I.

A is for Anger

You may have noticed that anger is making a comeback for women. Or rather, *feminism* is making a comeback; if anything, Second Wave feminism fell over its Birkenstocks or Slut Walk platform heels, fractioning and infighting itself into oblivion over the notion that feminists were "angry," were "unsexy," were anti-men. For Generations X, Y, and Z, the phrase *I'm not a feminist but . . .* could often be heard as a disclaimer in college classrooms or drunken parties, before any tentative criticism of men could be voiced, as though toxic masculinity, rape culture, and misogyny were all entirely less embarrassing than to align oneself with Those Feminists: angry, hairy, frigid killjoys. Ironically, only since the 2016 election has a furious brand of feminism achieved mainstream vogue for the first time, with angry women taking to the streets (albeit often in bright pink hats) and exploding the Twittersphere with their collectively righteous burning of Any Fucks Left to Give in lieu of bras.

It might be fair to say that this is the moment I've been waiting for since the sixth grade. Except now that all this pent-up rage is finally here, loud and proud, I am not entitled to it exactly. For starters, I am too old—part of the problem, part of the internalized misogyny that led an actual majority of women my age, with my skin color, to vote for a pussy grabber over the most qualified presidential candidate in history. There's that, but I have also been beaten to the punch. As women are finally rising up en masse to denounce their widespread mistreatment by men, I am left naked, with no pristine red robe of Victimhood. Rather, I have cheated, I have lied, I have done damage, I have been selfish and ruled by my desires . . . in other words, I have often conducted myself *like a man*, despite being a mother, and hence have perhaps forfeited my claim on female rage, which carries with it the implicit assumption that women are morally stronger—that we would do things better if given the chance. But I have lost the arrogance of youth (though I cheer it from the sidelines)—I have lost belief in my own high ground, and so my anger hovers in the no-man's-land of displacement. Who the fuck am I to judge anyone? Or so my party line has gone, in the hopes that my kids, family, and friends will forgive my transgressions, will understand how sorry I am to have hurt anyone . . . will understand that I know myself to be a perpetrator here, an equal-opportunity dick.

What happens, though, if I cannot fold my fury neatly in a closet in favor of my scarlet letter? What happens if my affair has become inextricable from awakening to my own anger: a taboo force that scares me more than all the cumulative male rage I have seen and faced? I need to back into that space slowly before I can fully own it, before I can see its facets and understand what to do with it now.

I was about to say that if you have made it to **Adulthood** without witnessing male rage unleashed, then perhaps you will not understand what I am talking about—perhaps you will not know what it means that I do not need to be good to be furious. Then I realized the folly of that sentence. You have not made it to adulthood without witnessing male rage. The very best you can possibly claim is that you made it without that rage being directed at *you*.

A is for . . .
"**Art** cannot save anybody from anything," wrote Gilbert Sorrentino in perhaps the first sentence from a book that I ever underlined, ever committed to memory, suspecting it would somehow both belie and also exemplify the many truths of me. Who was that girl, barely nineteen, who knew so little of both herself and the transient, tumultuous world that unmakes and reforges us? Who am I, now, on

the other side of so much wreckage, still loving, still typing, still *here*?

If I believe that art can, in fact, save us, over and over again, then does it follow that I risk the audacity of believing that you might be the very one who needs my words to save your life?

A is for Anton (Chekhov)

"And it seemed to them that they were within an inch of arriving at a decision, and that then a new, beautiful life would begin," Chekhov concluded his seminal 1899 adultery story "The Lady with the Dog," which Nabokov considered one of the greatest pieces ever written. "And they both realized that the end was still far, far away, and that the hardest, the most complicated part was only just beginning."

So it was for me, some one hundred and fifteen years later. And there, I begin.

Affair

Death's Monkeysphere

> We can never know what to want, because living only
> one life, we can neither compare it with our previous
> lives nor perfect it in our lives to come . . . There is
> no means of testing which decision is better, because
> there is no basis for comparison. We live everything
> as it comes, without warning, like an actor going on
> cold.
>
> —Milan Kundera

Don't cry for me when I'm gone," my father recently told my
mother. "I'm ready."

My mother relays this to me at my upstairs apartment. She and
my father have lived downstairs since my husband and I bought this
house in 1999, but my father no longer comes to visit because he
can't manage the stairs. If we want to see him we go down there,
which doesn't sound complicated, though sometimes it is. My life
has become a series of fast-moving parts, each hurtling forward
while I race to catch up, forever on the verge of tripping. Sometimes,
I go days without seeing my dad. When I do bring the kids down to
visit, he's usually listening to the television turned so loud that nobody can hear anyone else speak. His TV is so blaring that although
our upstairs apartment is a duplex and my husband and I sleep with

a whole floor between our bedroom and my parents' apartment, we can usually hear the thumping voices of my father's crime dramas vibrating in our ears right through our pillows. Sometimes my mother makes my father put the TV on pause when the kids and I come down, but given that my father is essentially deaf, he doesn't hear us when we speak anyway.

This is absolutely hilarious to my twin daughters, who are eleven and not yet afraid of their own decay. "Hi, Papa!" one of them shouts at the top of her lungs to the other, and then the other hollers back in an old man voice, "Why don't they ever say hi to me?"

At one point, my dad would have been the first one laughing at this joke. When my maternal grandmother was getting old, and my mother asked her at a family gathering if she wanted a glass of wine, my nana jumped up in alarm shouting, "Lion—what lion?" My father did "Lion—what lion?" imitations for years. He also used to chide my nana for never eating anything but sweets. Her pantry was jammed full of Little Debbie snack cakes; her freezer spilled popsicles to the floor when opened. My father found it particularly batshit that she wasn't just addicted to sugar, she was addicted to cheap, crappy forms of sugar.

At one time, my father would drive my mother to New York on dates just so they could get a slice of authentic cheesecake—even in my teens he was known to hunt for the best apple pie all over the state of Michigan, just because. He knew which bakery in Chicago made the freshest doughnuts and drove across the city for a particularly fine custard cake. "If I ever get like that," he would say of my tiny, elderly nana with her dowager's hump, chowing on prewrapped brownies and freezer-burned, neon-colored popsicles, "just shoot me."

Now a big day out for my father is a trip a mile away to the Entenmann's warehouse, where he can stock up on enough processed coffee cakes and doughnuts covered in waxy chocolate that an

avalanche falls out of his freezer when we open it. He buys which-
ever ice cream is on sale. When my husband and I go shopping for
him and buy an ice cream he deems too expensive, he pitches a fit.

"Just shoot me," he would tell us.

But it's never that simple. You can't just snap your fingers and
disappear like a magician's trick. Sometimes you live to turn into
your mother-in-law. You remain trapped inside your body, unable
to walk, unable to hear, taste buds faded, increasingly incontinent, napping during the day and awake all night, in chronic pain.
Waiting.

I've come to think of this past summer as a season of death. An
old comrade from grad school, blithely handsome and the youngest member of my first writing group, died swiftly and painfully of
cancer that had been misdiagnosed for years as a blood-clotting disorder. Less than a week after his passing, my longtime friend and
surrogate sister, Kathy, just a month before turning forty-three, was
diagnosed with Stage IIIC ovarian cancer, already spread to her
stomach and colon linings as well as her entire lymphatic system.
Even my husband's longtime family dog, who never left his mother's
side as she wasted away from cancer and cirrhosis last year, was—
as though part of a sick plot twist—roasted to death in an Iowa
heat wave when accidentally left inside a car. Death has found my
monkeysphere, and amid it I am full of a thrashing kind of energy,
restless and nuclear with little need for sleep or food. Meanwhile,
thousands of miles away, my friend Emily is watching her son's system shut down bit by bit following a Tay-Sachs diagnosis, her life
consumed by the unexpected responsibility of shepherding her
beautiful boy to an inevitable death before his third birthday. My
youngest child is five. When I consider what Emily is facing, I get so
overwhelmed that I undermine other things happening around me.
How can I call it "tragic" for forty-something adults—people who

have traveled, worked, fallen in love—to be diagnosed with cancer when there are babies trapped inside their own bodies waiting for death? How dare I dry heave on my bedroom floor over an elderly dog, or even fear of losing my own dad—someone lucky enough to have lived for nearly a century?

What is the continuum of grief?

The writer with whom I've been having what is usually referred to as an "emotional affair" for more than a year sometimes quotes James Baldwin to me when I start spinning like this. Baldwin says that suffering "may be the only equality we have," and that all pain is real and not easily quantified or measured. Emily herself has emailed me a beautiful treatise on the importance of female friendships, and how the culture often undermines them as trivial, making an impassioned case for my right to love Kathy and grieve her shortened life expectancy. And these sentiments are true—of course they are. Who would want to live in a world where they weren't?

On the other hand, emotions, even strong ones, are not equal at all. I don't mean this in a Bukowskian no-one-suffers-like-the-poor or in Zora Neale Hurston's the-Black-woman-is-the-mule-of-the-world kind of way, even if those things are accurate. I mean it, rather, in a personal, I-would-push-my-father-under-the-bus-for-my-children sort of way. If something were to happen to my kids, the first and most appealing thing I can think of would be to take several handfuls of pills and disappear forever, so that I would not have to live in that kind of pain. I'm not saying I would do it. I *hope* I wouldn't do it. But it would definitely be on the menu of options, as it is daily for Emily. When I think of my father's impending death, I feel sad—I feel, even, afraid—but I do not think of killing myself.

What does it mean to love by degree? What does this say, too, about my place in my own children's love chain? Is this the cycle of life, then? To be prepared to be thrown under the bus, if necessary, by those you value most in the world?

I've been sleeping with a white-noise machine. At forty-four and forty-three respectively, my husband and I both started snoring a few years back, but this is more of a problem for me because I am an insomniac, whereas my husband falls asleep the minute his head hits a pillow. Actually, that cliché does not adequately capture my husband's supernatural ability to fall asleep whenever he is not adequately engaged in a situation—he has fallen asleep, during our eighteen years of marriage, at places like raves, nightclubs, and once while a spring was protruding from the movie theater seat on which he was sitting, so that although he dozed soundly through *Exotica* by Atom Egoyan, he stood up with a patch of blood on his ass that never washed out of those jeans.

What I have not told anyone about my reliance on the white-noise machine is that I need it not only for my husband's snoring, but for the sound of his breathing—a thing that never bothered me until the past few years. Even the sound of his mild sleep breath is enough to make me feel like clawing the paint from the walls, trapped in the dark insularity of our bed.

I cannot pinpoint exactly when my husband's noises began to feel like an assault. Lately, he buys meringues from Trader Joe's and sits at his computer popping them whole into his mouth one by one, sucking on them with a slurping sound I could swear echoes off the slanted ceiling of our shared office. I have been known to sharply order him, *Stop that, stop sucking on them that way, it's driving me crazy!* It is impossible to say whether the fact that I am instructing my husband on how to eat, or that he heeds my agitation and revulsion not at all and continues to buy tubs of meringues to slurp at will, is more indicative of the state of our marriage.

The man I've been emailing almost daily is someone I have known in some capacity for more than a decade. I published a short story of his when I was first editing a literary magazine that now includes a book press, where we're also publishing his next novel. We have "reasons" to talk with each other, given that I am his editor. It would also be accurate to say that male-female friendships are common in my artsy circle. My forty-something friends who teach elementary school, are social workers, or work in offices don't seem to socialize as much with members of the opposite sex anymore, except as couples, whereas I have always had a lot of male friends. This is nothing new.

Except, of course, that this male friend confessed to me a year ago, while I was in Kenya with my family, that I was the part of his day he looked forward to the most. *I've realized that I'm a little in love with you,* he emailed. *I hope that can be ok. Why can't people sometimes be a little in love, without it meaning they're going to have an affair or run off to Cuba?* His confession shocked me, even though I had nursed a more benign crush on him for several years. According to the universal laws governing the friendships of people who are both married and not to each other, I knew I was now supposed to slowly back away, to distance myself to prevent things from getting out of control.

I am not, however, a woman prone to thinking of things as "out of control." After all, he is in California, and I have met him in person only three times in the thirteen years we've been crossing paths. Being "a little in love"—minus Cuba, minus an affair, minus even being able to meet for coffee and stare at each other—is hardly a bomb threat, is it? Years ago, before we had children, my husband and I lived apart for about a year while he was working overseas, and although I wrote to him daily, he emailed me not once—why shouldn't I enjoy the attentive correspondence of an interesting, talented man? It isn't as though we are sexting or sending dirty photos or asking "what are you wearing?" Our emails are long meditations on the slippery nature of happiness and whether contentment is good or bad for art (good, we both conclude, though he says that nothing is more mysterious to him than a "happy person," which I, of course, claim to be), and amusing or disturbing stories about past relationships and our parents. At forty-five, the roughly dozen years he spent in the thrall of addiction figure far more prominently in his stories than all the thirty-three clean years combined—a fact that makes him both highly entertaining and also a bit of a precocious boy-man, even though he is two years older than I am, born on the same date, June 22. It is all perfectly safe, if safety includes my stomach surging like my body could cause a citywide power outage every time I open my email.

My husband and I still have sex. We still go on dates. We still take family vacations. Nobody could call us "estranged." It's just that for the past four or five years, significantly predating my emotional affair, we seem to speak different languages, that old feeling of connection refusing to click into place, constantly getting stuck in the wrong groove. Maybe this is just what a long-term marriage looks like. Does my husband even think anything is wrong? He swings between chilliness and volatility lately, and I find myself acting overly polite toward him, like he is a customs official or a cop, knowing things will go more smoothly if I am "nice." I used to be so intense that I exhausted him with my attempts at engagement. When I look at the early years of our relationship (when I loved him madly), the woman in those memories strikes me as a needy little dog perpetually trying to jump up on a too-tall couch, yapping the whole while. I don't know what to make of the fact that my happiest marital years now also make me ashamed of myself. When we were first living together, he complained that I was *too intense, too much*, and three times made noise about breaking up, but then committed, became acclimated to my perpetual pursuit. If he's noticed I'm no longer chasing, he hasn't said so.

Our marriage exists in shorthand these days: brief layovers between the consuming storms of jobs and kids and sick and dying parents and friends. If anyone asked either of us, we would say that we have a beautiful, happy family, and in so, so many regards we would be telling the truth. But it's what isn't on the page—what resides in the white spaces between words—that tells our story of things lost.

My father sees mice. In addition to being on a dozen strong medications, he's also got macular degeneration that can cause him to hallucinate spots. For several months now, he's claimed to see mice scampering across the floor, to glimpse their droppings in corners, so my husband investigates these claims but never finds a trace. My mother, always quick to cater to my father, leaves little pieces of Entenmann's cake in areas where my father claims the mice have been, to see if any crumbs go missing, but this only results in scraps of stale cake littered around my parents' (already-not-winning-any-awards-for-cleanliness) apartment. Finally, we call in my cousin Gink, who used to be a rat exterminator for the city and now runs his own pest control business, and Gink confirms there are no traces of mice in my parents' apartment, or even in our basement.

Still, my father reports on the mice's activities almost daily. They come out mostly, it seems, when he sleeps. In addition to seeing them, he also—at night—hears them making their little mice sounds, and feels them scampering over his body in the dark.

He begins to sleep with the lights on.

Soon he moves out of his bed entirely. My parents have had

separate bedrooms since I was five, but my father now moves into my mother's double bed, driving her out to the living room couch. One day, when sitting on the toilet, my father calls to my mother. He sticks his foot out in the air and points at it.

"Look at that!" he hollers. "My big toenail was definitely longer yesterday. That damn mouse must have been nibbling on it in my sleep!"

My mother very calmly informs him that if he does not recant the completely deranged thing he has just said, she is going to take him to the psychiatric ward immediately.

Upon which my father sheepishly mumbles that perhaps the mice have not given him a pedicure, after all.

After that, my mother calls their longtime physician and gets a prescription for antipsychotic medication, and my father moves back into his bedroom.

My father has been institutionalized before. Twice. He's been on antidepressants since I was about twenty, after sobbing at our kitchen table for a couple of days straight to the point that he wet his pants, unable to get to the bathroom, and my cousin Gink, who then lived next door to us, had to come and forcibly put him in the car. Before I was born, my father went through a period in which he was convinced burglars would break into our apartment, so he stopped sleeping with my mother and took up a vigil on the couch. He became addicted to Valium and ended up hearing voices that told him to kill my mother and himself—*that* time, he checked himself into the hospital, no assistance required. While institutionalized, he begged my mother to leave him, but she wouldn't, even though her hair was falling out in chunks from worry and her doctor had to give her B_{12} shots to keep her from going bald.

Despite having been on Paxil for twenty-plus years, my father has grown increasingly high strung. He keeps a stockpile of food under his bed (mainly baked beans), even though my parents' pantry is overflowing, and decorative cookie jars on every flat surface of his bedroom, though none of the jars contain cookies. He spends his mornings reading *Star* and *People*, even though he used to be a fan of Royko and Bob Greene in my youth. He would be able to tell you every detail of Paris Hilton's latest sex scandal or Lindsay Lohan's rehabs and weight losses . . . except that he can't actually remember the details because he's on so much Norco. He usually reads these magazines aloud to himself, repeating most of the words multiple times at the kitchen table, giving my parents' apartment a distinctly *One Flew Over the Cuckoo's Nest* type of vibe. If he watches old home movies of my children, and one of them happens to be jumping or running in the film, he yells out warnings to the television set, afraid they will bust their heads open on the corner of the coffee table, or poke out an eye, even though they are sitting right next to him—the movie having been filmed six years ago—bodies intact.

Shortly after my father is prescribed this antipsychotic, my mother wakes one night to a loud noise. My father, who has dutifully resumed his place in his own bedroom, is writhing around on his twin bed, weeping hysterically. "John," my mother begs (I can hear her begging in my mind), "What's wrong, sweetheart, what's the matter?"

"We're all going to die," my father sobs. At further prodding he adds, "The kids are going to get old and die too, and we'll all be dead already—the kids are going to die, what's the point of anything?"

My mother fetches his walker and brings him to the kitchen table and makes him some warm milk and talks him down. In the morning, she calls his doctor again. It seems that she has made a mistake: when the doctor prescribed new medication, my mother thought my father was to take it in lieu of his Paxil.

"No," the doctor clarifies. He has known my parents since I was in high school. "John is never, ever going off the Paxil, Alice. He's on Paxil for life. This is to be given *in addition*."

My father had been off his Paxil for exactly two days.

How do we measure a life's worth? In laughter? In orgasms? In money? In how often we have been photographed? In children borne or raised? In the number of continents on which we have made love? In number of books published? In latest versions of iPads and iPhones? In jazz albums filling a giant trunk in the basement? In years?

We are all specks of dust against the specter of Time. Is ninety years so different from forty in the scheme of things? We are all the walking dead of history.

When I was in sixth grade, our teacher, a former actor named Albert Tortorici, showed us the movie *On Borrowed Time*, in which an old man chases Death up a tree. Mr. Tortorici went to school with my father as a boy, to the same underfunded Chicago public school I attended, just as I slept in the same bedroom where my father was birthed with a midwife in 1921. My paternal grandmother, when not birthing seven children, made bathtub gin in the basement and served as one of the (several) faith healers in the neighborhood. She spoke only Italian until the day she died. When I was growing up, Puerto Ricans had replaced Italians as the dominant newcomers to the neighborhood, but otherwise little had changed. Both cultures were Catholic, macho, food-oriented, suspicious of authority; both factions of the neighborhood were poor, with tentacles in low-level theft, gang activity, corrupt local politics, and, in the case of the Italians, organized crime.

Mr. Tortorici conducted his classroom like a gangster with federal immunity. He chain-smoked constantly at his desk and had been known to bite students, put them upside down in trash cans, and (once) hang one out a third-story window. He was the most popular teacher in the school. Mitchell School lore had it that Mr. Tortorici had been diagnosed with lung cancer a decade prior and given a few weeks to live, but not only was he still teaching, he lived to attend my wedding in 1993. He outlived all but one of my father's seven brothers (two of whom died as children in the 1918 flu epidemic and the rest of whom died of various heart- and alcohol-related ailments such as rupturing an esophagus while binge drinking). If Mr. Tortorici gleefully chased Death up a tree for years, then my father, who has also been half-dying for decades, seems to be begging Death to come back down and finally do the fucking job.

At last, Death is starting to listen. Almost nightly now, my father dreams of his dead brothers. My mother and I rarely figure in his subconscious. In the dreams, his brothers are still young: Emilio playing the sax; Joe a mildly powerful bookie; Frank on the front porch smiling and waving with his grandkids. In one dream, my father is forcibly taken away on a wagon across a barren white landscape.

"I never took my father out to dinner," he tells my mother, his voice thick with regret. "He worked himself to the bone for us and I never bought him a meal."

"You were a young man," my mother assuages. My paternal grandfather died before I was born. "You had your own life. You didn't know he would die soon. You thought you had time."

Mr. Tortorici is dead by now, too, of course.

We are on borrowed time with my father, I think daily. But of course, whose time *isn't* borrowed? My own youth has evaporated amid the business of adopting and having kids, teaching, editing, writing, cooking dinner, playing chauffeur to playdates and lessons, helping with homework, packing lunches, attending readings, composing and reading emails, taking Kathy to chemo, planning trips to new continents on which to make love.

How many walks down the stairs will I regret not having made?

•

Last month my son Lorenzo asked to see the house I lived in when I was little.

"Be careful," my father told us on the way out the door. "You don't want him to get shot."

It seemed a strange thing to say in reference to the neighborhood where he chose to raise me, despite my mother's perpetual urgings that they leave.

I put Enzo in his booster seat, and we proceeded to drive four miles due south on Western Avenue. We passed the church where I used to be an altar girl and first developed my terror of Hell. We passed the funeral home where everyone I had ever met prior to the age of fourteen held their family wakes—where someday people will gather to pay last respects to my father. We passed my first elementary school, Holy Rosary, which is now a vacant lot overrun with weeds. We passed the Head Start program for low-income kids, which I attended when I was younger than Enzo is now, and the shuttered corner candy store where you could go to play Pac-Man or buy drugs. We pulled onto my old street, which is narrow and one-way, flanked on the other side by the elementary school my father dropped out of in eighth grade to work at a factory, and from which I graduated and just last year returned as the commencement speaker: the inspirational One Who Got Out. That Getting Out was only the first in many steps of running as fast and far as I could to flee my roots, yet here I am again, four miles away from the crime scene of my youth.

Four scant miles, but this is nowhere my children would likely ever be. There at the west end of the street is where my cousin was murdered—shot in gang violence—seven years ago. Kitty-corner across the playground is the street where the legendary Mafioso Joe "the Clown" Lombardo lived throughout my youth. "Why don't you move out of here?" my father reportedly once asked him—"you've got more money than God." And Joe replied simply, "This is the only place on earth that I don't have to look over my shoulder."

I pulled into the Mitchell School playground, where all the teachers still park, and Enzo and I got out of the car. We walked to the playground fence, surveying my old building: a brick two-flat with an awning that used to be green but now just appears as a canopy of dirt and rust.

"Papa was born in that house," I told Enzo. "He lived here until he was almost eighty, and then he moved in with us. I lived here until I was eighteen, when I went away to college."

Enzo stood at the fence, fire-auburn curls against the decayed wrought iron of the bars. When I was ten and my father was in the hospital with a bleeding ulcer, on the verge of death as was often the case in my girlhood, my mother would come to this fence every day during recess to give me an update on his condition. She and I would hold hands through the fence, even though this was the last thing a new transfer student should be doing at a rough, urban public school, and my mother must have realized that as well as I did. She and I were apparently complicit in my social ruin. One day, however, she did not materialize at the fence. I deduced that my father must have died, and she was at the hospital, so I ran screaming from the playground across the street to the concrete steps (that did not seem nearly as short or ramshackle to me then as they do now). I pounded on the door yelling, "Daddy! Daddy!" even though there was no possibility that my father was home. Mr. Tortorici, who was not yet my teacher, came across the street to fetch me. Although he was a frail man with a long white beard and I was a pudgy child, he carried me back across the street, where I was taken to the school office so someone could reach my mother.

Some thirty-two years later, Enzo leaned up against the fence, staring at the little brick two-flat. The air was cold and the sky a dingy gray: the color palette I remember most vividly from my youth because my father convinced the neighbors that their tree roots were getting into our sewerage system, so a whole slew of them ripped up their trees and cemented over their tiny lawns. That my father persuaded several other families to do this alongside him seems preposterous to me, but indicative of his status in the neighborhood as a patriarch and a man of wisdom. One of my most vivid memories is of my father outside with his hose, spraying down the sidewalk in front of our house until it glistened like a bone.

Memories collided in my head like a movie montage gone wrong. A boy I grew up with was shot and killed on a bench in 1989, maybe twenty feet from where Enzo and I now stood. But there, just across the playground, was also where my beloved childhood friend, Angie, and I would take her boom box and listen to Melissa Manchester's "Don't Cry Out Loud" while lying on our backs looking at the few visible stars, playing the song over and over until it became the template for our lives. I held Enzo's hand. He looked up at me. The moment seemed ripe for poignancy.

"This place looks really old," he said finally. "It looks like zombies attacked it."

How do you measure a life's worth? This December 14, my father will be ninety years old. He never thought he would live to see his fortieth birthday. When I was born, he said he hoped to live to see me graduate from elementary school. Now it is possible that he will live to see my daughters graduate. When he was a boy, Italian girls didn't go out without chaperones. I would say that this was before people were shot and killed in our old neighborhood, but that wouldn't be true exactly. People were just shot and killed under different circumstances. The neighborhood has a long history of crime, just as it has a long history of family.

What is true is that my father raised me there oblivious—or volitionally blind—to the neighborhood's shortcomings, conscious only of its strengths. When I went away to college, he cried. I had betrayed the family. I wouldn't stay put; I would not learn what he was trying to teach me. He believed I didn't understand loyalty. I believed that too. I believed loyalty was a trap. I wanted to be Sabina from *The Unbearable Lightness of Being*. I wanted a life based on betrayals and escapes, and for a time, I created some sexy facsimile of that, although I felt it unraveling in my fingers even as I clutched at it ferociously. In the end, despite years in Madison, London, New England, New Mexico, and Amsterdam, I ended up back in Chicago with my parents living downstairs, just like my grandmothers— first my father's mother, then my mother's—resided upstairs from us when I was a girl. I abandoned my fantasy of myself as someone other than my father's loyal daughter, who would throw him under the bus for my babies just as he would have thrown his parents under the bus for me. The night his mother died was Christmas Eve 1980, and within hours of her death my father resumed our holiday festivities—though he was my grandmother's youngest, the one with whom she had lived after all her other sons left home—he did not take the time to mourn alone because he didn't want to spoil my Christmas. I have taken my father out to dinner plenty of times, but someday when he is gone I will nurse my regrets as he nurses his about his own father: *the things I could have done, the more I could have given.*

"Sometimes I see things that aren't there," I told my father in my twenties. "Figures walking into rooms and things like that."

"Oh, sure," my father assured me. "That happens to everyone."

"Sometimes when I'm lying in bed, I hear someone calling my name."

"That's normal," my father concurred. "That happens to me all the time."

"Sometimes my heart feels like it's racing and skipping beats at the same time and I can't breathe and my limbs go numb."

"Flower," my father said, grimacing at the thought of my vegetarianism, my feminism, my world of isms, "there's nothing wrong with you that a good cheeseburger couldn't cure."

I assumed, into my thirtieth year, that someday I would be institutionalized too—that insanity, in lieu of any money, would be my inheritance. Instead, adopting my daughters at thirty-two tamed me with joy, tamped down the edginess inside me, and for five or six years I felt so calm and content that I began to wonder whether I was more like my mother, after all: the reliable one, the selfless one, the one on the sidelines perpetually putting out fires.

Since Kathy's diagnosis, though—or maybe it dates back before then and I merely found a catalyst on which to pin the label of previously unnamable feelings—I feel myself unspooling, a hypomanic restless energy mounting. I change radio stations mid-song; I'm eating and sleeping less, something under my skin clawing to get out. Am I the lion in the house, after all this time, waiting to pounce? I run soups and pastas down the stairs for my parents' dinner, go back to collect greasy Tupperware. I listen to Kathy crying on the phone, sit next to her while the nurses put on hazmat suits to administer her chemo. Emily tells me she is getting a divorce. *If I am unhappy and my husband is unhappy but neither one of us speaks up, does anyone hear the tree of our marriage falling?*

The white-noise machine dulls the roar of Sabina's siren call.

Once upon a time, my father was a hero. He was trained to drive a tank in World War II, but his ulcer and bad back got him sent home before he could be deployed overseas. Instead, his heroism took place on quieter grounds. Years ago, while hanging out at his men's club shooting craps with his friends, a young woman, maybe nineteen or twenty, entered the club. She claimed to want a few dollars for the bus, but it is clear to me now, from an adult lens, that this probably wasn't what she really thought to achieve, walking into a crowded men's club full of ex-cons and soliciting money, then failing to leave when all the men began suggesting to her the things she might do to earn it. They were laughing, saying the things men said back then and still say now, and she was maybe laughing with them, the way some girls have to erase themselves in order to survive. Amid this my father stood up, took out twenty dollars, and handed it to her. "You need to leave now, honey," he said, and walked her to the door.

Another time, many years later, my father was having some coffee in the little eating area of Target when some scruffy teenagers came in. He saw them go to the counter, where one scraped together just enough change to buy a tiny personal pizza, and they all sat around a table while the one who had purchased the pizza ate. The way the others stared intently at the pizza was something my father recognized. Although he always managed to keep his own head above water, he had seen hunger in his life, and it was something he understood. He went to the counter and said quietly, "Give those kids whatever they want to eat, and I'll pay for it." The counter girl went up to the teens and told them they could have what they wanted, and they all ran up and ordered food excitedly. My father sat, drinking his coffee, while they devoured their food. He did not speak to them or tell them he was paying for their meal. He waited until after they had been gone for a while before he left. "I didn't want them to think I was a masher," he told my mother, laughing himself off.

He would never relay these stories to me himself. To him, it would seem like bragging.

I don't know how to reconcile these stories. They reflect the gentle, quiet father I grew up with, and yet that same father once told me, when a childhood friend was raped while she was passed out, that it "wasn't really rape" because she was drunk and sleeping at the boy's house—even though this boy's mother was right in the other room, and we had all known one another since grade school. He is the same man who has started to make comments about how my daughters' most curvaceous friend "shouldn't wear those shorts cut up to her crotch," with a tone that clearly implies that she—a twelve-year-old sixth grader—is *asking for trouble*. This same man, when my mother was on the rollercoaster of Weight Watchers and TOPS throughout my childhood, once suggested that they go to a Halloween party as "Robinson Crusoe and the whole week," and my mother laughed at the joke while my insides roiled. He is the same man, too, who very vocally supported Harold Washington for mayor of Chicago in an era when no one else in the neighborhood would support a Black candidate, and all the usually proud Democrats of our blue-collar world had started wearing Epton pins and voting Republican—a trend they would never quite reverse. I'd heard my father arguing with his best friend, Mario, on our front porch, saying, "Man, are you kidding me? You think if you cut a Black man, he doesn't bleed? You think if you hurt his kid, he doesn't cry? They're just the same as you and me, stop being a fucking savage and grow up."

My cousin Gink and his brother, whose father was dead; my childhood companion Angie, whose father frightened her; my oldest friend, Alicia, who now teaches at Mitchell herself and whose heroin-addled car-thief father spent her childhood in prison . . . the litany of young people who looked to my father as a stable force in their lives, as a father figure, is considerable. When we take him to a family wedding, men from the old neighborhood—past middle-aged themselves—jump up to help him to his seat, to get him a drink, to hover around talking about old times, to hold open doors.

My mother and I have suggested throwing a party for his ninetieth, where all the many people who love him could gather, but he won't hear of it. "Oh, Jesus Christ," he says. The trappings of socializing—having to maneuver around with his walker, possibly falling down as he often does or not making it to the bathroom in time—have been added to the long list of things that make him anxious. His world shrinks, month by month, day by day. Although he can still read, he can no longer recite the alphabet or remember the order of the letters. Only Lindsay Lohan and Paris Hilton, on the pages of his morning *Star*, remain as some reminder of wider terrain.

He is on a journey across the white barren land, inside himself. We stand on the periphery and watch him ride away.

What is love? Is it possible to love by degree? If a love is not the greatest of all loves, is it love at all? Is a life lived to ninety more "full" than one lived to forty-five? What if the life lived to ninety was consumed by anxieties, by illnesses, by complexes and regrets? Where does quality intersect with quantity? But what defines quality anyway? Is existence itself "quality" enough?

After we watched my husband's mother die slowly, unable to speak, vomiting on herself if she tried to sit upright, her flesh an empty sack loose around her bones, I told my husband, "Kill me if I get that way." After listening to my father scream at a god in whom he does not believe, begging for death on his eighty-fifth Christmas when he broke his hip and my husband, mother, and I had to change his diapers while the antibiotics ravaged him with explosive diarrhea, I promised my husband, "I'll make sure I have enough pills in the house when the time comes. Don't wait too long—do it quickly when people will still believe it's possible I've done it myself."

My husband looks at me patiently, perhaps pityingly, when I talk this way. He knows I seek to escape the indignity of death just as I once escaped my old neighborhood. He knows I grew up with the mistaken impression that cleverness could exempt me from anything, but middle age teaches nothing if not the lesson that *nobody* is exempt. Several times a week, our phone rings in the middle of the night because my father has fallen again on his way to the bathroom, and my husband, no doubt as beleaguered as I am by the multiple needs pressing down upon us, heads dutifully downstairs to lift him back into bed. Will it be my husband or me someday, making phone calls to paramedics, to our children and their partners, needing assistance with the other?

We are all the walking dead of history. This goddamn place looks like zombies attacked it.

It is late fall, my father's ninetieth birthday careening toward us. Mario, whom he has known since they were three years old, just had his leg amputated and has been convalescing at home. My father has avoided going to see him because he can't stand the thought of Mario without a leg, and it is easy to avoid things when you are almost ninety, disabled and incontinent and seeing nonexistent mice on the floor. But now Mario's sister has died and my father has to attend the wake. My mother, who did not know how to drive until she was seventy and learned only when my father's feet failed him on the brakes and he ran his car into a pole to avoid hitting pedestrians, drives him to the funeral parlor. At the door, my father sees Mario in his wheelchair. Other men rush to get a chair for my father and place it beside Mario. They sit: two old men who used to play in front of the house we were all raised in, when they were younger than my son. They talk: the two of them with legs that are missing like dead brothers, or that no longer work. I have no access to the specifics of their dialogue, but I know there is laughter. I know they call each other "Baby" like Frank Sinatra, as they always have. They are historical relics from a day of covered bridges downtown and chaperones for young Italian girls. Through some accident of mistaken identity or grace, they are still alive.

That same day, only four miles north, Enzo has his first kiss. In the coat room of his classroom, like generations of kindergarteners before him, he asks a pretty blond girl he has known since preschool,

"So, do you want a kiss?" and she says, "Sure." When I ask if he kissed her on her cheek or her lips, he shrugs at me and drawls evasively, "Oh, I don't know . . ." Since the start of the school year, he has already had four fiancées. As my father and his friend Mario sit in the funeral parlor foyer, my son gets ready for bed, excitedly reading aloud from the Magic Tree House series. We "snug" together in the darkness, and he twirls a strand of my hair around his finger absently as he makes the jerky breaths that precipitate sleep.

His life is contained in this moment. In the moment of his first kiss. In the moment of sleepy breath and Mommy hair. In the moment of his brain's voracious recognition of symbols on a page: letters that form words that form language that form story. My father's life exists within that single frame of laughter with his oldest childhood friend, as they commemorate yet another death—"doomed," as Faulkner wrote, to be the ones "who live."

Now. Buddhists tell us to live in the moment, but the moment already contains us, whether we want it to or not. "When I find myself laughing at something now," Kathy tells me in her tenth week of chemo, "I feel conscious of it more, and I'm grateful." She did not choose this gratitude or perspective. Like Emily, in an instant she would trade her knowledge for her old, blithe ways. Nor will wisdom save either woman from anything: just as Emily's son's death is inevitable before his third birthday, so ten days before my father's ninetieth birthday, Kathy will have her last night on earth. While I am alone in a California hotel room saying aloud, "I have never known such desire," into the void, after having had dinner alone with my email correspondent for the first time, in Chicago my father waits for the mice to descend on his body; Kathy feels her fiancé spooning her as her Klonopin begins to anesthetize her enough to sleep; and my husband, trusting me entirely, retires to our marital bed alone, no white-noise machine required.

In that Schrödinger's box of uncertainty, *my* entire life is contained. In that in-between space, I am both having and not having an affair; Kathy is both living and dead. When I wake in my hotel bed alone, two hours behind Chicago time, Kathy has already been carried away in the cart of my father's dreams. That morning, before the phone call comes from her fiancé, I dwell in the relative peace of my frantic, overly busy life for the last time, before descending into the throes of both grief and feral lust: a dangerous state for a woman, one that makes her feel self-immolating and invincible at once. Kathy, Emily's son, my father, and the woman I thought I was—watch us all shoot brief and bright against the same vast sky one last time. Vibrant, singular, miraculously ordinary, full of love and pain we flash. Then, one by one, we are out.

Substitute Beauty

There is no control group. I don't even want to talk about "female sexuality" until there is a control group. And there never will be.

—Maggie Nelson

You and Angie, whom you worship, periodically tie each other up with orange hair ribbons made of puffy yarn and watch the bound person try to escape. You are five, maybe six years old. Your mother, who babysits for Angie weekdays while her mother waits tables and goes on acting auditions for roles she never gets, doesn't interfere, because she is in the kitchen doing dishes in a pan of gray-beige water, smoking Salem 100s, or lying down in the back bedroom with a migraine. Sometimes she says, "It's a bad day for kids!" and you and Angie know not to bother her. If the orange-ribbon game had a name, you don't recall it, but sometimes, along with your slightly older cousin from next door, you and Angie also play Mean Babysitter and spank each other until your butt cheeks turn bright. When your cousin isn't over, this game evolves into another, "Red as a Tomato," which is divorced from any offending babysitter: a pursuit in its own right. Angie can play "Red as a Tomato" without making a sound or ever jerking away from your slapping hand. You try to emulate her in this, as you do with everything, and find to your surprise that unlike hitting a ball or crossing the monkey bars or climbing fences or being picked for teams by the boys on your block, in this game you can give Angie a run for her money—this, a denial of pain, you are good at too.

The bondage game and Mean Babysitter and Red as a Tomato are all Angie's idea, but you never question them, because you have played imaginary games for as far back as you can remember. With your mother, your games have characters with names and more complex identities than Angie or your cousins have the attention span to sustain. You beg your mother to play these games in bed at night, because you sleep together now in the back bedroom while your father sleeps in the living room on the daybed, where he can watch the front door for burglars. In one game you play with your mother, you get to be Angie and she has to be Gina. Gina, you tell your mother, is Angie's older sister and is "fat and ugly and cries all the time." You are not (yet) overweight, but your mother is. In real life, your mother cries a lot and so do you, but these are not the traits of heroines. Angie has long, nearly black ponytails that trail behind her when she runs, whereas your father recently made you get your unruly dishwater curls cut into a pixie, and on the weekends when Angie isn't at your house, you draw pictures of the character version of her with her airborne hair, a cape, and a big A on her chest. In the drawings, Angie is always escaping from Bad Men: across tightropes with flames licking their braided twine; swinging on vines over bubbly swamps full of alligators.

You go to Holy Rosary school a few blocks away, where you learn about cursive writing and Hell, but Angie attends the bigger, ramshackle public school across the street from your house, where the kids all seem loud, wiry, and half-feral. Some make out with each other on the benches lining the fence during recess, and other times fights break out, even between girls. You are afraid of those kids, but when you're playing outside with Angie, sometimes they wave or come talk to her, and Angie never seems intimidated even when they're older—even when they're boys.

In some of your drawings, the character version of Angie has lost a hand from a previous misadventure, when an alligator bit it off. "Ask me if I cried when my hand fell off," you command the actual Angie, tucking your hand inside your yellow windbreaker sleeve and trying to spread your make-believe world beyond bedtime enactments with your mother. You have to give Angie this direction three times before she distractedly does it, and you shrug coolly and say, "No." You are not sure if the payoff was worth the setup, but Real Angie did not cry when she fell off the Giraldis' fence and broke her arm last summer, and you imagine that she never cries when her father takes the belt to her, whereas you cry if your mild-mannered parents so much as look at you crossly. "Spoiled," all your cousins call you, even though your family never has much money either, but you're an only child of parents old enough to be your grandparents so you own toys, children's books, and have your own bedroom—a walk-in closet under the stairs—even if you don't actually sleep in it.

You begin writing your very first book: *The Danger Adventures of Angie*, which turns into a series of chapter books, the folded pages tied together with string. You rename the embarrassing older sister from Gina to Miriam, knowing there is something humiliating about giving her your own name. You draw elaborate pictures and dictate the words to your mother, until soon you are able to write well enough to keep up with your own ideas. Your mother keeps these early efforts in a giant box in her closet, and when she is dead you will find them.

First, though, before you were any kind of writer, you were a pretender. First, before the books (either handwritten on pages torn from a roll of butcher paper, or the books you would publish), you were simply someone fine-tuned to escape. First, before you had any inkling of writing your way out of the captivity in which you were born, there was simply Angie, and your desperate desire to inhabit her skin.

Angie's mother is young enough to be your parents' daughter. She dyes her hair red and wears it in a shag cut and has a rabbit-fur jacket. She is popular with the other women in the neighborhood, even though she does weird things like call herself an actress and venture outside the neighborhood by herself frequently while Angie's father, a long-distance truck driver, is away. She gets away with her eccentricities because she grew up here, attended the same school Angie attends (and your father attended), and was known as a great beauty of her generation until she had Angie before she was twenty. Your mother, who isn't Italian or from the neighborhood, is often left out of the other women's coffee klatches, although your father has more status in the neighborhood than Angie's, who—like your mother—is an outsider, a customer randomly seated at Angie's mother's station in 1967, who ended up knocking her up and marrying her, in that order. Your value relative to Angie's, though, extends further than your parents' respective positions, and even further than the way the mothers on your block all rave about Angie's beauty—"even prettier than her mother was"—while you have frizzy curls and an overbite. The real magic surrounding Angie is the way she is respected rather than teased by the boys—the way even adult men speak of her admiringly as "tough" and a "tomboy." She can hit a ball over the fence and do more chin-ups than most of the boys on the block, and when she takes to wearing a jean jacket over a white T-shirt most days, instead of making fun of her the other kids start calling her Fonzie. Angie doesn't spend her time covertly writing books about other people, inadequate in her own skin—she is out there living the kind of life you imagine for your characters. Even her father is like a Bad Man from one of your games, always yelling and using his belt, and for reasons you will never fully understand, this thrills you and makes Angie seem still more special, glamorous and important.

(The Important Girls of history—those worthy of obsession: Joan of Arc, Anne Frank, Freud's "Dora"—are so often targets of male violence.)

Every night it goes like this: you lie in your narrow bed under the stairs, casting spells to turn yourself into Angie. (A witch named Maria—one of your many imaginary friends—lives in the narrow space between the dresser and the wall, but she is not involved; this is your secret.) In your memory it will seem this went on for years, though probably it was more sporadic than that—you lie very still, counting backward from ten, telling yourself that when you get to zero and open your eyes, you will be Angie and Angie will be you. The problem is that you will never know if the game works, because if you are Angie, you won't know that you used to be you—you won't know it only happened because of a spell you created. You will just think you've been Angie all along. For years you play this game fanatically, watching your friend for signs that she has become you in some way, that her flame has dimmed or her reading improved, but nothing changes. Eventually you realize the preposterousness of your spell and stop engaging in it. You are not Angie. Changing places with people isn't possible in real life—it happens only in old movies like *Freaky Friday*. You are no longer a little girl and know better than to think you can bend the world to your will with a wish.

By this time, Angie's mother no longer goes on auditions, has started bartending an evening shift for better money. Angie has her own house key and doesn't need a babysitter anymore, even in the summer. When her father is away, she eats dinner alone, puts herself to bed. She is "not allowed" to have people over, either when she is by herself or when her father is home, so for a short

time, you don't see much of her anymore. Then Holy Rosary closes
due to underenrollment and you end up transferring into Angie's
fifth-grade class at Mitchell School. Her friends are the cool kids,
the ones who run fast and swear casually and already wear eye
shadow. One tells you that Angie must feel sorry for you to let
you hang around so much; another makes fun of your "ten-dollar
words" and says you think you're better, even though you think
exactly the opposite.

In short order you come to realize that a game is more satisfying
when no one else knows about it. In a game with more than one
player, you have to respond to things your friends or mother might
say, and these things often don't match the dialogue in your mind—
the way you want the story to go. So although you still play imaginary games with others, you also begin to engage in them when
no one knows you're doing it. You are always an orphan or a run-
away, always in danger from an abusive authority figure, and always crafty, tough, the kind of protagonist who lives by her wits
and schemes. You create worlds inside your head: your elementary
school is Sunnyside Orphanage, and you and your new best girlfriend, Alicia (who also loves the public library and is also hopeless
at sports), are orphans named Karen and Genevieve, always trying
to break out of its oppressive confines. There are thirty-six kids in
your sixth-grade class, so you don't bother to name all of them, but
some you assign alternate identities in your mind: Debbie is Anna,
Karen's rival; Pasquale is Patrick, her oldest friend and secret crush;
and Angel is Frank, who loves Genevieve, even though in reality
people say Angel likes you and you are alternately terrified and
thrilled that this might be true. Although you are in the same classroom, every time you encounter each other in any direct way, Angel
mutters, "Hi, Gina" under his breath, and your heart starts flipping,
even though you don't actually like Angel back. Your teacher has

arranged you in a kind of hierarchical order of intelligence and academic performance, and you are in the second seat, while Angel is in the last row. Still, you know enough about the world by now to understand that if a boy likes you, you are supposed to be flattered, honored even. Angie has had several boyfriends already she has "wrapped to," which means French kissing and maybe more but you're afraid to ask.

Angie doesn't have a secret alias in your classroom games because she would have to be Karen, given that Karen acts exactly like her, and that wouldn't work because you are Karen in the game. Only Alicia knows about these characters because sometimes you play Karen and Genevieve together in the back bedroom of your house, but she doesn't know you play more or less constantly, without her involvement, all day at school . . . that you have taken to signing your diary "Karen," or that you have started writing novels about these characters in secret. You accumulate 200 sheets, 300 sheets, 450 sheets of the brown, jaggedly ripped paper your mother buys to save money.

When you pretend to be Karen, and write about her, she appears to be your polar opposite, based on someone else entirely. But the longer you write about her, the more you act as her no matter where you are, the more things begin to click into a certain kind of place: you feel yourself becoming someone else. Not Angie, of course, but a facsimile of Angie by another name, the symbiotic Angie of your desires. Your shy insecurity morphs into a sarcastic bravado; you become class president; you lose thirty-two pounds even though your mother has never been able to manage it. You stop crying.

It seems important to stipulate this as a key element of your pretenses: for more than a decade you stop crying, even when alone.

"And there were all those poems about women, written by men," Adrienne Rich writes in "When We Dead Awaken: Writing as

Re-Vision"—"it seemed to be a given that men wrote poems and women frequently inhabited them. These women were almost always beautiful, but threatened with the loss of beauty, the loss of youth—the fate worse than death. Or, they were beautiful and died young . . ."

But what happens to the young girl who isn't beautiful? What happens to a girl who grows up under a male gaze that renders her inconsequential, with nothing much of importance to lose?

You watch your mother's body expand, the flesh under her chin become puffy. On the walls of your apartment are old black-and-white photographs of her in Greenwich Village in the late 1950s, looking like a young Isabella Rossellini. Your mother once won a contest for the "best legs" in her neighborhood when she was in high school. Although you have lost weight (too much, some of your concerned teachers have taken you aside to say), it hasn't rendered you beautiful. Your acne, your hair that makes one of the boys at school call you a sheep and bleat "Baaaa!" to you loudly in the halls, your too-big nose and underdeveloped breasts remain. You are becoming hairy, everywhere, your mornings spent in front of an illuminated mirror plucking your face, applying concealer, bleaching the hair on your arms so that you can be presentable, so the boys at school won't make fun of you for daring not to make their dicks hard. Although you are old enough to realize that the girls they call "ugly" *do* make their dicks hard too, just in a different, crueler way.

You are old enough to understand that your future—a selective-enrollment high school across the city; the hope of college someday—looks brighter than your mother's ever did, than Angie's does. You are getting old enough that you no longer want to "wrap to" any of the gang members and aspiring criminals you know anyway, so it would only make life harder for you if they all desired and pursued you, as they do Angie. Still, trapped in your developing body, sometimes when you are in the bathtub and naked, you find yourself pretending that Angie's father is making you bend over so he can use his belt. You stand up and brace your hands on the wall and a current races under your skin. In real life, Angie's asshole father holds no interest to you at all. He is just some Tall Man who is alternately absent or yelling, who smells of yeasty beer and once abandoned their dog on the side of a highway. He is everything you want to leave behind in your burgeoning desire to get out of your neighborhood. Still, no matter what you tell yourself consciously, you can't seem to shake your body's belief that somehow male cruelty has the power to make a girl important. That only through the violence of a man can you be made visible and special too.

Many years later, you will come across a quote from Eleanor Roosevelt about her biggest wish being that she had been born more beautiful. By then, you will be aware that she had affairs with women, that she more or less ran the United States when her husband was ailing, that she was arguably at moments the most powerful woman on the planet.

That even Eleanor Roosevelt could not seem to escape the need for approval under the all-seeing male gaze feels like one of the saddest and truest facts you will ever discover.

For everyone except professional actors, sex is the only realm of the Sanctioned Imaginary. No one finds it strange if someone admits to "fantasizing" during sex that their partner is somebody else: a rock star, an actor, the hot neighbor. If you were to admit to doing the same thing while at a family barbeque or out to dinner, however—especially if not only was your partner "someone else" but you were too—the public perception of the situation would quickly shift such that the pretender seemed . . . unbalanced, at best? Only in bed can adults make believe, either together or privately. In worldly circles, even rape fantasies and extreme BDSM are understood as "play," with the potential for catharsis. Sex is simultaneously our most judgmental yet forgiving arena.

In his short story "The Hitchhiking Game," Milan Kundera alternates points of view between a young man and his girlfriend on the first day of their vacation, as they embark on an ultimately disastrous (of course—in fiction only things gone wrong are interesting) game of role-play wherein she is a flirty, sexually experienced hitchhiker instead of her usual modest self, and he, acting out some version of himself that his girlfriend fears most (the kind who likes such women and knows them well), is progressively goaded to become more and more callous, tough and misogynistic, surpassing any behaviors of his past, to become the girl's worst nightmare and sexual fantasy combined. They end their disastrous encounter— which Kundera wryly remarks took place on the very first day of their vacation, leaving them thirteen days together remaining— with the girl postcoitally weeping on their motel bed, calling the man's name and saying, "It's me," while the man has to call on compassion from "very far away" in order to bring himself to comfort her.

What if the young man and the girl were playing this same game with no intention of fucking at the end of it? Well, of course there would be no "story." Kundera knows sex to be the most understood domain of the Imaginary, but if pushed further, it can be argued that many adults find eroticism the exclusive domain of the Imaginary, the endgame without which make-believe lacks relevance. Whether the dominatrix's "dungeon" or more mainstream environments like Renaissance fairs or cosplay conventions, there is rarely explicit identity-play among adults that does not contain some (at least underground) sexual element.

You, however, have never been to a dungeon, to a *Star Trek* convention. These outlets of communal make-believe and social sexuality hold no appeal. Your games, the older you got, became more and more private; the last time you recall anyone else actively participating, you were in mid-high school and you and Alicia deliberately had a marathon of "playing characters" before deciding to give it up forever because you were "too old." The characters you played were loosely based on the nighttime soap opera *Dynasty*, and she played one teenage female character while you played the entire rest of the cast. It was like rehearsing for a play as understudy to every role, but a play you had also written and were directing. Years later, both of you married to WASPy men and raising children months apart, she will tell you that when you played the male characters, she found you attractive and felt like she had a crush on you. Maybe it was the reason you stopped. You had reached an age where the Imaginary could no longer exist without the erotic.

When actors enter a role fully in their private lives, it isn't sexual: it's called method acting. Though considered excessive in some circles, it is lauded in others, part of what makes actors "artists." But of course the method actor has a clear and concrete goal: to become the character to be played on film or stage—to inhabit this other persona so fully that they really are that person in their own mind, no longer acting but simply being.

When the film stops shooting, is it difficult for method actors to return to their real lives? Once there is no longer a point to their pretense, either sexual or professional, does the game ever remain seductive merely for its own sake?

You and Angie take different buses, in different directions, at different times of day to get to and from your respective high schools. In the course of a few months, your life transitions from not being able to escape the constant, thick presence of everyone in your neighborhood to scarcely seeing anyone within its confines except your parents and Alicia, who commutes to high school with you. Does Angie still hang out on the corner in front of Fiore's grocery store with the girls your mother calls "fast" and the older boys who scare you? Fiore's is not on your commute route, and if she does, you no longer hear word of what happens there. Your neighborhood has become little more than a crash pad, so it is with both surprise and a sense of inevitability that you open the door one evening to Angie's old knocking code and find her on your porch with no overnight bag, asking to sleep over on a weeknight. You are even more surprised at the speed with which your mother acquiesces— your father is out, and you watch Angie eat fast, overlapping bites of leftover chicken cacciatore, reminiscing with your mother about the long-ago drives your parents took the two of you on, as though she and your mother were the ones who sat together in the back-seat, leaning against each other in half-sleep on the drives home. Leaving homework undone, you follow Angie when she crawls into the double bed in the back bedroom, trying to keep to your own side of the bed, but although she'd been jittery all night she is asleep in seconds, her limbs sprawled everywhere like when she was a girl, and you remember the way you used to put a Kleenex box on her face if she snored, your casualness with each other's body—the way you sometimes woke up spooning her: the only time you will ever sleep deeply and comfortably on the outside of a spoon. Now you will never be able to sleep next to Angie's radiating presence—her difference—except you must have, because the next thing you remember, your mother is at the front door arguing with Angie's father, his incessant knocking already the backdrop of your shaken-off dreams. "Angela!" he bellows, and Angie opens her eyes like a spy who was only ever pretending to rest and says, "I don't want to get your mom in trouble," before she stands and goes to him, still in the nightgown you loaned her. It is past midnight, but your father still isn't home, which isn't exactly normal but is not unheard of enough to register beyond the fact that you and your mother stand alone together at the front window, watching helplessly as Angie's father slaps and pushes her still-slight frame down the sidewalk, her stumbling illuminated by streetlights and your pale nightgown billowing out when he shoves her, until they disappear from view: the last time you will ever see him. Rage and envy mingle in your chest until you can barely breathe. "Call Daddy!" you demand of your mother, and then, "Call the police!" to which she shakes her head sadly and makes noises of pressing her tongue inside her mouth in ways that don't know how to find words. "You're complicit!" you shout at your mother before rushing back to the back bedroom, Angie's clothes discarded on the floor in a pile. But complicit in what? Was Angie actually running away from home, like Karen and Genevieve from the orphanage? If so, her father has the *right* to claim her, doesn't he? You feel like you should cry, but instead you can't stop thinking how dramatic and intense Angie's fourteen-year-old life appears, while all you do is homework or babysitting or taking the bus with Alicia to see rated-PG movies.

After that night, Angie avoids you, or maybe you avoid her, ashamed of what you have witnessed, of her once Fonzie-like invincibility transformed to fragile girl bones in your cheap nightgown. You knock on her door to return her clothes, but her mother answers and says Angie isn't there, and acts as though Angie even being at your house at all, much less returning home in your sleep attire, is perfectly normal. Though you live less than a block apart, once again your paths rarely cross. Soon enough, you are yearning for Forenza sweaters to wear backward and a driver's license to take you farther away; soon enough, you discover alternative music and underage dance clubs and boys' hands down your pants and vodka in soda cans; soon enough you are a "summer girl" and a hostess at a pancake joint and you rarely traverse your neighborhood farther than from the Grand Avenue bus stop to your front door. Soon enough you start speaking of college as a given.

Still, that night Angie ran away—just as when you were a little girl casting spells in your twin bed, but now restless in your uneventful, almost-woman skin—you would have changed places with her instantly.

At newly eighteen, you identify with Janis Ian's ballads of unloved women, with Dolly Parton's plea to Jolene that she "cannot compete," with the notion of yourself as always the bridesmaid, excluded on the fringe. But by nineteen, you identify with characters like Kundera's Sabina, with Anaïs Nin, with the idea of an artistic, traveling life collecting experience and lovers, the complete antithesis of the female lives you grew up seeing as role models: wearing housedresses outdoors and all cultivating the same short helmet of puffy hair before they turned forty. You begin to keep a list of men you've fucked or let go down on you; you lecture your roommate about learning to orgasm and send her to her room to masturbate; you find yourself getting into dance clubs for free and bought drinks by handsome Brits. You overhear a friend say about you at a party, "She exudes sex," and wonder how this can be true when you never had a single date in high school.

You do not wake up one day and find yourself afflicted with beauty, like some woman in a movie who removes her glasses and is suddenly Julia Roberts. Your polycystic ovarian syndrome will, well into your twenties, wreak havoc on your skin with bouts of cystic acne, and your breasts are as small as ever and your nose still decidedly Italian. But there is starting to be something underneath all this that only certain men can sense, like dogs hearing a whistle too high for human ears, and these men begin falling, one at a time, in unrequited love with you. They say things to you like "You're such a free spirit," and "You're really intense," that seem to be at odds with each other, that make you feel on the one hand that the image you are trying to project of yourself against the blank wall of men's bodies is "working," and on the other hand as though you are nebulous, a hologram, a text rendered meaningful only through the interpretation of its readers.

Your first relationship is with a slightly older Brit who educates you about music, vegetarianism, and Amnesty International, and fucks you four times a night because he rarely sleeps. He pays for everything when you visit him in Newcastle, regularly taking the train from London, where you are studying, to stay at his house, and he sends you mixtapes and rings you on the pay phone down the street every Sunday at a designated time. You've met his mum, who prepared the blandest curry you will ever taste, and all his mates. Still, when he packs for Greece in front of you he puts Fetherlites into his bag as though it has never occurred to him that you might mind. In your own picture of yourself, you don't mind either. You have a boy you call Nudist in London, who tells you you're beautiful and brings you a rose sometimes when he picks you up, and who fucks you like a small-brained animal, muscles rippling through his thrusting body. When you go out with your friends you pick up other men, too, occasionally stealing hash chunks from their bathrooms. Still, when your British not-exactly-boyfriend goes to work in the mornings, you write him seven-page letters about your feelings and cry to Sinead O'Connor's "Troy," and sometimes you are stupid enough to leave these letters behind once you have taken a train back to London, though he never mentions finding any of them. You are lonely.

Back home in Chicago, the loneliness doesn't disappear. You travel in a pack of other lonely girls to happy hours and ladies' nights where you get into clubs for free; you let yourself get hand-cuffed to the bar at a club where women can have unlimited drinks if they'll play along; you gravitate, in one-night stands, to men skilled at mixing cruelty into flirtation. Back at college, you have a bad trip when some Australians you squatted with in London are passing through and give you weed from some connection in Baltimore, and your body ends up turning into a pillar of salt and you tremble uncontrollably for about four hours. The next day, during an exam in psychology, when asked what major theory Freud developed in Paris, you write, *Freud never went to Paris.* Your body gets smaller and smaller; you develop a phobia of unopened packages of food and can eat only if someone has already opened the bag or the can or the box and consumed some. You write in your journal one night, your senior year of college, *I know I'm not eating enough, I know I've got problems with food, but I don't want to talk about that.*

After you graduate college, you go out for Thai one night with Angie, before you head off to Europe to backpack and work. Her father ran off with some woman in another state years ago, and she and her mother now live alone in a basement apartment on the neighborhood's busiest street, bars on their windows that showcase the feet of passersby. Angie's once "foxy" mom, not quite forty-five, has grown as heavy as your own mother, with a crone's thick white spittle in the corners of her mouth. Angie's hair is short and hard with gel, and she's a head taller than you despite always being so petite as a girl. At the restaurant, she only glances at the northern Thai menu before ordering what you order and then not eating it because it's "too spicy." When you hug tightly in your parents' car, outside the basement apartment you already know you will never see again, she tells you without looking at you that for your entire childhood she was frantically jealous of you and wanted your life.

You are old enough to have deduced by now that of course this was the truth—of course she was—and yet it remains among the most shocking things anyone has ever said to you.

•

By the time your British boyfriend dumps you some thirty seconds after coming in your mouth; by the time you're down to 98 pounds and regularly spending days lying on benches in Battersea Park calling your self-starvation "penance" for some sin you cannot name; by the time you're working as a bartender in London where pub regulars ask if you'd like to "come home and see my ceiling," and you're shacking up with a South African hash dealer with whom your first sexual encounter would now be defined as "date rape," you no longer expect to stop pretending someday. It has become simply a part of who you are, as inextricable as having labeled yourself a feminist by sixth grade in a woman-hating neighborhood; as inextricable as the compulsive ways you read and write; as inextricable as the fact that you consider yourself "selectively heterosexual" in that you have little interest in men as a wide-scale gender, but the few times you've fallen fast and hard—as you just have with a young American you met in a train station in Avignon—the object of your infatuation has always been male. You pretend in the same ingrained, hardwired way that your sexual fantasies have deep (if now uncomfortable) roots in your childhood games with Angie, though whenever you attempt to trust a lover enough to act out these fantasies of being spanked or tied up, things are more awkward and painful than fulfilling. Like loving and pitying your mother in equally intense measure, pretending seems organic to you, as insurmountable to exorcise as the way the hairs on the back of your neck prick up in fear if a man walks behind you on a street at night. A permanent, archetypal condition.

You are driving to Florida with the man who will soon be your husband. It is 1992 or so, and your fiancé's grandfather is dying of Lou Gehrig's disease. You are driving down from New England to see him, even though he can no longer communicate and your fiancé is not particularly close to him and seems to have no strong feelings about his imminent demise. You are doing what the callous young do, making a vacation out of it, with other stops to visit friends and see sites along the way. You are maybe twenty-four years old, on a road trip with the man you love, and for whom you relocated to a tiny town in rural New England: this journey should be an adventure. But like the characters in Kundera's "Hitchhiking Game," your road tripping is not enough for you; in your mind you have a whole other scenario worked up: you are Kendra, a character from the novel you are writing, and you are taking a trip with the much-older married man with whom you have been having an affair, as he drives down to Florida to see his dying father from whom he has been estranged for years.

Needless to say, unlike the games of make-believe with Alicia when you were younger, you do not call your fiancé by a false name. You do not (despite it being the early '90s and the diagnosis undergoing a weird resurgence) suffer from dissociative identity disorder; you are not under any delusion that you are really living the scenario in your head—that your fiancé is a fictional character married to another (fictional) woman, or that your name is Kendra. When your fiancé speaks to you, you smoothly answer him back, inhabiting your normal identity. Sometimes you talk for an extended time and you forget all about the game. But once he falls into silence and you are staring out the window again, watching the highway roll by, looking at your young neck and jawline in the side mirror, listening to Tears for Fears on the CD player, you sometimes slip, without even having to decide as much, back into being Kendra—back into writing dialogue and scenes in your head about the Floridian trip with your older lover.

Maybe you believe this will someday end up in a book; maybe you don't. You are thirteen years away from even publishing a book. If this is method acting, it is not for any professional goal. Likewise, although once in a while you cry late at night about Angie and the things you now understand about her life or the way you ruptured apart when you fled your neighborhood and left her behind, you no longer have her specifically in mind when you imagine anything. You change your name, your vantage point, your plotline, the way other people have too many drinks or do drugs: to avoid pain, to escape themselves, or to make things seem bigger. Reality, enhanced.

Your fiancé, assuming he is enough to hold your interest given that you are going to marry him, has no idea you are even doing this.

Some years later, when you are in graduate school for your second master's degree, you will fall in love with the French feminists, in part for their strident insistence that women are more than one thing. Some, like Luce Irigaray, give creatively ludicrous rationales for this, such as women having two labial lips, constantly rubbing together "in communion," hence it is in the female nature to be dual, whereas the phallus, by contrast, is singular, linear, logical. By the time you encounter these works, you will be married and living an entirely different kind of life from your childhood—you will be prone to saying things like men and women are not so different from each other, that everyone is the same inside; that all this "Mars" and "Venus" nonsense just sets feminism back by positing the sexes on opposite sides of a fence, alien to each other. Yet you are obsessed by the French feminist concept of multiplicity, as though for the first time you have a template for the overlapping Venn diagrams of yourself that have never made sense—for the first time, you have a language for the way that you don't feel neatly contained under your own skin, your own name. The French feminists are fond of "play"— linguistically, sexually—associating it with artistry, and here, too, you feel the recognition of a previously unnamable thing.

The French feminist movement of *l'écriture féminin* teaches that women writing their bodies can change the world. It may be fair to say that you have never wanted to believe anything in your life more than this.

After you leave her behind in your old neighborhood, abandoning her for your burgeoningly bourgeois adulthood, Angie becomes:

a)   A stripper and junkie.

b)   A bank teller who has four children before you have even finished your first master's degree.

c)   A radical lesbian separatist who now lives on a commune of women in Oregon.

d)   The singer in a punk band who gets murdered behind a club after a gig and whose killer is never caught.

e)   All of the above.

f)   It does not matter what Angie becomes. The point is that you left.

You marry four days after your twenty-fifth birthday, on the three-year anniversary of the day you and your husband met. For your honeymoon, you go to Europe for a month, during which time you are ecstatically happy. You make love in a cheap Italian hotel near Portofino with the window open, street traffic outside mingling with your moans; you go to a punk club in Prague; your husband takes photos of you in front of statues, graffiti, stone walls. He doesn't tell you that you're beautiful, although he sometimes compliments your eyes, your smile, your ass, as though these individual features may redeem you. He likes to pass himself off as a man who doesn't care about such things anyway, though when he is secretly angry about something, he finds ways to dig at your appearance, like telling you after your bachelorette party that you could never be a stripper because your breasts aren't conventionally attractive and then pointing out which of your friends, including others with small breasts, could be strippers, until you cry as though becoming a stripper is your goal. Still, someday you will be able to tell from all the photo albums of your marriage that he did think you were beautiful then: that no matter where the two of you were in the world, you were always the most interesting site to him, the place to which his eye gravitated to document, and this will break you in myriad ways so that you can't look at old photo albums anymore.

But of course none of that has happened yet. Right now you are newly married, and your husband is the smartest man you have ever known, which sharply differentiates him from the men amid whom you grew up. Your life, in a small college town, is cozy and full of gentle pleasures. In your graduate student housing, on the east coast far from where either of you were raised, you and your husband make homemade yogurt and bread together, and you pick him up sometimes at lunchtime to do a strange low-impact aerobics class for free at the university health center, or go to the one Chinese restaurant in town and eat thick, succulent wedges of eggplant with brown rice. You have married Richie Cunningham, on whom you always secretly had a crush while Angie was so obsessed with Fonzie. Except this Richie's mother has a British accent and went to boarding school, of all things! Both his parents have graduate degrees. Your husband is working on his doctorate; you are employed part-time at a foster care agency, and in truth, economically, you are not yet much better off than your parents, who were below the poverty level when you started college, but everything else about your married lifestyle feels like a whole other universe.

You did not marry your husband despite the fact that, occasionally, he does things like throw a telephone across the room while screaming or punch the wall or shout obscenities at you. You grew up around men who boasted about going down to the South Side of Chicago during the 1968 riots and busting Black men's heads. You grew up watching kids come to school covered in bruises from their fathers or their mothers' boyfriends, no teacher ever saying a word. Your elementary school did not have a counselor; you didn't know what the Department of Children and Family Services was. In your fledgling work as a therapist, you are focusing on foster girls because you have some sense of wanting to "give back"—some sense of survivor's guilt that you flew away while so many of your childhood peers, including Angie, remained behind. Your husband is, by any definition, a good catch. He is not just smart, but ambitious, generous. He cooks you breakfast in the mornings to help you with your hypoglycemia and you watch *Thirtysomething* reruns together on your futon at night. He isn't much of a drinker; he has never used drugs. The first time you had sex doggie-style, he worried you would think he was degrading you and that it was unfeminist, although thankfully he got over that one pretty fast.

Kathy has been annoyingly vocal in her concerns that he is "not the right guy for you" and that she "always pictured you with someone else," but you know this is just because she is still pissed off that when the three of you went camping, he flew into a rage and screamed at her, and feel confident that in time she will get over that grudge and learn to love him, and you will be right about that.

It would be neat and clean to say that your husband's occasional bouts of fury make you feel important—capable of arousing his deepest, uncontrollable passions—the way Angie's father's abuse made her seem more interesting and special, but that would be a lie, a false reduction of a complicated story designed to make every piece of an unwieldy puzzle fit. The truth is that nothing about your husband's temper strikes you, initially, as unusual or problematic. The foster girls you work with grew up with fathers who made them shoot the family pets if they "misbehaved," or invited friends over to fuck their daughters in exchange for drugs. The domestic violence survivors you've worked with have stories about having been held captive in cabins in the woods while their abusers placed dynamite next to their heads, or have borne babies by their fathers. In Houston, one of your close girlfriends from college is living with a man who slaps her around, and you write her a long letter about her need to value herself more and how she should not put up with that shit. Sometimes, for work, you drive around to neighboring towns and give presentations at high schools about dating violence and how to recognize it.

It does not yet occur to you that when your husband screams at his parents in a restaurant and races out onto the street, abandoning you there with them, that someday it will be you he is screaming at in public places, pushing his chair violently away from the table to stalk out. It does not yet occur to you that the way his face gets bright red and full of blind rage when he stands over you screaming during one of his "tantrums" is the way he will look someday standing over your nine-year-old daughters. These episodes happen, at first, so infrequently that you do not even consider them a significant part of your relationship. If anything, in those early days, you often roll your eyes at him when he behaves this way (which only enrages him further, which leads to more eye-rolling) and talk slowly to him as though he is a small child to be humored.

You have been around dangerous men your entire life, and they are nothing like your husband. These outbursts of his are just how men are.

What happens when the very thing that once taught you how to survive—how to escape—suddenly stands between you and your life? Not only should your "pretending" have long since fallen away as a childhood game, but your fantasies of being overpowered, punished, hurt strike you as deeply incompatible with your politics, your public persona. Your attempts to act them out with your husband have often been stilted and resulted in your feeling "humored"—in your husband talking to you in a throaty voice that doesn't resemble his and saying contrived things of the *You like it, don't you?* variety while belting you. This makes you cringe even though when you look at the words themselves (You. Like. It. Don't. You.) there is nothing inherently offensive or even (you are the one into this, after all) incorrect.

Except maybe you don't like it. What is the difference between "like" and "need"?

It's the late 1990s. Andrea Dworkin with her all-intercourse-is-rape rhetoric is fully out of fashion and Mary Gaitskill, heroin chic, and postfeminism are in. Daphne Merkin writes about spanking in *The New Yorker*, Madonna brings BDSM to the mainstream long before *Fifty Shades of Grey*, and you are very well aware that part of feminism is supposed to be sex positivity, whatever you happen to desire. But the coping mechanism that once helped you survive a hostile environment is also inextricably tied to your romanticizing things that were nothing to aspire to—Angie's life of being abused by an angry, power-hungry adult man—and transforming her pain into your private psychosexual drama.

You are ashamed, so ashamed.

The French feminists—especially Hélène Cixous and Catherine Clément—also take up the mantle of "hysteria," that condition doctors and psychoanalysts historically so adored slapping onto any woman who stepped out of line—any woman whose body manifested dis-ease with the constricted roles available to them. Cixous, who proclaims, "the hysterics are my sisters," posits them as some of the original feminist outlaws, as rebel riot grrrls (much as feminist theorists have often done of the so-called sorceresses), focusing on their upheaval of the patriarchal system rather than the upheaval of the so-called hysterics' actual bodies, which were usually mangled and ruined, vis-à-vis what is most likely an inextricable mix of gendered oppression, undiagnosed mental and somatoform illnesses not yet understood in the era, and the syphilis virus, which led men and women of the period alike to "go mad." If the hysterics were anyone's guerrilla army, they were butchered, dissected for the theories of medical men, before they could even reach the battleground.

Women's bodies, of course, have always been understood as the battleground, and sometimes the only means women had to fight with was their capacity for self-destruction. The hysterics lost their voices, walked with limps, were unable to swallow food, were sent for rest cures that shrank their lives further and made them worse. Roughly fifty years after Dr. Walter Freeman "treated" schizophrenic women (the hysteric's heirs much more so than sexy French academics like Cixous) by traveling across the United States lobotomizing as many as thirteen women in a day, Thelma and Louise would at least take a handful of men with them before driving off the cliff, but the outcome remains surprisingly similar: a body count of women.

Cixous implores all women to turn breast milk into ink, to invent a new language for female experiences inarticulatable by the Father's Tongue. And although you find holes in the appropriation of the suffering hysterics by privileged academics, writing the female body remains your battle cry: you turn in forty-page critical papers when eight pages would suffice; you produce two books in your master's program, the subject of both boiling down, perhaps, to the link between female dis-ease and disease. It is the late 1990s and you contain fucking multitudes; your breast milk would be ink if you didn't also have polycystic ovarian syndrome, which renders you infertile; you and your impassioned graduate school papers and plethora of publications would be a sign of Cixous's victory were you not also afflicted with interstitial cystitis, were you not also cutting yourself, were you not also feeling, before the age of thirty, trapped and middle-aged in your marriage. You hide behind other names: no longer Karen but now Kendra, K.C.—your (derivative of Karen in their K initial) fictional female characters. You write the truths of their bodies because the truth of your own feels too revealing.

You chronicle one doomed Ophelia after another. So, it seems, does every woman writer you love. In one way or another, every single one of your heroines drives off a cliff.

How, perhaps, could it be otherwise? How, when the very concept of *l'écriture féminin*—an idea designed to liberate you—defines the female body (bodies that comprise more than 50 percent of the human population) as outside every language we have ever known?

For almost a decade after adopting your daughters in 2001, you and your husband practice so-called vanilla sex almost exclusively . . . or, at least, if vanilla might be overstating it, at some time during this period, you throw away your spreader bar; you lose the key to your handcuffs and they sit in a forgotten drawer in your bathroom; when your husband tries to spank you, you usually stop after a few playful smacks that don't really hurt, redirecting his attention with some other sexual act you know he prefers anyway. Though throughout your twenties you chased and even seemed to tire out your husband with your desires for a more psychologically engaged kind of sex, an eroticism of the mind, a sense of play and collaboration that never quite clicked (*Dear Abby, Dear Sugar, Dear Fucking Hélène Cixous—I've had lifelong spanking fantasies, so why don't I enjoy it when my husband, who has thrown me into a wall and called me a fucking bitch in public, hits me for fun?*), after becoming the mother of daughters—in particular daughters who have already, at their earliest infancy, suffered deep ramifications of the patriarchal preference for male children—you feel a wall fall down between you and those old longings.

The first five or six years following this change are the most harmonious and uncomplicated phase of your entire marriage. You feel relaxed, relieved of a burden even. It feels incredible to no longer passive-aggressively struggle for whose sexual preferences will be given priority—to feel yourself locked in an unspoken game of granting each other sexual favors like patronizing trading cards, and to instead give yourself over to your husband's simpler tastes, the rote nature of long-married sex that holds few surprises but also the guaranteed pleasures of knowing each other's body like a road you could drive in the pitch dark. You and your husband often congratulate yourselves together on how well your sex life has survived parenthood. *Look, Angie, at my perfect life! Look, Karen, at how far I've come.*

Your desire shuts down within a year of Enzo's birth, like someone turning off a faucet. Is it lactation hormones, weight gain triggering old body issues, some mild case of postpartum depression? Or is it that this is the same year your husband's mother is diagnosed with terminal cirrhosis and cancer, the same year your mother has a heart attack and stroke, the same year your first book comes out, the same year your husband's rage begins a four-year ascent? You are thirty-eight. You blame your lowered libido on "maturation," middle age, the pressures of being in the "sandwich generation," and indeed many of your women friends express the same things happening to them. You make certain to nonetheless engage in sex regularly with your husband. You want to be a good wife. You want your husband, who seems stressed and withdrawn, to be happy. You still believe implicitly that by making him happy, you will be happy too.

What you know now: There are ways to cheat without cheating. There are signs you are not living the right life for you, even if your life looks almost unfathomably pretty and privileged compared to where you come from or in other people's eyes. There are ways the body screams truths when the voice lies. Dis-ease manifests in the bladder, in the back, in the ovaries, in the jaw. Grinding your teeth down flat until you need a night guard and then braces for your

TMJ, you nonetheless refuse to stop giving your husband (who is famously well-endowed among your friend group ever since a trip to a nude beach in Spain in the late 1990s) head, even when the dentist agrees that it may be exacerbating your TMJ and headaches; even when your girlfriends stage an intervention over drinks and tell you not to do something your body isn't accommodating well just because "men like it." Rather than taking their advice seriously, you defiantly view your perseverance as a point of pride, even as—no longer only once in a great while—your husband's voice more and more frequently joins the cacophony of male rage in your ears.

"Why can't you ever support me?" he sometimes screams when he is angry. You moved east to live with him; dropped out of your PhD program to follow him to Europe and then raise your children; you do almost all the child-rearing, cooking, coordination with teachers, doctors, parents of other children. If anyone in your household is sick, you cancel out-of-town trips for your writing, push back deadlines, stay home in deference to the fact that your husband is the one earning the money. You attend his business dinners and holiday parties, make peace with his difficult mother and drive frequently to Iowa during her illness. During the years he spends shouting this at you, you don't understand what he means—it feels genuinely, at that time, as though your and your children's lives all revolve to a significant extent around your husband's career, your husband's moods, your husband's needs.

It does not occur to you until later that what he was really screaming was *Why aren't you genuinely interested in anything I care about?* You are going through the motions of being an almost Stepfordly devoted wife, but something unsettled and bored has set in. You rarely fail to have dinner waiting for him, but when he talks about his work, about the men's group he has joined, with their "warrior names," your eyes are, more with each passing year and without your even knowing it, already on the door.

•

In her essay "Grand Unified Theory of Female Pain," Leslie Jamison discusses the fact that pain that is "performed" is "still pain," acknowledging the devastating realness of the many ways women have been oppressed, repressed, and abused, often to the point of death, throughout the centuries, both off the page and on. "The moment we start talking about wounded women," Jamison writes, however, "we risk transforming their experience from an aspect of the female experience into the element of the female constitution."

If Angie was your model for learning to hide your pain, to obscure it behind bravado and swaggering charisma, then Kathy, like a woman in a Jean Rhys novel, wears her suffering like a heavy coat she never takes off, even at parties. Sometimes you and your friend Tori privately lament that it is impossible for anyone to go more than fifteen minutes without Kathy finding a way to work into the conversation that her father blew his brains out inside their house when she was ten. She casts herself, you and Tori like to say, "as the tragic heroine of her own life." Kathy's existential sadness, until she is around forty, seems to you almost a kind of performance art for an audience that never goes home—the precise inverse of your own performed resilience, imperviousness, contentment. If Angie always seemed like flint, then Kathy is a perpetually wounded bird who (literally) bruises easily: an embodied litany of mistreatment and bad luck and windowless basement offices and public transportation and drinking alone in the dark while listening to other doomed women like Billie Holiday. Kathy often strikes you as a cautionary tale of what happens when women confuse their suffering for identity—internalizing that malaise is what makes them interesting. The more you watch her performing her (very real) pain, the more your own reflexive smile remains plastered to your face. Kathy is . . . interesting, yes—you have written a couple of stories based on her fucked-up life—but she is often seen as pathetic or desperate by men and even by her own girlfriends. If Angie taught you anything, it is to be allergic to pity.

You tell no one about the rumbling fault lines in your marriage. One night, on the porch of a friend's farm, drinking gin and tonics, Kathy asks you, "Who do you talk to about your problems?" She is asking, you know, *Who do you favor over me?* but the question throws you on a more primal level, and you stammer disclaimers and deflections, make noise about how when you're married your spouse is your primary confidant. There is something deeply discomforting to you that the real answer, just as when you began pretending to be Karen some thirty years ago and stopped crying for a decade, remains *no one.*

The year you turn forty, your pretending escalates for the first time in more than a decade of slippage, and you find yourself splintering off occasionally—usually when you are alone, but sometimes with your husband too—fragmenting into your latest novel's protagonist, Mary. It is the mania, you tell yourself, of finishing a draft; this often happens when you are in the throes of a book's completion and know you will have to leave your characters' world soon. But at the age of forty-two, on a bucket-list dream trip in Kenya with your family, you are *still* pretending to be Mary, dividing your attention between what is real and what is not, that old equator you cannot seem to stop straddling. Why has this escalated again, here in middle age? You are old enough to know that at this point you are exercising choice—that you are volitionally participating when you could just stop. But you do not stop. Instead, you breathe in the familiar air of escape while your husband screams at you on Manda's Diamond Beach, a flank of jaded islanders standing by nonplussed at seeing a woman put in her place—while your husband waves his arms and shouts and then stalks off away from you into the sand, you remember this safe house inside your head and let it in on purpose, *fuck it, fuck him.* Inside the confines of another fictional woman's skin, you cannot be hurt; you cannot be disappointed; you cannot wonder why you are putting up with behavior you orchestrated your entire life in an attempt to flee. Yes, you remember this: the oblivion, more soothing than rum and gingers, better than any drug you've ever tried. The water is always warm in here. Come in.

The options available to women who step away from patriarchal expectations: saints; sexy self-destruction artists; badasses who refuse to flinch or recant as the flames men light burn them into legend. But you aren't any of these things. You are in your forties, spending your days at Chuck E. Cheese, five to seven children trailing behind you like so many adorable ducklings. "If I had searched the entire world to find you a husband," your mother sometimes says of her practical, responsible son-in-law, "I would have picked him. Now I'll never have to worry about you."

When you ask a female colleague whether you expect too much out of marriage if you still want to actually desire your husband, she laughs almost manically and says, "Hell, yes."

"Fake it till you make it," Kathy liked to quip sardonically, until her diagnosis fell like a dark curtain and instead she sobbed, "I can't do this, I don't know how to do this, I don't want to do this anymore," every day, over and over again on the phone for four months straight until she didn't have a choice anymore, and died.

What happens when self-erasure has been the norm for so long that the You cannot find its way back to I?

The night before Kathy's death, when we were both forty-three years old, I experienced full mind and body lust for the first time since . . . when? Had I ever desired anyone with this laser-beam intensity, or rather had I been so consumed with wanting to be desired that I couldn't tell the difference? Certainly I had never wanted to eat a scab off anyone's arm, my stomach a bubbling lava of inappropriate joy even though all I'd done was talk to my Not Yet Lover across a table. I felt half-mad with burning want—if given the chance, I might have traded years off my life just to share the air in a room with him a few hours longer.

Now my best friend was dead, no more air in any room for her, no more years off her life to trade. Everyone else who loved her was home in Chicago comforting one another, while I was in another man's hotel room two thousand miles away in Palm Springs, listening to him play guitar to soothe me. He was too shy to sing in front of me, but he held me while I sobbed. I took the lorazepam I'd brought for the flight home and drank an entire bottle of red wine for the first time since college. I told inside stories about Kathy—*Is there rice involved; No matter what you do, use the word "salve" in a sentence*—broken up by periods of weeping and almost catatonic silence and frantic wondering whether I should somehow try to get a flight home in the middle of the night instead of the next morning when I was set to leave anyway.

At some point, it became clear I was not going back to my own room, and he turned out the lights and spooned me—me fully dressed and him in long johns—until I fell asleep, but we both rested fitfully, rolling together and clutching each other like drowning animals. Right before the break of morning light, I drunkenly told my Not Yet Lover that I wanted to kiss him, and he, who had missed me so much while I was in Kenya that he declared his love over email, said, "I don't think we should do that." I was scorched, though the pain of Kathy's death soon crested again and obliterated my humiliation, just as I had hoped to obliterate my pain momentarily with the taste of his mouth. The following day I got on a plane back to Chicago, every place he had held and touched like illuminated track lighting on my body, flashing the way to an exit sign on a burning plane, humming, ready to blow.

By the time I got home, however, I felt grateful at having been rebuffed. I understood it had been done out of love, the way a man in an old movie puts a woman to bed and covers her up even when he knows he could have his way with her. I had never in twenty-one years with my husband kissed or even held so intimately another man, fully dressed or not; I had never made a first move on anyone, even before marriage, always waiting to be pursued. For days after Kathy's death, when I wasn't sobbing on my stairs or trying to comfort her fiancé, I emailed my Not Yet Lover about my gratitude that he had not taken advantage of my grief—how I had not been in my right mind.

I was not in my right mind.

Of course I wasn't.

Except what if it's also true that after that day—December 5, 2011, the day my best friend died and the day I realized I was madly in love with a man not my husband—I never once felt even mildly tempted to pretend I was anyone else again?

The hysterics may be our sisters, but they are not anyone's role models. That is just another distortion of the Father's Tongue, right next to those Jean Rhys or Marguerite Duras or Kate Braverman or Sylvia Plath or Kathy Acker or Mary Gaitskill texts we revere as feminist— that electrifyingly document our feminine bodies and truths just as Cixous demanded—but that somehow ultimately confirm the patriarchal narrative that women have to be miserable to matter.

When you are a woman, you see, the cliff first saves you and then kills you.

When you are a woman, there is no primer on how to jump but not end up dead.

I am not Angie. I am also not Karen or Kendra or Mary. But they have all come to me, a Greek chorus of doomed, wild women, when Gina was not a body I could inhabit, when I needed them to survive.

When Gina was the name of the foil: the fat, cowardly girl-child who cried a lot in the background, who believed she would never have access to the heroine status granted to the Beautiful and Doomed, and who was too young to understand that club of tragic damsels as an equally toxic card trick of patriarchy: *you are special; we can't take our eyes or our cocks off you; see us watching in rapture while you burn.* When I was caged in my old neighborhood, waiting to see what girl I'd gone to school with would be raped or shot next; when I was trying to save other girls as a neophyte counselor without understanding that I needed to recover from the possible PTSD and survivor's guilt of my old neighborhood before I would be psychologically whole enough to withstand bearing witness to so much more female pain. When I was afraid of my husband's rages, but even more afraid to step out of the comfortable box in which I felt heart-poundingly grateful to have found myself at his auspices, it being so preferable to the other boxes I had known.

Days after Kathy's death, I went with my family to buy a Christmas tree.

I bought all the holiday presents as usual, sent out our electronic holiday card consisting of a slideshow of the past year, including our trip to Kenya. I sent one to my Not Yet Lover and his wife, whom I had met several times and who had always been kind to me. When Kathy's fiancé gave away her things, I took a dress I knew she loved, but it didn't fit so I sent it to my Not Yet Lover for his wife to wear as though the dress of a dead woman could make up for my having tried to kiss her husband. At night, I masturbated on the floor of the office my husband and I shared, under a skylight window in the weak moon glow, thinking of my Not Yet Lover's hip bones and crying after I came, believing I would never know the weight of his bones on mine and telling myself I should be glad.

About a month after Kathy's death, at a White Elephant party that was a tradition among our friends, we all drank too much in an attempt to turn our mourning into raucous fun, and did uncharacteristic things like give one another foot massages and dares, and I kissed a woman friend of mine I'd known since high school for thirty or sixty seconds while everyone else watched and took photos, and afterward my husband and I came home and had the most wanton, adventurous sex we'd had in at least ten years, an affirmation-of-life, no-inhibitions sex, but it felt like salt rubbed into my raw desire for my Not Yet Lover, like a lottery check that arrives at an old address too late to be cashed. Though I would try—too hard, too cruelly—to use my husband's body to fuck the desire for my Not Yet Lover out of my pores over the ensuing months, I would fail at everything except the realization that, while I had been busy plastering on a smile and trying to find happiness through making other people happy, some essential core of myself had already left the building and could not be summoned back.

By the end of February, when my Not Yet Lover came to Chicago for a conference and I picked him up at O'Hare, I got out of the car to greet him even though it was freezing, because I didn't want to miss the chance to hug him. He was staying in our basement, which my husband and I had dubbed "The Visiting Writer's Suite," and through which many touring or conference-going writers before him had passed. This time, no one was dead thousands of miles away so that I was stranded with only him as comfort; there was no longer any acceptable reason for us to hold each other all night, or really for any period at all beyond hello and goodbye hugs. So I took off my red mitten and—for reasons I couldn't explain—swept the woolly, flap-eared hat off his head to touch his newly short hair while he stood holding his guitar case and luggage in the cold. I opened the trunk of my family's SUV to put his things inside, and there in the Arrivals lane in front of bleary people waiting for shuttles and rides, he backed me up to the edge of the car and kissed me so hard that we half-fell together into the trunk.

Then we got into the car and, my mitten still off, I held his delicately ruined hand, conscious of every centimeter of our touching skin—my skin, his skin, only ours—and steered the car back toward the city.

The Counterevidence of Love

Like a stone shot out of a slingshot
In the dead of night in the dark
The slingshot could not control the stone
—Edward Hirsch

Circumstantial Evidence:

My body knows something is wrong before I figure out exactly what it is. I walk into the master bedroom to find my twelve-year-old daughters crying in my bed, side-by-side, the duvet up to their chins. It is July, consistently stuffy in the upstairs bedroom despite central air. Kaya and Mags are of the sort who often don't want to wear a coat to school in February, not the kind to need a blanket in the dead of a humid Chicago summer. More than that, though, they do not cry much, don't like overt displays of emotion. Are they sick? But something in the way they're acting makes it clear, even as I go through the motions of feeling their heads and asking if they feel all right, that sickness isn't the problem. My stomach knows already what has happened, because there is only One Thing that would explain this, but my brain doesn't want to acknowledge it, sends me on an errand to the bathroom to get them each one Ty-lenol. Still, my body is ahead of my mind. As if on autopilot, my hand scoops up my iPhone—on my bedside table, left unattended that morning while the girls watched TV—and takes it with me to the bathroom.

Notifications for the most recent text messages from my lover, which I have not yet read, do not show up on the home screen.

What is it in us that makes us pretend not to know when some-thing terrible has happened? What is it that makes us tell ourselves idiotic things like the iPhone is glitching, or that I must have seen these messages and forgotten them? I forget none of my lover's mes-sages. I read his messages over and over, which is a time-consuming task given that we email and text each other upward of fifty—sometimes more than seventy—times per day, and most of our emails, as well as maybe half of our texts, involve a great deal of scrolling down. We do not use text messages in the way they were intended to be used: *c u soon!* We have, in the five months we have been sleeping together (or the seven months since we began debat-ing sleeping together, or the year and seven months since he first declared his love, or the past twenty-five months since we became "best friends"), written tens of thousands of pages to each other, sev-eral would-be novels apiece.

I never leave my phone unattended.

Except clearly, that isn't true, as it was just there, unguarded, on my bedside table, where my daughters—who I did not take for all that interested in what their mother might be texting to one of her middle-aged friends—have obviously gone snooping, and gotten more than they could have prepared for.

How has this happened? I always delete his texts.

Except of course, I have to read them some twenty times apiece first, which means that they are not always deleted *immediately*.

I thought I was being careful. My lover claims with complete confidence that his wife would "never" go snooping on his phone; that she "isn't like that." Of course he also thinks that she has no idea we are having an affair, whereas I am certain his wife is fully aware and has simply decided to pretend otherwise, hoping it will blow over, suspecting that were she to issue an ultimatum, she might not get the answer she wants, their daily life instead becoming a mutual artifice that they volley back and forth to each other like an invisible ball across an invisible net. My lover says he knows his wife better than I do, which is indisputably true, as I know her barely at all, and that he would "know if she knew." Still, I believe with no humility of doubt that I am right.

I am a person like that: a reader of people, a knower of such things.

But what difference does that make when, like many people gifted with a certain insight about other people, this has had little bearing on my capacity to make terrible, reckless, irrevocable mistakes in my own life?

The Information:
We are a family, and it is July, the kids off school for the summer, me not teaching. Where was my husband when all of this was taking place? Maybe he was out on an errand; maybe he was watching TV downstairs? All I remember is that he couldn't have been working a full day, because we had plans to go to the beach with another couple and their children later. All I remember is that Mags would *not* come to the beach, period: she insisted on staying home. Kaya, on the other hand, though taciturn and silent, put on her suit and came along.

My stomach, on the ride to the beach, falls down a thousand successive elevator shafts. What will happen? The first question, the one looming above all others: will my daughters hate me forever? But there are other questions, too, of course. Will Kaya blurt out right here in this car what I have done? Is this how my husband will discover my duplicity? Why have I never checked whether infidelity influences child custody in the state of Illinois? Will my husband leave me and take my children away from me? Will he throw me out of the house, throw my parents out on the street, zip my children up tight with the privileges his money brings, and brand me a criminal, a bad influence? My brain spins, trying to grasp some control of the narrative, but I have no control.

I feel like vomiting while we unload the car, spread out towels and sand toys, greet our friends while I smear sunscreen on my pale, auburn-haired son. Kaya lies inert on a towel, speaking to no one. I claim the need to go to the bathroom so that I can walk a good distance away from the others—I ask Kaya if she wants to come, so that I can talk to her alone, but she declines, clearly wanting nothing to do with me. I am afraid to go to the bathroom, leaving her alone with my husband. But I said I needed to go and so I do, bringing my bag—my phone inside—with me.

It is like trying to remember what happened during a fire, while smoke clogged my lungs and I clawed at doors, trying to get out.

Did I call my lover on the phone, or did I text him? I believe I called him, though maybe I texted first to ask if it was all right to call and he said yes? We were not in the practice of calling each other unannounced. I remember hiding behind a tree, behind the concrete restroom building some far distance from our innocently bright beach towels, and telling him what had happened. I remember his guilt, his horror at being a part of something that would hurt and scar my children. He kept saying, *I'm sorry,* though my lover tends to apologize so compulsively that it is almost possible to edit out his apologies subconsciously, like when other people clear their throats or pepper conversation with "like" and "um." I remember telling him that I wasn't sure how far back in the text stream they had read, but that some of the yet-undeleted texts were much worse than the garden-variety-affair texts one might expect:

In one series, I am going to the gynecologist to get tested for STDs because I have a lump on one of my labia. It seems likely that affairs can . . . cause such things . . . even though my lover, having been in addiction recovery for many years, has been screened for every disease on the market numerous times, and has been with the same woman for nineteen years and she has no diseases. Still, I have this bump and I am nervous, and at my nervousness my lover, chronic apologizer, begins to spin that perhaps he *does* have an STD that was somehow never identified over two decades of medical testing, and has transmitted it to me, and saying how he would never forgive himself, and as is often the case, I end up, in the texts, having to talk him down and reassure him.

In the next series, I am at the gynecologist's office, and I steal two empty vials from the lab while waiting to have my blood drawn. My lover and I have an ongoing joke about wearing vials of each other's blood around our necks, which, even though the joke is half-serious, we obviously could not do given we are both married and given that these vials are as long as a human palm and not aesthetically pleasing. Still, I snatch them, and we text about each pricking our finger and exchanging our blood, having it with the other always, hiding it somewhere it won't be found, and somehow what began as a joke takes on a life of its own, transforms into an urgent need to become blood siblings.

In another, we discuss what to do if it turns out I do have an STD. I will have to tell my husband, of course, how such a thing came to pass. We decide that if this happens, I will tell my husband that I slept with my lover only *once*, on the December night Kathy died. If I say it happened the night my best friend died, I explain in the text, I will seem deranged with grief and not responsible for my actions, so my husband has some chance of forgiving me.

In the next text stream, I don't have an STD—the gynecologist proclaims that my bump is merely an ingrown hair. Even my HPV test comes back negative, which is shocking given that, prior to meeting his wife, my lover fucked more than one hundred women during his punk rock junkie days, and something like 80 percent of the population has HPV. Somehow, though, it has eluded both him and me, so we are euphoric that everything is okay, that his twenty years of medical testing was (surprise) accurate after all, and so we immediately and shamelessly begin to plan the ways we will ravage each other the next time we are together.

On the phone, behind the tree, I explain to my lover that I have to guarantee my daughters that our affair is over, and that my husband is sure to find out. My lover is crying a little but understanding. He is always understanding, a man prone to saying such things as *Whatever you need* and *Is there anything I can do?* and meaning them. Of his some hundred lovers, I have never heard him say a bad thing about any of them, excepting one he sold several guitars to visit in Europe only to have her break up with him the day of his arrival. *Why couldn't you tell me this on the phone?* my lover apparently yelled at her—the only "fight" he has ever had with a girlfriend in which he did a bunch of yelling and carrying on. *That seemed rude*, she told him, because she had money, a *lot* of money, and didn't understand that regular people don't want to save up to fly to Europe just to be dumped.

"I understand whatever you need to do," he tells me now on the phone. "I'll love you forever, whatever you decide."

This is my way out. This is the moment—after getting myself in too deep—that a door suddenly opens up in the fabric of the universe and offers itself to me. I can walk through this door, right now, and never look back. I can confess to my husband what I have done and throw myself on his mercy, make any promises that require making, and I can—despite my fears that he will throw me and my parents out onto the street—in all probability resume my life. My husband and I have been married—owning property, raising children, embroiled in each other's dysfunctional families—for a very long time. Lives are not unbound so easily. If I am contrite enough, he will probably forgive me, if for no other reason than that forgiveness is easier than ripping apart everything we've built.

An escape hatch has opened, but I can't feel relief. All I can feel is that this is the worst day of my entire life. Worse than the day Kathy died; worse than the day my mother had a stroke and I had to spoonfeed her in the ICU while she mumbled incoherently about men taking her down to hell in an elevator, and then I came home to nurse four-month-old Enzo, every energy draining from my body, every force sucking me dry. Worse than the night I learned we had lost the heartbeat of my first pregnancy, and I sobbed in the dark while my husband spooned me, his grief also palpable but never insistent or overriding my own. Worse than any of the three years in my twenties when I was suffering from interstitial cystitis and my bladder felt filled with battery acid to the point that I had started cutting myself and sometimes contemplated suicide, though that was before I became a mother and the door of suicide closed irrevocably to me. Worse than any of those things, because strokes and miscarriages and pulmonary embolisms and autoimmune conditions are uncontrollable forces in the universe and not a pain I caused. I have never in my life done a wrong of this magnitude, caused this much wreckage. To my twelve-year-old daughters, whom I promised to give a good life; to my husband, who made such a life logistically possible; to my son, not even yet in first grade and believing he is safe. My lover, having been an addict, is familiar with self-loathing, but this level of wanting to rip off my own skin, to turn back the clock, is new to me. My muted footsteps, padding back to the blankets of my family near the shore, thud in my own ears like *I did this. I did this.*

Plea Bargains (Unsubmitted):
For the past five months, since we kissed at O'Hare and escalated our emotional affair to something explosively physical, I have been

telling my lover that his wife and my husband have the right to know what we are up to so that they can make an informed decision as to whether they wish to stay with us. I'm not sure what this "informed decision" might look like, I admit. An open marriage? A pass to visit each other once a year, like in *Same Time Next Year*, one of Kathy's favorite films? Intensive marriage counseling with the intent of shutting the affair down and everyone, by mutual agreement, concurring that it was all for the best and helped put our marriages back on track? I can't get past the part where "we should tell them," because my lover doesn't want to tell his wife, and so honor among thieves takes this option off the table: it is clear that neither he nor I can confess without the consent of the other, and potentially bring both marriages crashing down.

My lover's wife is sick with fibromyalgia and chronic fatigue, and the reason he doesn't want to come clean is that he does not want to "cause her more pain," which is obviously not consistent with the fact that he is fucking another woman, but there it is. That is who we are—my lover and I, and of course much of the human race—capable of both compassion and cruelty. We did not invent infidelity, even though when you are in the midst of it, it feels like you did. We did not invent shadow selves or double lives or Neruda's "dark things" loved in secret, "between the shadow and the soul." Much of the literary canon to which we have both devoted our lives revolves around forbidden love and its consequences. "Adultery is a most conventional way to rise above the conventional," as Nabokov said.

My husband is not sick. He is an able-bodied man who has most of his hair and a successful career. There is no logical reason he should have to contend with a wife who is in love with another man and cheating on him. But our beautiful Enzo, constantly smiling and gifted with what my husband and I sometimes dub "the mental illness of happiness," is only six. Mags and Kaya were abandoned in a train station in China at 3.5 pounds apiece, and I cannot bring myself to fracture their family and their sense of belonging once again. My disabled parents are financially dependent on us—and by "us," I mean my husband, because I could better support a family by working at McDonald's than on what I make per year. *Our son is so young.* So slowly—over the past five months—I have started telling myself a different story, convincing myself that not telling my husband is *for everyone's good.* Thanks to my silence, my children have an intact home, my husband and I both get to see them every day, and my parents are secure and comfortable. Maybe my long-distance affair can just be a secret within myself, something I keep just for me. Would that be the worst thing anyone has ever done?

These are the stories I tell myself now. This is who I've become.

Establishing Motive:

Ladies and Gentlemen of the Jury, you may be asking yourselves: *Did this dumb bitch leave her phone unattended on purpose, half-hoping her husband would bust her?* Might I have been seeking to relieve myself of the burden of my guilt without having to actually take action? I don't remember even fleetingly wishing to be caught, and I certainly hope, in the case of a subconscious desire, I would still have been savvier about orchestrating the proper audience for a "discovery." That said, looking back on my actions, at my level of carelessness, I, too, am suspicious of the defendant in this story—of what that woman's intentions were.

That July day, however, my daughters crying silently in the bed, my brain is merely animalistically dividing into a split screen: on the first screen, computations spin as to what could be upsetting my daughters so terribly, since it cannot be—*oh god please don't let it be*—that they have found my texts. On the second screen, the one smart enough to know that there are no other computations, fight or flight takes over and my only coherent thought, flashing repeatedly, is: *How the hell do I get out of this?*

Strategy #1, the Angry Man Defense:
Less than a month before that terrible day at the beach, on another continent entirely, my friend Jun, with whom our family was staying in London, took me aside and told me that my husband seemed "so angry," scary, like he might be violent. She asked, "Are you safe?"

I was taken aback by her question, even though I knew the incident to which she was referring. Earlier in the day, my husband had shouted at me—and in fact at her—on a public street, in front of our combined children, because the directions Jun insisted on taking to the Tate museum were wrong. Nobody was listening to him about what needed to be done, so he screamed at us, and stormed off to walk at some distance from us, silently fuming for the next several hours.

I'd been embarrassed, but the truth was that my husband had been doing this kind of thing for so long that it had not occurred to me that Jun or her daughter might be alarmed. That day in London, it had already been twenty years since the time he'd screamed at Kathy on a camping trip in New Mexico. It had been eleven years since he'd slammed me into a wall in China while we were there to adopt our daughters in 2001, and I thought for the first time, *Oh god what have I done?* We'd had our share of fights, even of prolonged marital discord before then, but that was the first moment I felt trapped. How could I expect to adopt my daughters if their new parents broke up on the trip? Surely no one would let me leave the country with them. And so I did not dash out of our hotel room for the airport. I stayed and worked my hardest to forget.

It had been some five years since, driving home from his parents' home in Iowa in the early years of his mother's illness, I said something that set my husband off as we were parking at a rest stop.

He unfastened Enzo from his car seat roughly, shouting at me about the something, yanking Enzo out of the seat. When Enzo began wailing, I grabbed for the baby, infuriating my husband further. He often accused me of "judging" him, thinking I was better than he was—of not accepting responsibility for the ways in which my behavior "triggered" his rage. We went into the rest stop, KFC and Taco Bell and Subway beckoning, still sniping at each other, me carrying Enzo, our daughters trudging behind us. I thought the worst had already happened, but once in the rest stop my husband escalated, swearing loudly at me while the other road-trippers listened with horror or interest, averting their eyes. And then he *left*, still screaming, waving his arms as he sometimes did when the fury took him: Mags and Kaya and I standing in the rest stop alone, Enzo on my hip. Kaya and Mags were crying, though within a year or two they would no longer cry in the face of their father's outbursts but begin responding with rage of their own, meeting him fury for fury with a ferocity I could never muster. Even that day, I tried to behave as though everything were normal as I bought the children lunch and we took it outside, unsure whether we would find the car in the parking lot or gone.

Ladies and Gentlemen of the Jury, he had, my husband, left us the car. Maybe it is that simple: why I never left. The anger was like a demon inside him that he alternately hated, justified, and feared, but he was a man who, even when afflicted, would leave us the car.

I buckled the children in and pulled out of the large parking lot, with no idea where my husband had gone. There were not many roads at the rural rest stop, and soon enough we found him walking along one, still, as we approached him from behind, talking to himself in agitation. Often after fights, he would mutter things under his breath: things he wished he had said or self-admonishments or both, stewing. I pulled the car alongside him, and although we were not even in the state of Illinois, he waved me on, shouted some more, refused to get in the car. *Should* I have driven away then? Our son was not injured, had long since stopped weeping. My husband's toxic mother was terminally ill and he was in a fog of grief he couldn't articulate. Should I have just driven on, back to our home in Chicago, called a lawyer, changed the locks? I did none of those things. I slowed the car to a crawl, following his jerky steps, imploring him to get in until he did.

Two years before our London trip: my husband, shouting and swearing at me while running through the halls of an Embassy Suites in Manhattan, the night we got the call to say his mother had died. I'd nudged him in the middle of the night to ask him to shift position because he was snoring, and he exploded, screaming, waking the children, who were used to his explosions but started crying anyway, stuck in such close quarters with us in a hotel room rather than safely downstairs like at home. Looking back: how *could* I have woken him on the night his mother died, to complain that I couldn't get to sleep, to tell him to roll over? Maybe I deserved his wrath for being so selfish. But our children did not deserve to hear him screaming that way, cursing like the world had conspired to do him wrong, on the night their grandmother died or on any night. If I behaved badly, the healthy, reasonably functional thing to do would have been to wait until we were alone before yelling at me.

He never hit me. Never in twenty-two years had he hit me. (Why do I feel such a need to stipulate that? Am I trying to protect him, or myself, from what you will think if he did?) Yet could anyone have faulted me, really, if I had left after any of these incidents? If I had said simply, *I tried, I'm sorry, this just isn't okay and I can't live like this.* Could even *he* have blamed me, deep down?

Correlation vs. Causality:
What is the relationship, though, between a sequence of events and an ultimate result? Am I saying that I would never have slept with

my lover had my husband never slammed me into that wall in 2001? No, alas, I am not saying that at all. I suspect I still would have. I suspect that there is not really a scenario in which I could have met my lover and maintained faithfulness to another man.

But maybe that is only a romantic construction. The past is inextricable from the present. It cannot be undone.

I wanted so badly, for half of my life, to heal my husband's mother-wounds. I wanted to love him so well that the cyclone inside him would still. Suffice it to say that from the get-go this was both an impossible task and one I failed. Did I confuse loyalty with fear, intimacy with dependency, unconditional love with a savior complex? Or were both things true, equally, at different times?

I stayed too long. I stayed long enough to become the Asshole in the story.

Breaking and Entering:
One terrible action begets another. The first time my daughters leave the house without me, I see Mags's diary lying around as it often is, and I do what I have never done before—what I have never even been tempted to do before, being a writer, a compulsive journal keeper myself, and valuing that sacred privacy without question—I open it.

I found out something terrible about Mommy. She did something really bad.

Fear makes people stupid. When I read these words, I actually tell myself that perhaps they have not read my texts at all, merely found the pack of American Spirit I've hidden in the pocket of my jean jacket. I quit when I was thirty, but since the affair, both my lover and I have started smoking again. It began with our finding a cigarette on the floor of a diner together, untouched, a siren song just for us the night before Kathy died. We lit it in the parking lot and passed it between us, fingers brushing, our mouths touching that way first, delirious with intimacy.

When I finally ask my daughters directly, I ask them—yes, I truly ask them—whether what they found out is that I have a hidden pack of cigarettes, or whether it is "the other thing, on my phone."

It turns out they have also found the cigarettes. It turns out that you can hide things from your preoccupied spouse, who has grown inured to your presence, but you cannot hide things from your daughters, who watch you, who shadow you, who memorize you, trying to learn how to be.

"But it's the other thing," one of them says.

We are on our way to the grocery store, but I have pulled over to the side of the road with one in the back seat and the other shotgun, captive, forced to talk to me. Mags has already started to cry, knowing I have tricked them into being alone with me and am now going to say things they don't want me to say aloud. They clearly want nothing more than to pretend this had never happened, but how can I allow them that? Part of me wants nothing more—I have deleted all the texts already—part of me wants nothing more than to do what I believe my lover's wife is doing, and just tacitly and mutually all agree without words to bury our heads in the sand and stay very still, avoiding a minefield. The other part cannot stop myself from forging on.

"Do you know who he is?" I ask them.

"I think so," one answers.

They first met my lover a year and a half ago when he stayed in our basement, and then again five months ago. Everyone in my household knows him. Enzo was three when they first met, and they took to each other instantly, Enzo following him around the house and sometimes even out onto the porch. He had even come with me to preschool drop-off, on a day there was a case of lice and drop-off was an elaborate affair with things being cased in Hefty bags inside the children's cubbies. My Not Yet Lover and I then went to breakfast, where he talked about his regrets over never having children.

Neither he nor his wife had wanted any for a long time, until it seemed possible that maybe they did, but she was in her mid-forties by then and ill and it was lucky they had no kids, because she was in bed most of the time now and could not take care of a child. She could not make it to a friend's play or reading on time, or keep a dinner reservation, or sometimes make a flight or check out of a hotel by the deadline. He had already been his wife's caregiver for several years, and adding a child to the mix would have undone him and he knew it. His bipolar was of the ultradian type—rapid, rapid cycling—and even medicated there were times when it was all he could do to take care of himself, teaching, publishing books, writing and recording music, touring with his band, doing the things his wife couldn't do anymore around their house, though he did some of them badly and things had fallen into disrepair. *I would have wanted to have a baby with you*, he told me, but remarkably this comment didn't strike me as particularly odd. He is that sort of person—the kind who appears to have no boundaries at first, who you have to get to know incredibly well to understand that his guileless openness is in part a defense to protect the deeper, more closely guarded things about which he is almost pathologically private.

I thought of having a baby with him, then, and of what he and I would look like at school functions, with his frayed jeans and tattoos and unlaced banged-up black boots and the retro-punk chain connecting his wallet to his belt loop. It seemed an amusing, tender thought: a path not taken. It did not seem to me a Serious Thing.

Now I ask my daughters to name him, and his name is harsh on their lips, an obscenity.

I don't want to be a danger to you, he wrote to me before we were even lovers, after his Kenyan love confession. But by the time someone is saying, *I don't want to be a danger to you*, it is of course already too late. Did I honestly not know that at the time?

Here in the car with my daughters, there is not one single choice

I can make that would be the Right Thing. The Right Thing would be to have never had an affair. The Less Wrong Thing would be to have had a better fucking password on a phone that I never let out of my sight. Here in my car pulled to the side of the road, to my half-weepy, horrified daughters, I say a series of cowardly things. That I have been having a terrible time since Aunt Kathy died. That sometimes grief makes you do regrettable things—causes you to make mistakes.

"Fine," Kaya says. "But if you were going to make a mistake, did it have to be with a pervert?"

"It's over," I tell them. "I love you two and your brother more than anything or anyone in the world. I ended it. I've already told him."

"Was he upset?" one asks.

"He was relieved." This seems like a lie, but maybe there is truth to it, too. A cloud of torrential guilt, parting.

Now what? Now what?

"Do you want me to tell your father?" I ask. A manipulative question, I see that now—the forcing of my disruptive, wildly ricocheting balls into their court—but in the moment I've lost my sense of anything other than preserving stability, the status quo. If I tell my husband, I think he will forgive me in time, but there is no guarantee. Marriages have ended over far less, and ours is already long-strained, fragile. The truth is: I have been with my husband for twenty-two years and in some ways I know him better than I have ever known anyone, and in other ways, he is a completely unpredictable stranger to me.

What if I tell him and the marriage ends? What if that happens "because" my daughters spied on my phone and discovered a secret, and to prevent them from carrying that secret, I instead make them carry the fact that our lives have all been blown apart as a consequence of their discovering my lie?

My fear permeates the car with a primal, animal smell; my words sound straightforward but are loaded with codes. Even as I am promising that I am willing to tell their father everything, isn't it already implicit that I will do so only if they demand it of me? Otherwise why are we here, my daughters averting their eyes as I interrogate them about what they know, what they want—why am I not having this conversation with my husband instead of two twelve-year-olds? Finally, one shrugs defiantly, mutters that she doesn't care one way or another what I confess or don't: it's my business, my problem. The other, having heard my insistence that the affair is over, mumbles something like, *Why would you tell him? He gets really mad.*

And it is that easy. That easy to hear this small offering and seize it: case closed.

"But I don't want you two carrying this secret," I protest, with the desperation of a woman has already gotten what she wanted— one terrifying door slamming shut—only to watch a new door swing open to reveal yet another loaded minefield. And so I grasp for the only thing I know how to say truthfully, directly: "I also don't want you two lording this over me so that I can't parent you normally because you have dirt on me. I don't want to worry every second that if I piss you off or don't give you what you want, you'll tell your father. If he's going to hear about this, it should be from me."

"Jesus," Kaya says, like it has just occurred to her that her mother might be a ridiculous person. "We aren't going to tell him!"

And Mags: "Seriously. What would we say? We barely even talk to him."

What do you do when behind Door Number 1 is the biggest mistake of your life, and behind Door Number 2 is the other biggest mistake of your life?

Now, from where I'm telling this story, I see clearly that the better choice, the only choice, was the one that was at least honest. Now, from where I am telling this story, I bear the knowledge that in my biggest moment of truth, I chose the wrong door.

"Okay," I tell my daughters—my girls who imprinted on me at nine months of age, who I had to carry on my hips to use the toilet throughout their toddlerhood; my daughters who trusted me to be a better person than I am. "It's over, and he agrees and is relieved. You know he's married too, so he was already feeling guilty. It's over, and if I'm not going to tell your father then we probably shouldn't talk about it much among ourselves."

"I don't want to talk about it!" one accuses, and the other on her heels, "You're the one talking about it!"

For the next thirty-three months, we never bring it up again.

Prosecution Exhibit A, the Bad Mother:

How did I get here? I have spent my entire life trying to be a good daughter, a good friend, a good wife, a good mother. Now I have joined those Other ranks: the mothers vilified by history, from Medea to Queen Gertrude to Mary Tyler Moore's brilliantly chilly portrayal of Beth in *Ordinary People* to my own dead mother-in-law, who so scarred my husband. I don't want to be here—*please, someone, take my name off this list*—it's all been some kind of mistake. How do I find my way back to some less wrong door, a path to repairing the damage I have done?

One blinding truth: I love my children more than anything else. If I had to choose—in a world where I had to choose only one thing—I would choose my children over either my husband or my lover.

Of course, we no longer live in such a world, that world of Mamah Cheney running off with Frank Lloyd Wright; that world in which a woman's choice of another man over her husband meant she must abdicate her children and run off in exiled disgrace. Though the stats vary by year, nearly half of American marriages end in divorce. Conservative estimates indicate that 30–60 percent of all married Americans have engaged in at least one act of infidelity. Are all these people dooming their children to terrible lives? My husband, my lover, and I all come from intact families in which during our childhoods our parents were so unhappy that perhaps they *should* have gotten divorced.

Wait: when did we start talking about divorce? What divorce?

Ten Counterarguments:

Marriage is a private island. Its language does not translate to the common tongue of any mainland. Every marriage has its own dialect, its own logical paradigms, its own implicit bylaws. A relationship cannot be by and large "happy" for more than seventeen years and then divide cleanly in two until it is reduced to its worst moments. Perhaps anyone who has been with the same partner for nearly a quarter century could easily make a list of "justifications" for the loss of love, the slow erosion toward a blank space where closeness used to be that sometimes opens up to infidelity.

The simple truth is that my husband was an "angry man" when I met him, when I married him, when I decided to adopt and then have children with him, so I can scarcely, decades later, point a finger at his anger as a radical impetus for . . . anything. The fact is that for a very long time, I fully believed that the good of being with my husband outweighed any bad. I loved him, with all the complications that implies, and although I'd had some mild flirtations, I had never considered myself remotely "in love" with any other man. My husband was mine, for all his imperfections, and I his, for all of mine. We were a Given.

There is the Angry Man narrative, the Bad Mother narrative, even the Cheating Whore and They Were Never Compatible to Begin With narratives, but there is also this:

1) The time in our twenties, when I was claustrophobic while getting an MRI and my husband came and sat at a chair next to my feet and held my toes, one by one, each for one minute, to signal to

me how much time was passing and how soon I would get out, and how at that moment, he seemed like the kindest person I had ever met, and I believed that no one could ever know me better or care for me as he did.

2) Making love in the garden of our cliffside hotel on La Gomera in the Canary Islands, after dark, small pieces of gravel digging into my hands and peacocks still roaming in a distance; making love on our hotel's beach chairs after midnight in Mexico, and though we went to Mexico often and I no longer recall clearly which trip or even which part of the country, I remember our collusion, our thrill; making love in the walk-in closet of a friend's vacation home in Green Lake, Wisconsin, with the voices of our other friends benignly discussing celebrity gossip magazines and where to go for dinner drifting through the door; making love in our first, garret apartment in Amsterdam, me straddling his lap on the love seat with Tori Amos's "Blood Roses" in the background; making love on the staircase of our first house in Chicago, when my husband was home briefly from his work overseas and I had come fresh from the salon, hair blown out, bikini line waxed, mani-pedi'd and decked in red underwear to greet him. The way it seemed, having met so young, that we'd grown up together, both of us running from everything that had come before each other, moving too fast for that old pain to grasp at our ankles, dashing into our shining future holding hands.

3) Our overlapping laughter on a train departing Marrakech, two years before we adopted our daughters. We had outrun some scammer on the make, trying to get us to pay him for some imaginary guide service. The man had tried to follow us onto the train but had been evicted, and as the train pulled away, my husband and I fell into each other cracking up, high on our escape. "I live by my wits," my husband said at one point, and it was hilarious because he was so methodical, so careful, so practical—because he didn't live by his wits at all, really, despite being brilliant. It was funny because it was

so untrue, yet in this instance had been, and had worked. We were fellow adventurers, partners in crime, there on that train, though in our real lives in Chicago, we would soon become fewer and fewer of those things.

4) Him walking with Mags on his shoulders, weeks after our return from China, tall and young with the weak spring sunlight shining on him like an understated spotlight. Looking at my husband with whom I had spent the last eleven years of my life (yes, the same husband I had weeks before contemplated leaving in China before adopting our daughters), in the dingy strip mall parking lot of Babies R Us, and believing that every single thing I had ever dreamed of had come true—that no one in the history of the world could ever have been as happy as I was. That this was exactly what I had always wanted my life to be.

5) Coming downstairs in the mornings on weekends, when he would "let me sleep in," to find both girls, maybe three years old, happily sitting on their father's chest while they watched a *Star Wars* marathon on TiVo, and feeling so giddy that I couldn't get it up to protest that maybe *Star Wars* wasn't toddler-friendly.

6) We were relaxed parents in that way: casual, informal, and a little 1970s about such things, and yeah, I liked that too.

7) Spending weeks scouting out a secret grotto near my husband's suburban office, bringing objects of significance to decorate it, finding a pastor, making a reservation at a nearby hotel, and then trying to trick my husband into a "hike" to the hidden grotto (even though I was wearing a skirt), where the pastor was waiting to renew our vows on our ten-year anniversary. See us in the photos of that day, our smiles shining, my husband's eyes mildly stunned to find himself with a wife fond of grand gestures and romantic excess—a wife who writes him love poems and throws him complicated surprise parties with colleagues from work he didn't know I'd even heard of. See him there, arm casually around me, knowing why he

loves me, feeling loved in return. If I went back to that grotto now, would there still be some trace of us—some object of our history, now wrecked from a decade of turbulent Midwestern weather—left behind to remind me of who we were then?

8) Weekends in which my husband and Enzo had video game marathons, built Lego, dashed out for trips to the neighborhood barber to get cheap haircuts, or spent whole days exploring the Museum of Science and Industry with geeked-out pleasure. How I swelled with gratitude and relief over their easy, seemingly effortless bond, the kind my husband had struggled to maintain with Kaya and Mags as they grew beyond their toddlerhood and—ironically similar in their reserved, introverted, and hot-tempered nature—began to clash with each other. I thrilled to see my husband experience a child who lavished love upon him guilelessly and without self-consciousness; a child who ran squealing toward the door when he returned from work, and though my husband and I were having problems, there was nonetheless a sense of our family now having a place for everyone, and that our daughters long-standing favoring of me had been smoothed over by the ways Enzo—whom his sisters treated like their beloved baby too—united us all under a single banner of Family.

9) Dancing with our children in a château in the Loire Valley. The children had thrown rose petals around the room to surprise us for our nineteenth wedding anniversary, and were blaring the Smiths' "How Soon Is Now?" because their father loved that song, and they were too young to understand that its lyrics are all about unbearable loneliness and not particularly applicable to a celebration. It was June 26, 2012, the first trip to Europe we had ever made with all three of our children, and our first time in France, the country where my husband and I first met. Although only days prior, Jun had confronted me about my husband's potential violence, now we were all safe from her meddling here in the French

countryside; now we were all laughing and shamelessly waving our arms in the air and the moment, frozen in time, is perfect: is better than if the song had been appropriate, even. In some list of the Greatest Moments of My Life up to 2012, this would be in the top ten.

10) Hold on, what is this last story doing in my husband's and my Greatest Hits montage? It doesn't belong there—not really. Because as I am dancing, I have already been sleeping with my lover for four months.

The prosecution rests.

Strategy #2, the True Love Defense:
The night before my daughters found the texts between me and my lover, I'd hidden in that same master bedroom where I would find them crying, headphones plugged into my iPhone listening to a song my lover had written and recorded for me. My heart surged like it could power cities, my legs sparking and weak, as they always were when I spoke to him . . . or thought of him . . . or read his words. *I have not gone longer than a minute without thinking of you in months*, I had written to him recently, and it was no exaggeration. I was consumed. Even his mumbled *Okay* on the recording, before beginning the song, moved me. I felt undone, gutted, flayed open, overflowing, unseemly—though in my daily life I seemed to be conducting myself normally. No one had ever written a song for me, and it intoxicated me. To be Suzanne, to be Sara. I sat cross-legged on the chaise as far from the door as possible, my headphones on to keep the sound of him private despite the room being empty, his voice and guitar vibrating into my body, suffused.

In the montage of *the Great Moments of My Life up to 2012*, this, too, is in the top ten, though like dancing to "How Soon Is Now" atop rose petals, it is tinged with dishonesty and secrecy, and

I've started to lose track of whether this makes a moment better or worse.

What do you say I call this one early, then? Let's face it: nobody wants to hear the True Love Defense anyway.

Coerced Confession:
What if I tell you, here, that even my retelling contains both purposeful and unintentional holes? That only one of my daughters was actually in the car with me that day I pulled to the side of the road, while the other and I had already had a more prolonged interaction about my texts, my secret affair, inside our home, in private? What if I tell you that I have put them both in the car not only as a writerly device, to avoid two "scenes" that cover the same repetitive ground, but to protect my daughters' privacy about who said what—that I have abridged, mixed up, blended their words or left them undesignated to get to the bottom line of "plot" without further dragging them into the spotlight? What if, too, I no longer trust my memory, and have had to text them—now at college—to confirm that certain things happened the way I remember; what if I admit, even, that I didn't initially *recall* just one being in the car and that only in our texts from separate states, years later, do I recollect that basic fact?

If my memory of these events is so clouded by trauma, shame, and fear, then what can I assume about the memories of two girls who were not even yet in high school?

Or maybe none of that matters—who was in the car, who was at home—if the end result was still nearly three years of silence. Like a family orchestrating itself around the collusive denial of one member's addiction—like the dynamics of my husband's family growing up amid his mother's drinking—what came to characterize us most, even when we were laughing, even when we were celebrating holidays or on family vacations, even when we stood with our arms around one another posing for photographs that presented a curated image of Family, were the things we didn't talk about, the things we never said.

And in those things, my husband never got a vote. His life forged on, now with three members of his family holding knowledge to which he had no access. Maybe all that matters is that during all the time I was worrying about what this secret would do to my relationship with my daughters, I should have been worrying about what it would do to his.

Closing Statements:

The night I realized that something crucial was broken in my marriage occurred about three years before my affair began. We were visiting my husband's parents during my mother-in-law's four-year illness. Things were never good during visits to my in-laws— my husband tended to revert to a sulky, silent version of himself from childhood, and sometimes, particularly before his mother's diagnosis, loud, vitriolic fights broke out between him and his parents or his brother (or his brother and their parents, or his mother and me, and so on . . .). On that visit, his mother was already dying, though, if far more slowly than Stage 4 cancer combined with late-stage cirrhosis would seem to indicate. She was still active enough that we were able to leave our sleeping children with my husband's parents and go out for a date night to the one restaurant in town we loved: a Thai place with shockingly good sticky rice and mango and a cute shop of imported goods in the back.

Things were already in a state of disrepair. My husband had joined a men's group the year of Enzo's birth, the sort that bang drums in the woods and have warrior names, and his conversation had started to take on a scripted quality such as "My need is that you _____, but my want is that you _____," and "My judgment is _____," and it was making my skin crawl in a way that made us both unhappy. Like joining AA or starting graduate school, involvement in this men's group made some of the men's marital relationships stronger, and left others floundering, with the noninvolved partner no longer recognizing her spouse, feeling someone cultlike and dogmatic taking the place of the old familiar. My husband loved the group and had tried to involve me by inviting me to ceremonies or suggesting I do a weekend with their women's chapter, but I had no desire to do any of these things, and I was at best tolerating his newfound behavior and hobbies, resentful over the erosion of the man I had chosen to marry: the man he was trying his hardest to no longer be.

The thing was: for a group he had now been in for some three years, an organization that was supposed to help men get in touch with themselves, the results had been . . . mixed. Since his mother's cancer diagnosis, my husband had grown increasingly withdrawn, having explosions far more often than in the past so that I was walking on eggshells, and then, in what he called my "morally superior way," judging his men's group as not being successful if his behavior was more volatile than ever. He was doing constant "work on himself," but things just kept unraveling. For a couple of years now, he'd been obsessed with global famine—with how the world was going to face a massive environmental crisis within the next five to ten years that would weed out much of the earth's population. He talked about buying land, becoming self-sustaining, saving cash, all the things we needed to do to protect the children and ourselves from this approaching Armageddon. My husband was an intimidatingly intelligent man with a tendency to be nicknamed things like "Michael Jordan" at any company he joined. He also read science journals voraciously and claimed it was already too late to turn back—that before our children were grown, the crisis would hit.

He was scaring the living fuck out of me.

My need is that you <u>stop talking about the end of the world</u>, but my want is that you <u>start acting like the guy I married</u>.

My judgment is that <u>if you and I met now, we would never even end up on a date, much less with three children together</u>.

We were seated upstairs in the cavernous warehouse-styled restaurant at our familiar Iowa date-night spot with aesthetically pleasing hardwood floors and ceiling fans. We sat at our table, ready to order drinks, and I looked at my husband, at his blue eyes that at times were like dull glass and at other times sharp, deep sea, and I begged him, *Please can we not talk about the end of the world tonight?* Please.

Please can we just have a normal dinner? Can we just have fun?

I could tell he was irritated, but he agreed.

It lasted five minutes. Maybe ten. Maybe I'm lying (we have certainly established that I am capable of lying) and it lasted an hour.

The dinner ended in tears. I could not pinpoint exactly when it had become true that my husband and I were no longer capable of going on a walk or for a drink or to dinner without discussing the imminent collapse of humanity. I knew only that it had started quite some time ago and become pervasive enough that I had to beg in advance for a one-night respite, which apparently I was not to be granted. It was not even that I didn't believe him, although that night I played Devil's advocate, as I often did. But what was it that he wanted from me—for our lives? His work lay in cities, consumed most of his time. We did not own or approve of firearms; we were not farmers—I could barely keep a tomato plant alive. Nor were we policy makers or environmental activists on the front lines, throwing our bodies in front of natural resources to save the planet. Were we supposed to defend our hypothetical land, our imaginary crops in this apocalyptic future—aim a barrel at starving neighbors trying to steal our food? Where was all of this supposed to unfold anyway, when it bore no resemblance to our reality? If the horror was all so inevitable, I argued relentlessly, why couldn't we just try to live our lives in the moment, snatch what joy we could, hope (knowing how facile I must sound to him) for the best?

What does it mean to love unconditionally? Are you obligated to love someone when you are experiencing their behavior as emotionally abusive? Is emotional abuse real if the cause is grief or a mental health issue? Can something be a mental health issue and potentially true at the same time? Was it up to me to demand that my husband get help, when he was already spending hours every week working on himself through his men's group? Was it just more of my judgmentalness that I would dare demand a fun night out when, according to my genius husband, the world was ending?

One year, one month, one night, one dinner, you are just an ordinary longtime married couple with some problems, like everyone else. Then abruptly you blink, and the termites have attacked the foundation of your home, and although you kept thinking you could manage it, you kept finding small makeshift solutions that seemed to patch things up for a while, though you kept thinking you had it under control, suddenly it is too late.

We went to marriage counseling. We both liked our therapist; the sessions seemed constructive. My husband even had an epiphany about his temper eventually—shortly before Kathy died—and, with the determination of a man who has accomplished most everything he ever set his mind to, his behavior began to normalize. Although his outbursts didn't end entirely, they reverted back to some earlier stage of frequency so that it was no longer rational for me to claim that I was going through every day "afraid." We had normal conversations again. He stopped talking incessantly about doomsday scenarios. It isn't that I wasn't relieved—I was. After four years of my heart pounding daily, I no longer lived in an emotional war zone. But four years is a long time, even in a twenty-two-year relationship. Neither my husband nor I was quite who we'd been when Enzo was first born, before both of our mothers' health went off the rails. I tried, like Kundera's young man in "The Hitchhiking Game," to summon back my love, my empathy—to remember who my husband and I were supposed to be to each other—but I could not call back the way I'd felt about him when I moved to the east coast to be at his side, or in the Babies R Us parking lot, or that day in the grotto. And instead of being upfront about that and letting the chips of our altered marriage fall where they might, I turned to another man.

So I've promised my daughters that my affair is over, that our family is the most important thing in my world. They believe me, or feign belief to shut me up, and everything is supposed to proceed as normal now. But alongside the fact that I would choose my children above either my husband or my lover, another fact is emerging, inescapable, the only other thing I know to be utterly, unquestionably true:

Between my husband and my lover, I would choose my lover on every level—emotional, psychological, physical—every time.

Ladies and Gentlemen of the Jury, this is what it's like to know you're going to blow. To know even as you are making vows of fidelity that you are no longer capable of permanently fulfilling them. To know that no matter which path you choose, you are going to hurt some of the people you love most—to know you will hurt yourself, even if you no longer make that list of those deserving of your love. This is what it's like to know that the only way to have avoided what is now inevitable wreckage would have been to deny yourself this affair to begin with—to have chosen to remain the woman you once were, and to realize you don't want to go backward and be that woman again, even if she was a better person than you are now. This is what it is to have bitten the apple, and to understand for the first time why female desire and knowledge are the most feared and demonized forces in history. This is what it's like to be a destroyer of worlds: that woman, that apple, that serpent, all at once. Even if your Eden was partially imaginary, this is what it's like to watch the dream of it fade forever into the mist and to want to turn back the clock, to want to return, but also to never want to return, to ache to keep running. This is what it's like to have feared your entire life becoming your martyr of a mother, and to instead have become the monster under your children's bed.

This is what it's like to choose love.

Embers

This is a work of fiction. No person in it bears any resemblance to any actual person living or dead, etc., etc. London does not exist.

— Graham Greene

My lover lay on a dirty mattress on the floor, naked of course. His desert cabin was already scorching in April, swamp cooler not quite working, everything covered in a fine layer of dust that swept without mercy through the rickety windows. The picturesque pot-bellied stove aside, a snuff film would not have looked out of place at that cabin. Sweat made grit cling to his bare skin, while I kept in motion, clean but for my knees when I'd straddled his face, tightened my thighs around his head until he gasped for air while I came.

How we had waited for this day. Our affair was less than two months old—four days together in California, so far from my real life, seemed a miracle that might never recur. How we'd rhapsodized; how we'd plotted; how we'd planned.

I wore my nana's vintage garter belt that had never fit my mother, passed right to me. My fishnets were torn; the boots he'd been licking had dried and bore no trace of him on their smooth Italian leather. I'd be wearing them later to a party in L.A., and already

I understood that voltage would run through my body every time I thought of this afternoon, of his tongue, his mouth. I had never burned a man before (I had never fucked a man's mouth with the heel of my boot before; I had never clipped a wrist cuff to a thigh cuff before; I had never used a violet wand before; I had never known intimacy so beyond the domain of ego or language before), and his hand, just below his knuckles where I'd marked him, still sparked embers. Nothing but raw, open flesh yet, still we had been prematurely referring to it as Our Scar all day.

My heels clicked across dusty tiles before I scoured his bag for the unopened American Spirit pack strewn among cuffs, crop, metal clips. I lit one and brought it back to the mattress to share. I'd forgotten to untie him. There was no place to rest the smoke, so I simply held it to his mouth and let him drag. He had once gone eleven years without smoking, but he sucked in hungrily, exhaled as I brought the taste of him to my lips. He said, "I really shouldn't be doing this," and we laughed until we were snorting.

"You mean the cigarette, right? What else could you possibly mean?"

He reopened the scar before I saw him again, four months later, after I'd already ended our affair. I never got to see it in its original state, whole. "I wanted it bigger," he explained in my dark Chicago gangway, my husband upstairs and his wife in the basement just below our feet, waiting for him. We'd planned this visit when the affair was still in full bloom, as a kind of proof to ourselves that we could be "very strange best friends" and not let it impact our marriages, our roles in an overlapping literary community, but that was all over now. Since I'd ended it, my lover had grown obsessed with the schedule of when my husband and I had sex, begging me to email him when it was over so he could "stop picturing it in my mind" and relax into about a week's reprieve before it would transpire again.

He looked thin, hollowed out as he showed me his handiwork on the scar. "It's all I have left of you," he whispered in the gangway, illuminated by my neighbor's sensor lights that reminded me we couldn't hide anything anymore. "I hope you don't mind."

I thought of his feral beauty while my heel had slid in and out of his mouth at the cabin; of the way he'd smiled when I blew on his flesh like coals to keep the burn stoked—his Zen-like, meditative purr. He never even flinched. In those moments, he was perfectly content. How could I complain about his wanting Our Scar to be more prominent? If anything, I was envious not to have my own permanent marking, my own imprint of our short history on my skin.

Besides, I already knew that much about him: in between our widely spaced-out chain of transcendent moments, he always wanted More.

Wasn't it inevitable, after all, that I should have a husband, that he should have a wife? What kinds of people, by their mid-forties, don't have such things?

Many kinds, of course. But different breeds of animal than he and I.

There are so many ways to fail a person. In her classic text, *The Drama of the Gifted Child*, Alice Miller argues that adults do not "require" unconditional love—that only children can or should be promised that. To vow otherwise, she says, is to imply that our feelings would be unaffected even if our beloved became a serial killer. But rhetoric and cleverness had taken me only so far before he crossed my path, and Miller's logic made no sense in my paradigm of loving him. There were no bodies in his basement. He existed within a limited frame of options available to his nature. When we say that anyone is capable of anything, we are lying.

He was capable of lying—yes, that is one thing of which he was wildly capable. When it came to lying, we were partners in crime. He was capable of both grandiosity and of a self-loathing so singularly focused it veered toward narcissism: grandiosity's dark, less charming twin. He was capable of petulance and quick flashes of anguish over minor things, such as the time his wife failed to wake him up in time to make my morning coffee before I left their friends' house in Michigan, where we had all spent the night. Even I knew she was right to let him sleep. He hadn't gotten a full night's rest in weeks at that point, gripped by the mania of finishing the book my press was publishing, the "product" that still provided rationale for our frequent contact. After chauffeuring his wife and me from Chicago to Traverse City after some thirty-six hours awake, he'd finally fallen into the black undertow, and no one in her right mind would have roused him. Still, he sulked around the lake house like a child, because coffee was all he had to offer of his continued devotion now. (Months later, however, he and I would have the exact same disagreement when I failed to wake him in time for a Starbucks run before we had to drive down the California coast, and I would find myself in a vortex of déjà vu so absurd I eventually wept in the hotel bathroom.)

That road trip in August: him, his wife, me, all in one car, driving to visit friends. See us all here, on a friendly vacation, Being Friends. Except now he was acting like a dick to his wife in front of me, because of me, petulant over coffee such that his friends must have thought he was coming unglued, but I saw a series of synapses connecting in his wife's eyes and instead of growing cold to me or starting a fight, she grew warmer, solicitous, *Keep your enemies closer.* He was capable of repetition, of the same miscommunications over and over, of ninety-seven apologies within the course of an hour, but we had known each other in some capacity since I was thirty, so this was not a revelation. He—intense, capricious, differently lit, his entrance to my life a *Wizard of Oz* moment: all the Technicolor switched on—existed, as we all do, within a limited range of options, and I knew I could love him through them no matter how the die of himself rolled. There are so many ways to fail a person (my simple nonaction of forgetting to delete a text), but loving him unconditionally may be the one thing I got right.

When I ended our affair, we'd already been apart for three months anyway. Between our first kiss in February and my daughters finding our texts, we'd seen each other all of twice. Yet now that we were over, he sometimes spoke of asking his wife for a separation, of moving to Chicago on his own to some shithole apartment just to be near me so we could "go out for coffee sometimes." He didn't comprehend that my not seeing him, my never wondering if we would run into each other while I was out in the world being the woman I was supposed to be, was the only thing holding me together. "Sometimes love just isn't enough to make something possible," I told him on the phone, in emails, in Michigan, trying to strike some note of closure, but is it any wonder this soothed neither of us?

After all, who wants to live in a world where love is not enough? If love isn't enough, what the hell is?

Even if he'd had children, I was a mother, whereas he would have been a father, and whether these two labels *should* mean the same thing—to the culture, to the parent in question, to the children themselves—in practice they usually do not. The rippling effect of unintended consequences, had my husband been the one to take a lover, even if he decided to run off with her, would bear stark little in common with any universe in which I did the same. The impact of a childless man leaving his wife who has already figured out he is in love with another woman might be emotionally devastating, but it would be more . . . contained.

My lover always hated binaries, but there is nothing in this life that isn't a choice. I wanted not to be the villain of my daughters' story more than not to be the villain of his. But if that sounded simple (it wasn't) from a distance of two thousand miles, here in each other's proximity, it was several mountain ranges worse.

Most of the ways to fail a person involve trying not to fail somebody else.

The night I shredded my journal over the trash bin outside his Chicago hotel, after he and his wife started snapping at each other on the way home from Michigan, after I decided that my daughters didn't need to see him anymore inside our home, after I searched travel sites and found them a good deal at a downtown hotel and dropped them off, I leaned over the giant trash receptacle near my entrance to Lake Shore Drive breathing fast, telling myself I was safe now. I had chosen what to protect, and it wasn't Us. A couple of weeks later, however, calling him from a riverfront park while Enzo played out of earshot, I rambled about the Madwomen of Modernism—how they had been erased by their husbands, their psychiatrists, their editors. I confided how angry I was at myself for perpetuating this system by having erased *myself*, of my own volition—for ripping the pages of us out of the world. Even before we kissed for the first time, we had more than eight hundred emails between us, now all deleted. Our friend S. had coined our correspondence Infinite Jest, and as I ended the call I imagined myself emailing my No Longer Lover/No Longer Best Friend someday, many years from now, when both our affair and his forthcoming novel were like specks in the rearview, to say an innocuous hello. Somehow, though we weren't managing it yet, we would have found a respectable distance, gone on with our separate lives, fallen loosely and then entirely out of touch the way people are meant to when there is nothing else to be done. *My long-lost Smutty Foster Wallace*, I might begin that email to his fifty-, sixty-year-old self, and the idea of this far-in-the-future exchange, when the longing and grief inside me might be tamped down into bittersweet, ironic nostalgia, kept me from screaming until I couldn't stop—allowed me to buckle my child into the car and head home from the river park. *Fake it till you make it*, again.

There should be more to show for us than a scar I burned into his hand, though. There was so much more to what we were than the heel of my fucking boot in his mouth. But things look one way if you stay forever, and they look a whole other color if you are the one to go. I remember the way he dropped to sleep in my arms, every single time we shared a bed, as though he had never had insomnia in his life. I remember how we used to laugh until our bodies convulsed, like the bad kids in the back of a classroom. I remember the way he could recite entire pages of Fitzgerald, and how the night we drove back from his cabin to Los Angeles, still sweaty and gritty under our regular street clothes, the hot wind blowing in my already wild hair, I felt alive to every molecule of air, the heights and depths of every sensation I had ever known. I remember the way he made filling my car up with gas fun even in February in Chicago. I remember love like we invented it.

I would beg you to find a way to love me even though I've walked away, but I know you do, and that hurts more, so instead I'm begging you to find a way to forget me, I wrote to him, trying for magnanimity, trying to act like someone who wanted to be erased, except people who truly desire erasure do not usually dole out advice about how to best forget them. Besides, like bodies in his basement or getting off the phone with me without saying *I love you*; like leaving a stray cat unfed in his yard; like ever eating Brussels sprouts again after the puke incident when he was six, forgetting was simply not in his range of options.

In Santa Cruz in October, we walked the pier at dawn, stood listening to the sea lions barking. The marine layer was thick, the air cool, though soon the sun would break through and the mist would evaporate fast. It had been six months since we'd touched—three months since I'd ended our affair—and it would be some five months before we were scheduled to be in the same city again in late winter for a conference. A friend's wife, seeing us together that weekend at events in San Francisco, in Santa Cruz—events at which we knew so many other people, we had deigned it safe to both attend—had said to her husband, *Are they a couple?* and later he would tell us that he had answered, *I have no idea whether they're fucking, but they're clearly a couple, yeah.*

We had been officially over for only three months. Three motherfucking months, after the way my daughters had cried in my bed: that was all I had in me to give.

But I had never seen a sea lion before. (I had never felt the texture of a man's toes in my mouth before; I had never licked a man's tears before; I had never felt the fragile pulse of my body's existence insist upon its will so primally before, reducing all of whom I thought I was to an exposed wire of desire.) Our leather jackets crackled together when we walked the pier arm in arm. He came with me into a shop to buy souvenirs for my daughters, and when the merchant didn't take credit cards and I had to borrow cash, he joked that the gifts were tainted by blood money. Afterward, though I never told him, I threw the small wrapped boxes away and bought them something else, though I'd already paid him back.

It was a slip, I told myself on the plane home from San Francisco. *A slip, not a relapse.* Five months still, until the next time we would see each other. Before driving to the airport, we'd wept into each other's hair in my cheap motel, like long-ago lovers boarding ships for opposite shores in a day before postal systems, telephones, computers. *At least we got to say goodbye in person this time*, I told him, and believed that I meant it. In five months, I would be stronger; in five months I would be better. This time I would not err. This time, I would last.

That day at the cabin, the embers of us still sparking in the skin across my lover's veins, he'd exhaled smoke and said, "I really shouldn't be doing this," and we laughed because few things feel so good as to be beyond one's control—because I'd spent my entire life believing that with pain came darkness, that with unconventional desires came shame, but between us there was none of that nonsense, no role-playing or repetitive compulsion of old wounds; no embarrassment or hackneyed artifice. Only this bottomless sense of adventure, the body our Mount Everest to climb while learning to breathe a different air, our intimacy a place of joyful safety and trust that made me question everything I ever understood regarding how to be Normal, how to be Good.

And we laughed to keep from crying, because he was right.

What Women Do

... And in the house
she destroys and she cleans; says at times:
"The asylum is nice. Where? Here!"
Other times she breaks down and cries.

—César Vallejo

I.
My father is banging on the wall with his cane.

This is what he does when he needs help. His legs don't work well enough to get up our back stairs, and his hands shake too much to dial a telephone. So with my mother temporarily in assisted living after a car accident, when my father needs anything he stands in the back staircase and bangs on the wall with his cane until I come down. He has one of those necklaces he can use to call the paramedics, but he usually doesn't wear it, and even if he did, the paramedics are not going to fix him some spaghetti or run out to buy him bananas or make his answering machine stop beeping. For a ninety-one-year-old man whose body has been attempting to expire since his early twenties, his wall-pounding stamina is impressive.

When I get downstairs, his apartment looks like a crime scene. It takes me a bit to figure out that all the blood is coming from his nose. A small wicker trash bin sits next to his chair at the kitchen table, overflowing with bloody tissues. Clearly he's been moving around the apartment, because there's a trail of bloody globules all around the kitchen island, including on the counter. There is blood on the telephone.

"How long has this been going on?" I ask. "Why didn't you call me sooner?

"Oh, Jesus Christ," my father says. "Maybe an hour. I thought it would stop."

When I was a kid in Catholic school, we had a girl in our class whose nose bled almost daily. It was like she had the stigmata in her nasal passages. Our teachers used to have her lie down flat on desks pushed together and would put a frozen knife alongside her nose (they kept one in the school cafeteria just for her, and different students would have to go downstairs to fetch it). This being the extent of my knowledge about bloody noses, I make my father lie down and put an ice pack on his nose.

Blood begins bubbling out through his mouth, spilling down his chin like a vampire.

I call 911. The first thing they tell me is not to put him on his back.

This officially confirms that everything I ever learned in Catholic school was a lie.

My father sits upright now on the side of his bed, waiting for the paramedics. His room looks insane, as usual. My mother is able to regulate his hoarding except in two areas of the house: the kitchen table, where he keeps stacks and stacks of old magazines and pulled-out pictures/ads, all of which are piled under the table and spread across the tabletop; and his bedroom, which has three clothing racks pushed into the middle of the small space, in addition to the food crammed under his bed and the senselessly nonutilitarian and strange knickknacks that litter every surface as closely crammed as sardines. On the floor are Hefty bags of clothing. When my father was a younger man—until his mid-eighties, really—he used to troll Marshalls and T.J.Maxx for sales and then take his purchases to the Italian men's club where he had hung out since I was a toddler, selling his wares to his friends at a small profit. "Michigan Avenue John," they called him, because my father has impeccable taste; he brought them cashmere socks, Polo sweaters, designer tweed sports coats.

After he lost the ability to drive, I began carting him to his club, but eventually my father lost interest. Most of the men he knew best were now dead. Plus, he didn't like people seeing how compromised his walking had become. He still went to the discount shopping venues because he didn't know anyone there, but without the club, Hefty bags full of unworn clothing with the tags still on began piling up. My mother periodically makes noise about garage sales or donating the clothing to charity, but whenever she tries to remove a single item, he pitches a fit. He had, at her last count, more than two hundred button-down shirts, although in the past couple of years I don't think I've seen him wear anything other than a white undershirt with stains on the front. It's not always the same undershirt, but with his shaky hands, they all accumulate stains pretty fast.

"These sweatpants," my father says, about the maroon pants he's wearing. "They're a large, not an extra-large."

I bought him these pants for his birthday in mid-December, which was also the day my mother got into the car accident that caused her exodus from our home and prompted my parents' longest separation in more than fifty-five years. My eighty-year-old mother was heading to Costco to buy a roasted chicken and cream puffs for our family celebration—his favorite things now that he will no longer go to a restaurant. She was turning left into the Costco parking lot, but before she could reach its haven, a speeding taxi zooming down a bridge slammed into her car. She was hit so hard that her vehicle spun entirely around and ended up facing backward in the other lane. Her car was totaled, her leg shattered in three places. She had immediate surgery, ended up in the ICU, eventually recovered enough to move to the hospital rehab wing, didn't make progress quickly enough to stay there, got transferred to a nursing home near our house, developed pneumonia, was told she needed a second surgery but couldn't have it until her lungs recovered, eventually had the second surgery, and was promptly forced to go back to the beginning of her recovery timeline: another six weeks before she can even put weight on her damaged leg.

When I am not cooking for my father or doing his laundry or dishes or going to the pharmacy to fill his prescriptions, I am at the nursing home, bringing my mother items from home and trying to cheer her up. One of her best girlfriends died during this ordeal, and my mother didn't get to say goodbye or even attend the services. Also, my father will not come to visit her given that he refuses to leave the house. My mother, who is usually accepting and good-natured to the point of passivity, is depressed for the first time since the Italian women in our old neighborhood used to shun her during my childhood for being a WASP. ("The hillbilly," my father's closest brother called her, because if she wasn't Black or Jewish or Puerto Rican or of course Italian, what else was there?) My father is depressed too since her medical incarceration, but he is always depressed, so this is nothing new.

"You don't take an extra-large," I tell him. "Your pants are always falling off."

"These pants are too tight," he says. "You have to exchange them for an extra-large."

I'm willing to bet that Lands' End isn't taking back a pair of sweats that my father has spent an hour and a half bleeding in, but I don't mention it.

•

If you were a paramedic and arrived to find a ninety-one-year-old man living in a room like my father's, I guarantee you would think some kind of elder abuse was occurring. What kind of people would allow an old man to live in these conditions? As soon as the paramedics show up, I half-expect the DCFS to call first thing in the morning to put my father in foster care, or to see myself on the nightly news, my Cruella de Vil sweatshop-for-elders exposed. I imagine trying to explain to the newscasters that my father will not let my mother and me clean his room, but standing in the blood-splattered hallway, watching a team of bulked-up men trying to fit medical gear into my father's hoarder's lair, this no longer seems like a reasonable excuse.

"I want to change my pants," my father tells them immediately. "This waistband is too tight. My daughter keeps buying me a large when I wear an extra-large." Then, contradicting himself for no apparent reason: "I've been dropping weight. They say no, but I know I've got the stomach cancer."

The stomach cancer. My father has been insisting for years that he has the stomach cancer, although he has been tested and retested and, truth be told, this is the healthiest his stomach has ever been. He spent the ages of twenty through seventy with a violently hemorrhaging ulcer that tried to kill him about once a year. When medical science revealed the link between ulcers and bacteria, he was put on antibiotics and cured, although he still insists on adhering to the diet he followed during the Ulcer Half Century, which includes a militant belief that anyone serving him a dish with even the smallest sprinkling of black pepper is tantamount to a murderer.

Hence, in the paramedics' eyes, my father is not only living in Harry Potter's cupboard under the stairs, but I'm letting him die of cancer, too, and purposely torturing him with too-tight pants.

My husband must have seen the ambulance outside, because he shows up in my parents' apartment still in his coat and carrying the leather messenger bag I bought him for Christmas. Quickly, it's decided that he will accompany my father to the hospital while I clean up the mess and get Enzo to bed. Although my father will not visit my mother in any medical facility, his long history of mental illness and brief history of old-man belligerence makes it unwise to send him off in an ambulance without an advocate. My husband is practical, responsible, and competent, and to the extent that the majority of our lives lately seem to be consumed with crisis management, we are a good team, but that reality hasn't stopped my ever-mounting aversions, not only to hearing him eat meringues but, since I ended things with my lover five months ago, to being able to regularly orgasm authentically or getting in bed for the night before my husband is already asleep. It is guilt, that much I understand . . . but beneath the guilt is also the resentment that he is the one standing between me and my heart's most heated desire, even though he is unaware there is anything to thwart. Unfair, cruel—I know all this and yet I feel a sense of relief the moment my husband departs rooms. This makes me despise myself, but since the Texting Incident I despise myself 'round the clock anyway, so what else is new?

We should go back to therapy. We have even talked about it a few times, but our division of labor is such that therapy falls under the heading of Things I Would Normally Arrange. My husband earns the money and pays the bills, and I manage all things social/emotional for our household of seven—when we've done marriage counseling twice in the past, I called the therapists, did phone consultations, made our initial appointment. Lately, when the topic comes up, my husband and I both agree that "maybe" we should go back, but then I let it slide and nothing happens. If we go to therapy, I'll have to admit not only to the affair but to having been caught by our daughters, or it will all just be more of the same lie, and I'm too afraid, too selfish, too frozen in indecision, too something. The more ashamed of myself I become for my silence, the more my emotional paralysis increases.

I imagine my husband, sitting next to my irrational father in the waiting room of the ER, hour after hour ticking by: my loyal husband, patiently tinkering with his iPhone, waiting to be of use, to handle things. For a moment, my limbs feel like lead. Then I push this thought from my mind and move, gathering cleaning supplies, dropping to my knees. I keep moving, until the dark, thick edges of my shame begin to blur.

Enzo appears in the back stairway, which empties from our upstairs apartment directly into my parents' kitchen, peeking around the corner to see what's going on. My daughters are at a friend's tonight, and though I urge Enzo back upstairs and he scampers off, without his sisters to supervise he is back again moments later, gawking at all the blood. I try to convince him that he should stay upstairs, but I've been down here so long and he wants to be with me, and I'm too exhausted to fight it. My six-year-old has become the only member of my household around whom I don't feel like I'm about to jump out of my skin.

My father's blood is already hardening into a sticky, gelatinous kind of wax. I attack it with spray cleaner and bleach wipes, crawling around on my hands and knees and scrubbing violently. It smears and expands like red paint before it releases, and I'm going through bleach wipes as fast as my father used tissues. For Enzo's sake, I try to make this funny—I make up a rhyming song about being an old man with a nose that gushes like a faucet. Enzo squeals laughter. ER trips and blood are a part of his lifestyle. Not that long ago, he and I took my parents to Dapper's, a strip mall Greek diner that is one of the few places left on earth into which my father will set foot, and before we could even get inside my mother lost her balance and fell backward and hit her head on the concrete with a thud that still resonates in my bones. Two women paramedics showed up and let Enzo play inside their ambulance while they were attending to my mother, who rode off with them on a stretcher while I took Enzo and my father home.

I scrub the blood for about half an hour. It's in strange places, as though my father's head suddenly spun 360 degrees, à la *The Exorcist*. Thankfully there is none on the ceiling, but that's about the extent of the good news.

Like Enzo, I am inured to this sort of thing. Blood scouring is not remotely the most disgusting thing I have ever done for my parents. Even my mother, the more able of the two, has had two knee replacements, two hip replacements, and several bouts of diverticulitis, all of which left her requiring assistance with toileting and random grotesque tasks such as stuffing an open wound with gauze as long as a small intestine, then, the next day, removing the gauze like a worm coated in bloody slime. During one bout of diverticulitis, she also had to wear a colostomy bag for three months while part of her colon healed. After dealing with the bag a couple of times, I drew a line and simply would not assist her with the maintenance of it, so she had to bring in an aide. Paying someone to deal with a colostomy bag so that you don't have to may be the best money you could ever spend—but that doesn't stop me for feeling like shit for refusing to cheerfully minister to my mother's shit.

Even on my knees scrubbing my father's blood while singing an impromptu rhyming song to make the body's decay palatable for my child, it is still never enough—*I* am never enough. My mouth waters with nausea, not from the blood but from self-loathing. Even before my affair, I was never selfless enough, never generous enough. No matter what I give, I will always fall short of what I—daughter, mother, wife—am supposed to be.

There is only one way to tell the truth, but there are myriad ways to live a lie.

•

That night, while we are snuggling as part of his bedtime ritual, Enzo starts to cry. I tickle his back, try to soothe him, promise that nosebleeds are No Big Deal and Papa will be home soon.

Enzo says, "How old will I be when you die?"

II.

My father has been home from the ER less than a week when he starts hallucinating intruders. First, it's a man staring into his window; then a group of menacing teenagers on the porch; and finally, armed men in his bedroom in the middle of the night. Although my father has been unable to get up the stairs to our apartment for more than two years, even with my husband's assistance, that night we find him in our kitchen at 2 a.m., shouting at us to take the kids and run.

If it is possible for psychosis to reveal the core of a person, without artifice or performance or the ability to care what anyone else thinks, then at my father's moment of greatest (albeit imaginary) danger, his most elemental impulse, like a mother lifting an automobile to save her child, was to protect his family. Maybe this is why my mother never left him. Maybe this is why he lives here in our house, despite being more than a little high maintenance, when most of my friends see their more innocuous parents only a couple of times a year.

Or maybe there is never a logical rationale for love.

Since before my affair, I've had a sporadically recurring dream in which my husband and I are hiking on a snowy mountain alone. It is the sort of hike where we should have pickaxes and elaborate gear, but we have only one small pack on my husband's back as we wander together in blinding snow, unsure which way to go, the path long covered like the roads snowed over to invisibility when we lived in rural New England. My husband and I wander, bickering about whose fault it is that we have found ourselves in this position, and suddenly, as instantly as it often happens in life, the flicking of a switch, my husband is screaming at me, waving his arms, face red against the stark snowscape, and swearing that I am to blame, that I've done something selfish and incompetent and now I've killed us. We are standing upon a precipice, the only way to safety a jump over a deep chasm to the other side where the trail is still visible. Calling me a fucking bitch, my husband suddenly takes off, sails on his longer legs over the chasm with our pack, leaving me paralyzed, knowing I cannot make the jump alone without falling. In some versions of the dream, I stay put: waiting for my husband to come back to himself as he always does, trusting him to return and find me and help me across. But in most versions of the dream, I stand watching the trail on the other side of the divide become rapidly hidden in the torrential snow, my husband rushing away from me, and I know that he will never find the path again in this storm—that by the time he regrets leaving me, there will be no sign of his departing footsteps either, and I will be lost to him forever, to die alone on a snowy cliff.

Freud, with whom I have had a love/hate relationship since college, says that dreams are not about fear but about wish fulfillment. Maybe, then, a psychoanalyst would say that I am not so much *afraid* of my husband's explosive temper and the damage it could do to me, as that some part of me *wishes* he would push it indisputably too far and force me to end my dependency on him, and fend for myself or die trying.

I don't know what the dream really means, if dreams mean anything at all. What I know is that I have an abiding fear that if our backs were against the wall, my husband and I are capable of turning on each other, of each pointing the finger of blame until the stronger of us cuts the weaker one off and saves himself. What I know is that in the subconscious of my dreams, it is always my husband who is the stronger party, who sacrifices me in anger. What I know: that as though in a preemptive strike, in reality I am the one who has leaped the chasm and run fast ahead, and now the snow has covered the road and I don't know how to find my way back. That alone would be terrifying enough, but what's much worse: I don't know if I want to.

My parents' doctor, himself starting to transform into an old man, calls to ask whether my father has been taking his antipsychotic. Without my mother to hand it to him, it turns out my father didn't even realize he was *on* an antipsychotic. And so in addition to managing the rest of my father's life, I take over responsibility for putting all his pills into Day and Evening organizers. Within a few days, my father's hallucinations mercifully go away, though of course he continues to sleep with every light in the house blaring as protection from the plague of mice.

When I ask my father's doctor whether he will write me a script for a few lorazepam, claiming anxiety about an upcoming airplane trip, he instead writes me a three-month prescription for a total of ninety pills. "You have," he says to me with a kindness that might crack me, "a lot on your plate."

It is during my mother's long exodus from our home that my new recurring dream begins. In this one, which I have nearly every night, almost *every goddamn night* for what will be the next three years, I confess my infidelity to my husband and we talk about all the experiences we have shared and all the mistakes we have made and decide to let each other go with love. Every morning, I wake with my lover's name as my first conscious thought, and for a moment in that half-dream state, I believe my husband knows—that I have told him the truth and everything is okay. Then slowly, inching up my body the way awareness of Kathy's death did in those early months, every firing neuron of joy dims and goes dark as I realize it has only been some Freudian wish fulfillment again, another of my cop-outs, and I am still a liar, still here.

•

The thing is: my daughters were in the car.

My mother's car, on her way to Costco, on her way to buy roasted chicken and cream puffs for my father's birthday.

My daughters, who weigh approximately eighty pounds apiece.

Mags was in the back seat. Kaya was in the passenger's seat. The death seat.

The taxi hit the car on the passenger side, completely smashing it. The airbags deployed. An airbag alone can, sometimes, be enough to kill an eighty-pound person. The passenger-side airbags in our car had been disabled since my daughters got old enough to sit up front. But in my mother's car, we never thought to do this.

My mother's airbag, it turned out, was old and semi-defective, a half-deflated balloon.

The brunt of the impact happened at the front of the car, because my mother, seeing the taxi's approach, froze in fear and hesitated enough—just enough—to prevent its full force from hitting Kaya's door.

Mags, in the back seat, was on her phone, and when the collision happened, she threw it in the air in fear. It hit her in the face and dinged up her nose.

Kaya got some bruises on her leg and the side of her cheek from the defective airbag, but was otherwise left unscathed.

I got the call about the accident from my daughters. "Mommy," Mags said into the phone, her voice achingly, agonizingly young, "Nana got in a car accident."

I raced to the site. Glass formed a terrifying mosaic all over the road. The taxi driver's passenger was injured and was being taken away in an ambulance. Paramedics were trying to get my mother out of the car. I don't remember much about the specifics of my mother's stuckness. I was rushing to the totaled car as if with blinders on, unable to see anything but my daughters. I couldn't stop hugging them.

I couldn't stop thinking of the way my stomach felt like I was falling down an elevator shaft when I heard the word "accident" from Mags's mouth; the way the ground dropped away like an earthquake casually cracking open its mouth of destruction.

Death is the only true ending. Everything else falls, to varying degrees, along a continuum of choice.

With my mother in and out of hospitals, rehabs, and nursing homes, between managing her care, looking after my increasingly weak and unstable father, and mothering three children (two of whom I fear daily will never love me again after what I've done), I fall behind in every manner of work. My business partner at the press is in the early stages of the longest and most contentious divorce I have ever witnessed, and I am turning myself inside out trying to avoid the same fate while paradoxically all but ignoring my husband, and both she and I are starting to fail miserably in our professional obligations. I barely spend time with my children because I am always rushing off to do something for one of the other of my sick and depressed parents. My parents—especially my mother—have been co-raisers of the children, have maybe spent more time with them than their father has, given he works twelve- or thirteen-hour days, moving up the ladder, supporting us, being all the things he believes a man should be. I can still hear my daughters squealing "Nana!" every morning when my mother would come upstairs for coffee before they started school, but it is around this time—my father verging on some precipice of psychosis and dementia, my mother morose and bedridden in a disinfectant-smelling assisted-living facility—that the kids begin to tune out, to avoid my parents, who seem to have become new and alarming versions of themselves overnight even if in truth this has been progressing for years. We are all new and scarier versions of ourselves, lately, except of course Enzo. What used to feel like magic, like a shimmering gold of extended family and dreams come true, is gone, and instead I now essentially have five dependents and a husband I'm doing my best to avoid and yet still fuck approximately weekly so that he can't point a clear finger at my negligence.

Like my parents' doctor, the other moms at my daughters' school apparently find my life so chaotic even from the outside, even not knowing the half of the train wreck I've created, that one attempts to organize a meal train for my family, but this makes me so profoundly uncomfortable that I refuse to allow it. I keep saying things like, "It's not like I'm going through chemo." I keep saying how they should save these kinds of community efforts for "people who really need them."

What I don't say, but mean: *This is my penance, and I cannot allow you to lift it from me.*

In literary tradition, as well as the mythology of most major religions, it is common to kill off children as a symbol of their parents' crimes. I do not believe in divine retribution or karma or any hand of god or fate that takes a sentient interest in the happenings of our world. But what I know: there are circumstances that unearth you irrevocably, that break you, that leave you never again an unbroken whole.

My daughters could have died in that car. They could have contracted head injuries that would have changed their futures. They could have come away never walking again . . .

Whenever I long for my lover's touch (which is always), I play the Could Have Been game to force myself into a fearful gratitude. My father's ulcer could have waited just long enough to rear its head so that he would have been deployed overseas and died in his tank on some European battlefield, in which case he would've never met my mother. I could have never been born, leaving my son to nonexistence and my daughters to be adopted from China by some Entirely Other People. Maybe they would be born-again Christians in

Naperville right now, immersed in Suzuki piano lessons and no-where near my mother's car or Costco on the night of the accident. Or maybe their referral to some could-have-been other adoptive family would have waited one month, two months longer, and one of my fierce, inextricable twins would've contracted some bug and died in a Chinese orphanage before her first birthday, leaving the other to live life as a "single," not remembering she even had a sister. But instead of any of that happening, here they all are—my family—for me to tend. Compared to the alternate realities that could have happened, how can I want for anything more in this one?

I let my daughters down. They were entrusted to me, and I hurt them, I made them cry, I made them frightened and unhappy and burdened, I violated their trust, and then I almost lost them.

If scrubbing my father's blood can remove just the slightest bit of blood from my hands, I will do it forever, and nobody should be allowed to send me a meal train as consolation. I do not deserve a meal train. I don't deserve anything.

When you hate yourself enough, there is a sharp tinge of satisfaction in unhappiness.

"I hope you're taking care of yourself," a happily child-free colleague keeps saying to me. "Ever since I've known you it's been one thing after another with your parents, your miscarriage, your friend Kathy. It never lets up!" She is a good friend, but when she talks this way, I want to slap her face. Her parents lost a child—her younger brother—and she of all people should know how inconsequential my trials have been.

Maxine Hong Kingston writes that in Chinese tradition, some-times mothers would loudly proclaim their children ugly or stupid so that no harm would befall them—so that the ghosts would not think them worthy of stealing.

I keep my head down. I watch my life shrinking by degree into the maw of need—children, parents; parents, children. Instead of resisting, I hurl myself into the contraction, the blood. *Move along,* I tell the ghosts of guilt who ricochet around my brain, who may be eyeing my children for the sacrificial altar for my crimes. *There is nothing exciting here to see.*

Please don't take them from me.

III.

In American culture, what we call a "good ending" usually means precisely what my father's been granted: a long life, a roof over his head, a devoted spouse, grandchildren running around. I would like to interrupt this program, this litany of my beleaguered winter and spring of 2013, to ask exactly what kind of gig it is being human if the best anyone can hope for is to end up like my father?

IV.

When my husband was living in Amsterdam without me, in the final year of the twentieth century, or whenever he went to Vegas for a conference or with friends, my father would snort things like, "You know what he's doing out there, don't you, honey? That's just how men are."

But I knew my father was wrong. I knew my father understood nothing of my husband's personal ethics, which had been part of why I'd married my husband to begin with, back when I believed with utter certainty that loyalty and fidelity were things we indisputably shared. My father didn't understand a man like my husband— he had come from a world where any Italian man with some money in his pocket had a *goomah*—from a world that had given him the madonna/whore complex that more or less ruined my mother's personal life for close to half a century.

When I try to tell my mother that my father is being a baby and a diva by not visiting her just because he doesn't want to be seen in a wheelchair, she hems and haws and makes excuses for him.

Persevering is what wives do. *Staying* is what mothers do. *Tending* is what daughters do.

I buy my father some XL sweatpants, so my mother will see that I took good care of him while she was gone. I put his antipsychotics and his antidepressants and his Norco and his potassium and his prednisone and all the rest of the dozens of pills that keep him alive and sort-of-functioning into his Day and Evening pill organizers. I do my duty, try to make enough for dinner that I can just give my father our family's leftovers, but my father was the family cook when I was growing up and has complaints about most of what I bring down to him (*your broccoli is always tough and undercooked*), so I start cooking him his own meals, things I know he likes, things he taught me to make by modeling them in the small apartment I grew up in, where no one ever had any privacy. Usually, when I bring him down plates or containers of food, my father, with too much time on his hands without my mother to talk to, says something to me like, "Why don't you ever wear tweed?" or "You should really get a pixie again," even though the last time he got his way on that front I was five.

Who are we kidding? My father was not going to eat anything from some goddamn meal train anyway.

I'd said goodbye to my daughters with no special sense of significance. We were talking cream puffs and chicken. There they are: one in the passenger's seat, the other looking at her phone in the back seat. Look, there is the taxi, picking up speed on the downslope of the bridge, heading straight for them. They could have died in that car, only five months after finding my texts, losing the years it will take us to heal from my mistakes—losing all the years they will spend growing into women themselves, growing beyond me, to live both loves and mistakes of their own. All the history we will make together could have disappeared in an instant, in the brunt of the approaching taxi just a few feet to the left or right of the point of impact. I fall asleep to mosaics of broken headlights, to my mother stuck in the car yelling in pain as I race by her, my Sophie's choice made, to scoop my daughters into my arms.

Every morning when I wake, I switch the white-noise machine off, remembering inch by inch that I've told my husband nothing; I've received no blessings to move on. It is all only ever a dream.

And where does lost love fit in among the *Could Have Beens*? Where does heartache, the kind of sting that coils perpetually in your stomach, a snake ever striking, weigh in on the scale of pains in this world? I feel like I could die of aching, but of course I do not die. How long will I have to wait, here in the longing space, before the hole in my universe shaped like my lover's body closes over?

Despite humanity's grisly history of war, famine, disease, corruption—despite the fact that not just death but pain and suffering and debilitation are fundamental parts of the human experience—our musicians, our filmmakers, our poets, and even our laws remain profoundly preoccupied with questions of love. Love is not a thing to be trifled with. My maternal grandmother was married twice and lived into her nineties, but until her death she never removed the simple onyx ring given to her by her first love when she was sixteen, before he was diagnosed with tuberculosis and headed west to a clinic, after which she never heard from him again. Nearly ninety years after those sleepless nights she must have spent crying in her girlhood bed for him, I wake with a start, sometimes in a heart-hammering sweat, sometimes jarred by a sleep orgasm in which I can still feel my lover, once transformed into a tree in my dream, his roots puncturing and intertwining inside my body. My husband sleeps beside me, the sounds of him muffled by white noise.

Some days, the Could Have Been game doesn't work. Sometimes

I can think only of the What Will Be, beginning with this: if my lover or I get rushed off to the ER in an ambulance, the other will not even be on the list of people who receive a phone call.

So many things, when you break them down, are about perception. So many things hinge on how we choose to interpret both our own choices and the immovable forces beyond our control. So much rests on having the wisdom, and sometimes the cold-edged fucking ruthlessness, to know the difference.

In terms of moral perspective, this much I know: when you are a woman, at times it seems as if opening your legs genuinely exceeds any crime that powerful men have yet to invent. How imperative it is in our culture that women believe just that. The face/slut/cunt that launched a thousand ships. How the very order of the world, of Family, of Important Men who need to make more money for the other men who already have more money, all hinges on women's piety, our faithfulness, our devotion to the hearth.

My mind whirls with car crashes and blood on the floor, yet I drench tights at the thought of my lover's mouth until I have to make wardrobe changes like Diana Ross.

What's the old saying? *Show me a beautiful woman and I'll show you a man who's tired of fucking her?*

Here's another: *Behind every Great Man is a woman who wants to chew off her arm.*

It has been a while since my father and I have engaged in what might be called a meaningful conversation. Generally, just as when I rang home during college and my father would pass the phone directly to my mother (actually, he rarely answered the phone at all), so when the kids and I come downstairs to visit and my mother is home, my father only even turns down the television if it's so loud that she complains she can't hear what we're saying over his racket. Generally—by which

I mean I've forgotten how long this has been going on, but it may be as long as my parents have lived here in this house—my father and I rarely talk exclusively, using my mother or my children as a conduit.

This was not always so. Because my father tended bar and kept unconventional hours in my youth, before he stopped working altogether, he was around the apartment much more than the typical father of his generation, and when he was home he was always in the living room or the kitchen, or on the front porch: accessible spaces where he made no particular effort at privacy. I could interrupt him anytime I wanted, ask him stories about the neighborhood when he was young, or beg him to read me the "funny papers." I remember long afternoons on the couch by our front windows, looking through the shutter slats while my father, stacks of newspapers knee-high beside him, lamented how no one baked potatoes in their piles of burning leaves anymore, describing those long-gone charred skins and the soft white meat inside with loving detail, or while he regaled me with a game my children still talk about, House on Fire, in which any new boy in the neighborhood would be lured into a game in which he was the "house" that was "on fire," and before he knew it all the other boys—the firefighters—had surrounded him in a circle and were peeing on him, to put the fire out. Although my father referred to his time alone with me as "babysitting," the truth is that we spent a fair amount of time alone, especially after my mother went back to work. While during my late teens and early twenties my father and I tangled some about my mounting feminism (this consisted mostly of my getting in his face, not the other way around), we never had any kind of falling-out or clear delineation of when we stopped talking to each other in any substantive way—when my mother became his proxy for all things parental. It happened gradually, such that I did not even notice it really—most of my friends didn't talk much to their fathers either—and it is only now that my mother has been in assisted living so long that I realize my father and I have forgotten how to manage ourselves as a dyad: that the only way he seems to know how to interact with me is through statements of contention or need.

A few times, while my mother is gone, I go downstairs and sit next to my father, nestled in his heavily indented space on the couch, to watch television with him. Maybe I should claim this happened more than "a few times," given how long my mother was gone, but the reality is that although I cooked his meals and arranged his pills and cleaned his blood—although I marched the children through his apartment frequently so that he could demand hugs and kisses and coo over their beauty each time as though seeing them for the first time—I did very little to meet my father's needs for substantial social interaction while my mother was away. And so I am stunned one night when I am down there just days before my mother finally returns, and my father says, as though he has never uttered a less-than-lucid statement in his life, "Flower, you remember when I used to ride your ass all the time about how you should go hang around the playground or Fiore's with all the other kids, and you wouldn't do it?"

Do I remember this? Of course I remember. Before I made my father cry by moving out of state to go to college, I had already disappointed him through my refusals to make even any vague attempt at teenage cachet in his beloved neighborhood . . . by biding my time inside scribbling and reading until I could fly away from him and everything his world represented.

"Sure," I tell him. "You wanted me to be popular like Angie and those girls. It's understandable. But I was . . ." and here a line comes to me unbidden from Arundhati Roy's *The God of Small Things* ". . . just not that kind of animal."

"I didn't know what the hell I was talking about," my father almost shouts at me now. I look at him, confused—even when we used to talk all the time, we didn't talk *like this*. "I thought it would help you if you went out like the other girls, if you got a boyfriend. You seemed lonely. But I was a chump. There was nothing for you there. I didn't know you were going to end up with a completely different kind of life—some kind of life I didn't know there was."

In a movie about a father-daughter relationship, this scene would take place a day before the father's death. This longed-for (so deeply, so wildly, that I had in fact not dared to long for it . . . never considered it imaginable) vindication of my choices, my pursuits, from my father would be the words to bring my entire life full-circle and grant me some previously elusive peace.

But in reality, my father is years from death still. Soon he won't be able to walk well enough to get to the toilet, much less bang on the wall with his cane. Soon he won't be capable of this sort of sustained introspection, and his life will disappear into a crack in his mind from which he will no longer emerge. My father and I will have years ahead of often ridiculous, often difficult interactions as his caregiving needs increase alongside my inability to meet them. And even now, there is a part of me—the same part that will not accept a meal train—telling me that my father's beautiful epiphany is misguided, is undeserved because my life isn't what he thinks; because the "different kind of life" he didn't know existed *doesn't* exist in some sense, at least not anymore.

But just for a moment, before I leave us to our respective unravelings, I'm going to step one inch to the side for a different view. Just for a moment, I'm going to see myself through my father's eyes that night: his forty-five-year-old daughter who looks nothing like the forty-five of our old neighborhood; whose life has looked like nothing he could have predicted, recognized, or even dreamed. Just for one fucking second, I am going to bathe in the light of his recognition—his seeing not just the 2013 me with a half-hidden face, but the me I have been for thirty-five years, who clawed my way somewhere new without a map while he did his best, out of love, to hold on to my ankles and drag me back. *Oh come on*, he used to snort when my mother suggested moving out of the neighborhood, *everywhere's the same—what are you, kidding? You think there's somewhere different from here?*

We are, my father and I, each about to keep sliding down an arduous hill, no possible traction to climb back up, no way of stopping until we reach bottom. But for tonight, this is one true thing: my father is proud of me. Not because I married well. Not because I gave him grandchildren. Not for my master's degrees or my books he doesn't read anyway. Not even for this house. He is proud of that young girl who resisted and refused his limited view of the world before any of these possibilities were even on the table.

It is enough. It is what I will be given, and for just a moment, I hold it close for that girl I used to be, who deserved his respect no matter what I may have done since. She is in here somewhere, still. She's in me. Maybe she is envisioning something even now that I can't yet see.

I am on my knees scrubbing my father's blood, singing, "There was an old man, blood squirted from his nose / La, la, la / And all the neighbors said it was like a garden hose / La, la, la."

Enzo giggles with mirth, even though later he will cry, as all children do at one time or another, wanting to know when I will leave him. He is yet unable to comprehend that by the time I do, there will be other people who surpass me in his heart, onto whom his worst fears will be directed. Someday, if he knows transformative adult love, if he is undone and remade by a lover's smile, by caring for babies whose need for him is total and obliterating, then, rung by rung, I will slide down the ladder of his heart until my death is bearable.

Dear god, let it be so.

The greatest lesson we teach our children is how to survive us.

I am on my knees scrubbing my father's blood. From here, I can almost believe in that old story of myself again: the good daughter, the devoted mother, maybe even the passable wife. I push harder to the point of quivering, muscle breaking down so that something new can form. *My story ends like this*, I tell myself—*here is my happy ending.* Just for a moment, I have dodged the bullet from my own gun.

Aftermath

Blow Your House Down

Something about amputating your arm
Because it bothered you
It was never a wing anyway

Something about amputating your leg
Because it hurt
You will never walk away from this

—Edward Hirsch

It was the season for treason. The first deep breath of Spring 2015. It was the season I just couldn't take anymore. Our hundred-plus-year-old house was being demolished for an extensive renovation—our first in fifteen years—and the walls had just been knocked down, siding ripped off, framing exposed. It was the season my husband and I took our children to a tacky Wisconsin water park resort during the worst of the dusty wreckage, the night we weren't allowed to breathe our home's toxic air. After a day of entertaining the kids, we left our daughters in charge of Enzo while we had dinner at the surprisingly elegant restaurant. It was the season of demolition, only three days into what would be a months-long process. It was the season that was supposed to be a beginning and instead became an end. The season my husband would come to believe I'd manipulated him into remodeling the house just in time to leave him, though I hadn't planned on leaving him, had never considered either of us moving out until some vague future point *when the kids were grown*, when my parents were dead, when the renovation was a blip in our memories. I didn't even expect to confess, that night or that year, much less at a water park on a family trip. It was the season for giving my lover no warning, for having no game plan of What Next after the bottled-up explosion from bubbling pressure inside my skin. It was the season for coming unglued.

At the surprisingly elegant restaurant, my husband and I drank more cocktails than was usual for either of us, especially him, laughing and talking in an easy manner I'd forgotten. It was the season a cloudy gauze suddenly lifted from my vision, and for the first time in three years or five years or eight years, I could see again how blue my husband's eyes were, especially when he wore a particular dark blue button-down shirt; I could see the way his smile lifted higher on one side of his mouth in the way I'd once often sketched, drawing caricatures of the two of us that we'd pasted onto green bottles we filled with homemade Kahlua and gave as gifts on our first Christmas cohabitating. We had been twenty-three, twenty-four. Now it was the season for forty-six, forty-seven. It was the season I hit a wall in the way a double life mandates not only lying to one person but to nearly everybody; I was alternately relieved and horrified that none of my friends seemed to notice I'd become a mere facsimile of myself. It was the season I realized how empty it is to hide—to be liked for being a blank slate, an empty receptacle, a reflective mirror off which others can bounce themselves. It was the season I feared that my daughters, now in high school, would never be able to have a functional adult relationship if their mother was a liar. Someday, would they cite me as the reason for all their pain, the way my husband talked about his mother? It was the season my blue-eyed, crooked-smiled, trusting husband was spending a fat wad of cash remodeling a house he believed he would die in, with me by his side. It was the season of accumulated dread from years of carefully parceling out sex I didn't want to have, with a couple of glasses of wine beforehand to get myself through it with good cheer and a headache in the morning—the season of artificial smiles and an underlying simmering snideness and derision to which I was not entitled but which leaked out of my mouth and showed on my face nonetheless. It was the season I lost control of a narrative I finally understood I'd never had any right to control to begin with.

It was the season I Could Take No More. Maybe you, too, have hit that invisible line in the sand, once or a dozen or a hundred times. It was the season I was overcome with disgust at the eternal Paolo and Francesca circular dance between my lover and me, of "ending it" and falling back together, moaning into each other's hair again and again—in early 2013 in Boston; in 2014 in Sausalito or Palm Springs or in his beat-up Subaru parked outside LAX—*I don't want to be without you*, the same old hand-wringing cycle of need and guilt and angst and the perpetual fear of discovery. It was true—I *didn't* want to be without him—but that didn't preclude the fact that we both made me sick. If at first the headiness of our forbidden passion was part of the rush, three years on, secrecy had become a poison albatross; it was excruciating, stomach-churning work to live this compartmentalized, this dishonest. It was the season the thrill of each other remained, but the thrill of sneaking around had long since gone.

It was the season to choose.

It was the season when, after years of Sphinx-like secrecy, I left increasingly blatant breadcrumbs—had been scattering them without much intention or control ever since, six months prior, my husband had privately told me at Emily's wedding (after first shouting at me in the hotel courtyard in front of my lover and his wife) that he knew I didn't love him anymore and was afraid I was only waiting for the kids to leave so we could become "a clichéd empty nester divorce." It was the season I could no longer pretend that ignorance was bliss, that my husband was anything resembling happy.

Over dinner at the surprisingly elegant water park resort restaurant, I talked about my lover to excess, waved the flag of our bond, but my husband took it in stride—seemed bothered not at all. (He had never been the jealous type—I'd so admired this about him once, but over time his lack of possessiveness started to feel synonymous with benign indifference, with a certain relief to "hand off" my emotional intensity to others so as to be relieved of the burden himself.) After dinner, we adjourned from the restaurant to an area outside with large armchairs, fireplaces, after-dinner drinks. Seated each in our own self-contained armchair, a small table between us, we were too far apart to easily touch and had to turn in our seats to see each other: a spatial arrangement reminiscent of an analyst's couch. Was it not having to look at him directly; was it the unusually lively nature of our dinner conversation; was it the crushing guilt of our expensive renovation; was it rainwater having filled the cistern of my body for so many years that I was a vessel running over; was it simply the goddamn booze that led me to utter Unsayable Things like *Marriage has been difficult for me for a long time* and *Monogamy is harder for some people than for others*, until at last my husband, not a jealous creature but certainly not a stupid one either, turned more sharply in his chair to see me fully and said my lover's name aloud. His name had flitted between us all evening, but finally my husband asked directly whether I was talking about him, and I said, almost casually, as though I had not spent more than three years in vigilant avoidance of revealing such a thing—my god, so simply in the final hour—"Yes."

Barely missing a beat, my husband asked whether I was in love with him, his voice also strangely nonplussed as though we had conversations of this nature all the time—as though we were a couple who commonly discussed our extracurricular romantic entanglements, maybe even used them as foreplay. Momentarily, in the fire-lit lounge, I felt like I was living one of my recurring dreams: that euphoria of waking and believing my husband knew and had given me his blessing, had either released me or granted me the freedom to pursue my own life. All at once, the dream seemed right in my hands to grasp: so close, so attainable. All it would take was my saying yes—*the truth will set you free*—and so I did, and though I held my breath for several seconds, the world did not stop spinning on its axis; the walls of the resort did not come falling down, water from the park flooding our lounge like the *Titanic*. Rather, my husband said more quietly, though still calm, *Have you slept with him?* or maybe *Have you had sex with him?* (how often I tried to remember later which phrasing he used: the euphemistic or the literal)—and I, who prided myself on being a reader of people, felt a jolt of elation that the worst had already passed: I had admitted my love and my husband was still sitting there looking at me, a worried but almost loving expression on his face, and so I affirmed again, "Yes."

It was the season I was wrong about everything.

It was the season my husband, who had been storming out of restaurants since the night he and I first told his parents we were engaged, abruptly rose to his feet, and all at once I knew my calculations to be delusional. I remembered, then, my father's old cracks about my husband's allegedly unavoidable philandering in Amsterdam, in Vegas, and realized in one fell swoop that it wasn't just that I hadn't believed my father, but that I hadn't entirely *cared*: sex with some random stranger, maybe even a professional, thousands of miles away felt abstract to me. But had my husband fallen in love with another woman and *then* fucked her . . . well, for some two decades, extending well into the time that I'd become unhappy in our marriage, such news would have seemed to crush my very bones—to freeze my lungs beyond inhalation, to end the goddamn world. That was what I had just done to him. My husband hovered uncertainly on his feet for several seconds, looming above me as he so often had, perhaps shocked, even, to find himself in this moment for which he'd long been rehearsing: an understudy for the role of the wronged man for a quarter century. Momentarily, I worried he might collapse—I said his name, cautiously, like to a frightened animal. But before I could attempt whatever weak words might follow, my husband bolted from the sexy cocktail lounge, this time without even shouting at me, and simply *ran*.

How many times had I chased my husband out of restaurants, begging him to calm down, to talk, to stay? How many times had he and I acted out theatrics like this for some petty reason—because I rolled my eyes at him or forgot to send him an email with our flight information or some other such banal transgression—until the season, like a self-fulfilling prophesy, I finally gave him just cause? Chasing him down an escalator to the basement of the hotel, part of me felt genuinely desperate to grasp him by the arm, to reestablish contact, but another part watched us both from an impartial distance like a predictable film, his familiar rage the inevitable conclusion of twenty-five years waiting for a catalyst. *Here*, the imaginary me hovering high above the escalator wanted to say as I watched my body rushing down to present myself in all my horribleness: *look how furious you at long last have the right to be*. A gift.

In the underbelly of our resort, my husband and I sobbed and fought and bargained and despaired. It was the season for ultimatums, for *It's him or me*, for demanding I never speak to my lover again and rededicate myself to our marriage. I knew what the Right Answer to such a justifiable demand was supposed to be, but it was the season I became incapable of giving it. It was the season for jealousy, for my flesh as territory, for my husband interrogating me on a long L-shaped couch in the hotel basement as to which sexual acts my lover and I had committed, demanding that I chronicle them all, that I tell him everything, and my shakily refusing to answer each pointed question. It was the season my period came unexpectedly, as if summoned by all this talk about my body's tidal forces, but my husband and I could not stop sobbing and fighting and bargaining and despairing long enough to find a tampon so I just wadded up toilet paper from the basement restroom and shoved the bulk between my lips to catch the sloughing-off insides of me. It was the season for thinking abruptly of Luce Irigaray and "When Our Lips Speak Together," for remembering that my husband had witnessed my intestines in a metal bowl during Enzo's birth—that he had seen the literal insides of me. How easy it must be, after something like that, to believe someone's body is part of your body, too, and you deserve to know everything, just as if your own hand committed a crime. It was the season my husband first looked at me like someone he had never met. It was the season he said quietly, when all the energy for screaming had drained, "How can you do this to me when we just started renovating our house?" and unbidden I recalled one of our favorite lines from *Unforgiven*, when Gene Hackman, about to be blown away by Clint Eastwood, says simply, "I don't deserve this . . . I was building a house." For years my husband and I had said to each other, off the cuff, *I was building a house!* It was the season every inside joke, every intimacy, became perverted, swerved ugly from my revelation.

It was the season we returned to the hotel room where our children were sleeping and woke them in haste to pack and leave, other ordinary families suddenly grotesque to us. It was the season I ushered my daughters quickly off to the side and whispered quickly, "That thing we never ever talk about? Well . . . I told him." It was the season when, in our frenzied exodus, we forgot Kaya's yellow blanket, the one I'd brought with us to China and rubbed softly against her face until she calmed, our first night in the Royal Dalton Hotel; the one she worried with her fingers or chewed the edges of to self-soothe when she was a toddler, until it became more of a frayed and holey (holy) rag. Amid the turmoil of sweeping what was left of our family into the car, my husband smacking the steering wheel and breaking down as he drove, we abandoned Yellow Blanket in a bed or among towels in the bathroom, and though I called the hotel six or seven times in the ensuing days to check on Lost and Found, Yellow Blanket was never seen again. It was the season for metaphors far too on-the-nose: demolished house, lost blanket. It was the season the story of our lives collapsed around us.

It was the season we were confined, all five of us, to the upstairs of our two-level home, one proper bed between us, extra furniture heaped in piles around our chaos, the entire downstairs draped in plastic tarps. It was the season we crammed the children's twin mattresses into what had been a hybrid of their playroom and my husband's office, closing the door tight between them and our master bedroom and pretending our walls did not have six ears. It was the season my husband and I made a million promises apiece that we would fail to keep. *We will always be a family* and *We will always be friends* and *You are an impossible act to follow* and *Your skin, oh god, your skin.* It was the season my heart felt bubble-wrapped, insulating me from the grief I knew I was supposed to feel. Instead, whenever I was alone in the car for even a few blocks, I cranked Beth Orton or Luscious Jackson or my lover's solo CD up to fifty; I sang elatedly, catching my own uncontrollable smile in the rearview mirror, my recurring dream banished for good. It was the season our workmen gave me dirty looks because our architect was in the same men's group as my husband and knew what I had done; I felt their eyes moving over me in the dusty air, assessing whether I was worthy of all this drama. It was the season of liberation and shame.

It was the season for confession, so my husband jumped in on the act, spilling demons of his own, from secret sexual fantasies to episodes of temper or negligence with the children to kissing a co-worker once in a long-ago car. It was the season we mistook honesty for mercy. It was the season of mutual accountability—a season as fleeting and rare as a leap year—and also sometimes the season of false equivalency to unanswerable questions about whose actions were "worse" and who had harmed our children more. It was the season that, instead of each trying to be our best self for each other and our kids, we tried to take solace in the amplified badness of the other to assuage our respective guilt, which is universally synonymous for the season when a relationship has Run Its Course. It was the season I recalled sitting in an emergency room with the toddler version of Mags, who had been crying in pain for hours, waiting for some doctor or nurse to tell me they had called DCFS because of her nursemaid's elbow even though I had no idea how her injury had appeared. That memory of my younger self—my terror that I would be falsely judged, as women so often are, and lose the thing I held most dear—that memory of my daughter's tears, not knowing why she hurt—it all incensed me until I threw up thinking about it while my husband was at work. *It had not happened—it had not happened—*I was an upper-middle-class white woman and no one had suspected me of foul play; my daughter had never been taken away; her arm was just fine now and had been for years. Still, it was the season of bile. It was the season my own anger terrified me so much I was more comfortable with his. It was the season my husband sometimes lamented, *I can't believe you're leaving me for a rock star,* and other times raged, *I can't believe you're so irresponsible you would put my life in danger fucking some junkie without a condom!* It was the season of STD testing, of inconsistency, instability, of the wild and reckless joy of release. It was the season I realized we never really know what another person is capable of or has secretly yearned for or done. It was the season of confidences between my husband and me when we should have both held our tongues.

It was the season Mags woke one dawn on her floor mattress

to find a beetle in her ear and she, once hysterical at any mild bug sighting even outdoors, had grown so inured to our degraded circumstances that she simply flicked it onto Enzo's mattress and went on sleeping. It was the season I told my husband that I loved him as a brother and didn't understand that as a slap. It was the season my husband took off his wedding ring and became my ex-husband. It was the season I kept saying, *Maybe someday I'm going to regret this*, and my already-becoming-ex-husband told me, more than once, *No. You won't.*

It was the season of six-hour conversations nightly, going over every minutia that had brought us here, every old grievance and indignation, my ex-husband often thanking me, between explosions, for "standing in the fire" with him instead of just shutting him out. It was the season his gratitude gutted me but I grasped it with both hands. It was the season Enzo rushed to jump onto our still-shared bed, begging his father to "stop crying, stop yelling, stop closing the door to have talks," and my heart flipped and cracked and shredded itself apart when our child's pleading had no impact. My body thrummed with *I did this, I did this.* It was the season my ex-husband took to OkCupid with a vengeance, racking up dates like balls on a pool table: a Spanish beauty; a woman who claimed to worship cock and in whose company he ran into a friend of ours, the sommelier who owned the restaurant at which my ex-husband was on his date. "I told her what happened to her also happened to me," my ex-husband informed me upon his return to our home, because the sommelier's husband had also been a cheater and had run off to New York after some unspecified length of a clandestine affair. It was the season when News Traveled Fast, which in the age of social media is every season. By the next morning, the sommelier's ex in New York, as well as a mutual friend in Los Angeles, had both texted me things to the effect of: *What???! You're getting a divorce!* and *OMG you're having an affair? With who? Why didn't you tell me?* It was the season when either my New York friend or my L.A. friend would only have had to each tell one other person, perhaps even one more between them, and by the next day half of our social circle would have pieced together the affair. It was the season my lover, who had as of yet said nothing to his wife about the hurricane blowing through my home in Chicago, stepped up to confess before anyone who knew her found out first. "I've already hurt her so much—I can't humiliate her that way too," he said, before getting off his phone to go have the Talk. Admitting to an affair his wife had secretly known about for years was one thing, but the revelation that he planned to leave her—to move out and make a life with me—was entirely another. *She went upstairs to fold laundry and has been crying for five hours,* he texted at one point. *I feel like a John Edwards piece of shit. I've never hated myself more.*

There are two implicit rules of adultery: first, do not call your lover's spouse on the phone and narc him out; second, do not confess to your own spouse unexpectedly and leave him flapping in the wind, at the mercy of your spouse's discretion. It was the season I kept saying to my lover, *I'm sorry, I didn't mean for this to happen,* and the season he never shot back, *What exactly did you mean to happen, then?* but we both knew he was thinking it.

It was the season my ex-husband and I attempted to go out to dinner "as friends" and it ended yet again with his slamming away from the table and calling me a bitch and running out of the restaurant. It was the season he would bring our car to a screeching halt and jump out, just a block from our house, and rush into an ebony night punctured by weak streetlights while I took to the driver's side and chased him, full of determination and déjà vu as he shouted, then texted, things to the effect of *I'm an asshole!* and *I should just get out of your and the children's lives and leave you alone!* It was the season I swore to this man I had slept beside for twenty-five years that nobody wanted that, least of all me—that his children needed him; that we all loved him; that we were still a family. It was the season I couldn't have imagined a time in the future when I would grow so terrified of him that convincing him not to just disappear in the turbulent darkness on that sad night would feel nothing like an act of humanity but rather the most dangerous of my many regrets.

It was the season my mother ended up in the ICU for her congestive heart failure and COPD, for the second or fourth or eighth time, a BiPAP machine attached to her face and doctors ushering me off to private waiting areas where they pressed power-of-attorney forms into my hands and fired bullets of questions: *Does your mother want to be intubated if the BiPAP doesn't work*; *Does your mother want CPR if her heart stops?* It was the season my ex-husband booked a solo trip to Colorado to meet up with his ex-fiancée from college, and maybe we both let ourselves imagine for five minutes that she was the one for him all along and I had merely been an overly long detour in the road of his life, my betrayal the release that set him free to return to her waiting arms. At the hospital, the amplified suction noises coming off my mother's face from the BiPAP thumped like some kind of experimental music. Her eyes were glued stickily shut. It was the season of my ex-husband pulling a suitcase out of his closet with a jerk, informing me that by the time he returned from Colorado I was to have all his things formally moved to the apartment we co-owned four blocks away. It was the season of "I am never spending another night with you in this house."

Here is a thing you don't know unless you, too, have left someone it nearly killed you to leave, and that is when you cleave from someone who doesn't want to break up, you have to find a cold steel core inside yourself to stand firm; you have to become a more unfeeling version of yourself, that same Stepford You who, in your naïveté, in the thrall of your first taste of honesty in three years, you believed you'd now cleanly left behind. You have to resist nostalgia, resist memory, resist the plurality of love. But at the finality of *never spending another night together again*, that façade of myself cracked, leaving only the unprotected, naked me under its shell. And so it became the season I sobbed hysterically, pleading, "Don't go, you can't leave like this—I'll do anything you want." It became the season of rushing into his closet and sinking onto its floor in a ball, a howling animal made as compact as I could get as though this would make him pack me, too. Instead, he said sadly, "Don't make promises you can't keep. Not anymore," and zipped his bag. It was the season he left the room while I screamed in blind pain on his closet floor. To get out of the house, he had to walk past our three children in the playroom, lying on their mattresses on the floor because there was nowhere else to go and already we were beginning to forget a time when rooms of our own had not been an unspeakable luxury—we were beginning to forget any season that did not always end in somebody's tears. As he passed the children, my ex-husband said to them, "Take care of your mother," and though Kaya and Mags pretended to sleep and ignored him entirely, Lorenzo leaped up and rushed to the closet where I was howling and took me in his May-warm arms, murmuring, "It's okay, Mommy, I love you, it's going to be okay." Never had I cried in front of my children before, even mildly. Always, I had striven not to be That Mother, whose children have to parent her, which my own mother, with her loneliness and marital neglect, often seemed to require of me. It had been a particular point of pride, all fourteen years I had been a mother, that my children did not have to "deal with my emotions"—that I was always able to put my game face on for them, even when my insides were rattling around. This was the season it became clear to me that my mother, whose life I'd always considered a monument to lost opportunities, had never made half the mess of anything with me that I had with my children—that although I had grown up in poverty and surrounded by violence and my parents seemed locked in a codependent stasis of mutual regret, in fact my tiny childhood apartment, despite our musical beds and my father's nine thousand locks on the front door, had always been to me a haven from the outside world. I had never slept on a floor with beetles in my ear, listening to my parents warring and weeping; I had never watched one of my parents leave and tried to protect my mother with my own body, believing I was all she had left in the world. It was the season I became a banshee with no control of the noises coming out of my throat while I huddled on a closet floor trying to tell myself I had no right to this, the keening of the abandoned when I had been the abandoner, and my daughters closed their eyes against the mess that was our lives, which we had imposed on them in such myriad ways that to count them all felt a never-ending hot potato of oscillating self-recrimination and blame. It was the season of wanting to be so, so many other things, but instead becoming this: a bad memory my children would never be able to get out of their heads.

It was the season I hired movers. By the time my ex-husband returned from Colorado, without any fantasy ex-fiancée on his arm and facing an uncertain future of whatever the fuck he was supposed to do without me, the movers were on their way. And so it was the season we stood together for the last time in what had been our daughters' bedroom before the renovation, the new, crisply painted white walls once an intricate mural of an Asian garden painted by a friend back when my ex-husband and I were both so goddamn painfully young, when we were about to fly to China and get our miracle girls and begin our family. Going through boxes still unpacked since the renovation, we came across the pink, blue, and white striped baby hat Enzo had worn in the hospital as a newborn, and we sobbed, simultaneously, wrackingly, convulsively, but separately now, without embracing, each encased in our own glass jar of pain. For what had been lost, for what was supposed to be our future but was Nothing Anymore. It was the season my ex-husband left me, after I gave him little other choice, after I had already left him in all ways except spatially, maybe the night at the Wisconsin Dells water park or maybe the late February evening in 2012 that my lover first kissed me in the pickup lane of O'Hare Airport, or maybe the night Kathy died, or maybe much longer ago at that Thai restaurant in Iowa fighting about the end of the world, without my even knowing I had done it at the time. The smell of Enzo's once-upon-a-time infant head mingled with the dust of that mistaken renovation, the sharp tang of paper box, the bacon our children had devoured that morning, the wet air of an approaching Chicago summer. It was the season our past and future commingled one last time together in the still-standing, beautifully remodeled, now irrevocably haunted house, the one I had blown down.

Big Blonde

I have already considered
the three philosophical problems
worthy of prolonged reflection: Why
are we here?
Is there anything to eat?
Where are our dead friends?

—Franz Wright

Years later, Kathy would claim we had met in the third-floor girls'
bathroom, but in my memory she and I first spoke during the
physics experiment involving razor blades. In both stories, she was
crying. In her version, she was crying because Max, the best-looking
guy in our class (or maybe the school), didn't notice her. In my version, she raced from the classroom crying when Max held the razor
blade to my wrist in jest, threatening to cut me, waiting for me to
flinch, and I'd said, "Go ahead, if it'll get me out of physics I'm all
for it," and he laughed, but Kathy fled into the hall. I caught up with
her in the third-floor girls' bathroom, but what she told me in my
memory wasn't that Max failed to notice her, but simply, "My father
committed suicide, that wasn't funny." While I stammered some
awkward high school apology, she held out her wrist—unnaturally

pale and delicate for a girl her height—and showed me a scar. "I tried to kill myself after he did," she said. "That's common. Kids whose parents commit suicide are at much greater risk." And in that moment, a friendship was born . . . a friendship for which there may be no better metaphor than the fact that, for the next twenty-seven years, we remembered its origins differently.

Soon after our bathroom encounter, Kathy took to calling me on the phone nightly to discuss her unrequited love for Max. At first, the gossip titillated me, but before long I began having my mother tell her I wasn't home. The nakedness of her desperation made me squirm—I wanted her to maintain some dignity. In my neighborhood, where I spent as little time as possible, showing vulnerability never ended well, especially for girls. I kept my cards close to my chest, subtly trying to urge her to do the same. But Kathy did not accommodate my desires on this front, then or ever. While Max, an aspiring actor, kept himself busy as an extra in Hollywood films and engaging in threesomes with older girls, hovering hopelessly out of both of our leagues, she continued to call me, to stalk me in study hall, which we also shared with Max, pouring herself into my hands whether or not I wished to receive her.

When I went away to college—the same college as Max, who had by then become a close friend—Kathy wrote to me faithfully. I believed she was "using me" to get closer to him, and in all probability, she was—at least initially. But then things shifted. Max intermittently receded, but Kathy always remained, a bawdy joke at the ready, a cigarette in one hand and a drink in the other. She made herself an indispensable friend. She had forgone college and was working in an office, and saved her money, scant though it often was, to come see me whether I was studying in Wisconsin or England or following a whirlwind romance to New England. When I threw parties in graduate school, seventy people crammed into my kitchen, Kathy was always the first to arrive to help set up, and the last to leave, washing dishes with me at 4 a.m. In our late twenties, she was by my side when I developed interstitial cystitis, accompanying me on doctor's appointments and running errands with me to pick up prescriptions. When I adopted my daughters, she became their first nanny, talking about them so much that other people assumed they were her children.

As the years passed, Kathy blossomed into a wounded, voluptuous sexiness. One of her quasi-boyfriends dubbed her "Big Blonde" after the Dorothy Parker story, and Kathy, with her literary aspirations, took this as a compliment in the same wholly uninvestigated way she believed Camille Paglia to be a pioneering mother of feminism. What this man actually meant, of course, intersected more closely with another friend of ours having once remarked that there was something about Kathy that made "men want to hurt her just because they know they can." She had a penchant for drunks, addicts, those living with other women, men who held her off to the side of their real lives. Her affairs invariably ended messily, in ways more embarrassing to witness than those old lovesick calls about Max. She would spy on her exes' apartments, write stalkery letters to their new girlfriends, and once I caught her rifling through my grad school notebooks because the Big Blonde–dubbing lover was in one of my seminars and she knew we passed notes when bored in class. She must have imagined herself as the central thread of our discussions, rather than Faulkner—rather than ourselves. Over a terse breakfast, I accused her not just of violating my privacy but of childish self-involvement: one of the few fights in our friendship.

By our thirties, however, all such melodrama had subsided to such a degree that I was almost nostalgic for it. In place of her self-destructive affairs, Kathy had slipped into a resigned celibacy, palpably exhausted and frightened by those twenty-something brushes with the edge of her own stability. She seemed afraid that she did not have what it took to withstand disappointments other women were able to weather with grace. For a full decade, she led a solitary life, working a safe job at a school staffed entirely by women, drinking Jameson and listening to Nina Simone in the evenings in her tiny apartment. And, of course, tagging along as an extra in my life: loving my children like a parent; nursing a nonthreatening crush on my husband (whom, after their rocky beginnings, she later took to joking she would marry once I—always sickly—kicked the bucket). At parties, she would give both my husband and me massages, would sit herself between us proprietarily until people muttered confusedly that perhaps she was our "third."

It was the sort of relationship that makes sense only from the inside, and even then, not entirely. The truth is that if Kathy's adulation seemed excessive, my acceptance of it—or, let's face it, embracing of it—was potentially even more mysterious. We weren't young anymore. Though I was neither beautiful nor well-bred, I had somehow grown, from our mousy high school days, into the kind of woman to whom certain things came easily, and in terms of traditional markers of a successful adulthood—higher education, work about which I was passionate, marriage, homeownership, raising children—it might indeed have been easy to conclude that I had "outgrown" Kathy—that, like Angie, I was destined to leave her behind. As my life grew busier to the point of bursting, there seemed scant explanation for why a lonely old high school friend remained perpetually glued to my side, insinuating herself into every corner of my pursuits, even taking over my mother's job of seventeen years when my mother at last retired. Some friends suspected that Kathy was "madly in love" with me, though I knew her attraction to me wasn't an erotic one. Other friends regarded my tolerance of her neediness as "saintly." Only those sharper observers of human nature recognized that she must be meeting some deep need in me, too.

At forty, Kathy broke her near-decade of celibacy with a turbulent affair that set off an intense depression. She sat at my kitchen table day after day, sobbing, shaking, drinking my scotch, popping my benzos, freaking out my children. And for the first time since high school, I, too, began to question why, exactly, I was allowing this in my life. Amid juggling the demands of career and family, Kathy often kept me on the phone for hours, analyzing every small detail of her past and psyche. For all her apparent hero worship of me, it became clear—perhaps it had always been clear—that I was rarely the topic of our conversations. I recalled how during those dark interstitial cystitis years in our late twenties, when I was dependent on painkillers and going to doctors, acupuncturists, osteopaths three or four times a week in desperation, as well as couples counseling due to the strain my illness put on my marriage, Kathy had told me with no trace of irony, upset over being jilted by some other unsuitable man, that I had "a perfect life." I was still four or five years out from becoming a mother and a decade away from having my first book published—did she mean merely my husband? Was marriage a trade up from health? I'd been borderline suicidal, cutting, unable to bear the thought of fifty more years in my agonized body: how could she be so blind?

Only two decades later would I see that she was not blind, merely trusting of the version of myself I volitionally fed her—had been feeding her since that third-floor bathroom where I never once admitted that I, too, thought about Max. In my twenties, I'd of course never mentioned the cutting. If anyone asked me how I was, I said, "Fine," smiling. When I went into remission from my IC at thirty, the clouds of my life parted, but from the outside, I probably appeared much the same. I had taken the ethos of playing it cool so far that even my closest friends had little idea what it was like under my skin; I was a Great Pretender, and Kathy my perpetually rapt audience of one. The deep need in me she was meeting—was it that she saw my life as better than it was, and that if I held tightly enough to her narrative, I might be able to believe it too?

Now here we were at forty. Despite my growing uneasiness, I saw Kathy through her depression, rejoiced with her when the antidepressants kicked in, then wrote the Match profile she used to meet the man who would become her fiancé. He gave her the happiest two years imaginable—the kind of blissfully gaudy PDAs usually reserved for high school; the surprise gifts that always perfectly reflected her tastes; the weekends away at Frank Lloyd Wright houses and fancy beach resorts she'd never been able to afford—before her sudden diagnosis of late-stage ovarian cancer pulled the magic carpet of her new life out from under her and sent her spiraling once more into the black night. This time, the depression did not loosen its grip. It sank its claws into her for four long, brutal months, until the December morning she died in her apartment while getting ready for work, blood smears on her telephone the only sign she'd been conscious long enough to know what was happening. For Kathy, there would be no "coming to peace" with her cancer, no gradual decline and acceptance. She died as she had lived: with her heart on her sleeve, full-throttle, and all too often alone.

In the last few years of her life, Kathy experienced both the greatest highs and lows she had ever known. And in the years since her death, I followed suit with the greatest highs and lows of *my* life, in ways set in motion by the loss of her, shaking me so far out of my role as the "perfect" friend/wife/mother that the woman Kathy used to know would begin to seem like a photo of a stranger in someone else's picture album. Would she even recognize me now, unmoored, sharing custody and living half-time in a small apartment alone for the first time in my adult life? In its confines, punctured by the mournful sounds of my weak iPhone speaker playing music to ward off the silence, I often think of Kathy: of her quiet, small spaces, of Jameson and Nina Simone. Without a husband and children to care for, I, too, sometimes have nights of calling a couple glasses of red wine "dinner." Out with friends, I, too, sometimes now hear the frantic lilt of my voice as I divulge more about my pending divorce than they probably wanted to know, and I remember how Tori and I used to cringe when Kathy, yet again, brought up things like her mother's chronic extramarital affairs and her family history of unplanned pregnancies ten minutes into any party. How little I understood, then, about the kind of sharp grief that pushes itself outside the skin, that lacks decorum, that will not be tamped down. Nights I'm alone especially, I want to pick up the phone and call Kathy not daily but hourly, the way she sometimes used to when she was the one with too much time on her hands. I want to say, *Can you believe this is real? I want to say, I am more myself than I ever believed I could be.* I want to say, *I'm scared out of my fucking mind.* My life—the less and less it resembles the one she knew me to live—is increasingly a ghost town full of her echoes. I began to understand her from the inside out only after she was gone.

What is devotion? What makes love mutual? Is equality an essential ingredient in friendship? In the years since her death, these questions have haunted me. It's become abundantly clear that Kathy was there for me in ways that no one—not even my husband or mother— ever had been: no detail of my daily grind was too banal for her to want involvement in it. I never had to attend an event or run an errand alone; she was perpetually available, tuned to my attentions like a little sister, seeking approval, studying me, emulating. The loss of her intensity left not a gap but a fucking crater—a loneliness that my other, more superficially "reciprocal" relationships could not seem to fill. At first, withdrawal from Kathy felt like it might kill me. Eventually, that same withdrawal—that loud void brought on by her unwelcome departure—snapped me out of the emotional autopilot that had become my life.

It is acceptable—expected even—to talk about how much we miss our departed friends. What is more taboo to admit is that Kathy's death woke me up in shocking, transformative, and ecstatic ways. The massive holes she left were not only a significant part of what forced me to realize how lonely I'd been in my marriage for many years, but the speed between her diagnosis and death pushed me to decide in one fell swoop to embrace how fleeting life is—to decide that in whatever time I had left, I would rather be a woman who regretted things I *had* done than things I hadn't, which perhaps remains the most complex decision about how to live that I have ever made.

Kathy met my lover only once, when he drove the two of us to LAX in 2006. It was the first time I'd seen him in person too, though I'd published him a few times by then, and Kathy made me sit in the back seat so she could sit up front and chat with him. Afterward, she always called him "Robert Downey Jr." and said he had a crush on me. But Kathy thought everyone had a crush on me, because she saw me through a certain flattering lens that made such things seem true to her, even when they were not.

In this case, I guess she was right. I wish she could be here to see that, too.

Paradoxically, I wish she'd been here to smack me upside the head at the bullshit I pulled along the way.

Except if she had lived, everything would be different. I would still have her. But maybe I would also still have all my artifices, the self-protective casing around my heart, the concern with how others—her high among them—perceived me. Maybe I would still be living my life on an imaginary stage, doing my best to project someone I believed everyone—Kathy included—wanted to see.

Kathy kept journals all her life, though like me she ended up destroying them. In her case, self-erasure was part of her performance of pain: she often burned her journals theatrically, informing all her friends she had done so and reveling in our protests and dismay. Still, those journals were real, whether or not they retain material form. In them, Kathy documented her body no less than I ever have, and I am certain they contained her private multitudes: her natural glamour and defiant woundedness; the way she made ordinary things like sitting in a cheap plastic folding chair in my tiny yard in Amsterdam feel like an "occasion" and yet, even in my photograph of her from that day, there was something irretrievably solitary about her. Her craving to be loved, sometimes flung at others with such velocity that it boomeranged back, pushing them away instead.

I have had to accept that my devotion to Kathy was in certain ways fueled by vanity—by the high of seeing myself as wildly more idealized and strong than I ever could be in reality. Since her death, this has stung, made me fear I was really the user between us, that I loved her wrongly and was not a good enough friend. Yet it is also true that I took her to chemo most weeks while her fiancé was at work. I loaned her money when she was in debt, bought her classes in massage therapy and bartending to help broaden her career options, let my kids watch hours of television while I talked with her about yet another disappointing lover, took her to the literary events she loved. And for twenty-seven fucking years, I listened to her, bottomlessly: something her self-involved mother and estranged older siblings rarely offered.

We laughed until we could barely breathe. We bought matching leather pants and wore them to baby showers. When I was hospitalized, she smuggled in flasks, and I loved her for it even when I was too sick to partake. When she sobbed in my car about her father during an east coast snowstorm, and we were rear-ended hard on the blindingly white night highway while I was comforting her, it never once occurred to me, even as I trudged painfully to the chiropractor for my whiplash, that I should have given her less focus in our perilous conditions, that I should have told her to wait for a more convenient time to come undone. We were friends. We were complicated, messy surrogate sisters. We had become that rarest of things, more rare than equality, I'd venture: unconditional.

Were we also fun-house mirrors for each other's images and needs? Of course we were, as is the way of people who grow up together. As is the way of people who understand that sometimes there is still a lot of growing up to do even at forty-three, when she was cut short. And yet: my love for her was stubbornly real. And yet: I wish I could thank her for the ways her skewed vision of me gave me the confidence to take on the world, making me more, even as the loss of her felt like a forensic blue light shining mercilessly on the invisible cracks left behind, not just in my "perfect life" but in me.

Would Kathy, once my biggest fan, like who I've become in her absence? I stumble forward while she remains frozen in time, until someday perhaps she would not know me on the street. The dead don't judge, but they also don't gratify, don't give permission. It's all on me now: these scars, these cracks, the tolls and beauties of my actions. I miss her more with every passing day because, just as words once written can never be unwritten, grief is not a thing that ends. Sometimes, though, it cracks us open and exposes the places we've hidden, and that can be a kind of gift. I learned to feel this heart-poundingly alive only once I learned from her how tenuous this life really is.

I wonder what would she say, if I could admit that it turned out she was my role model in the end? Kathy, who never could hold her heart back from her sleeve, who never played one fucking thing close to her chest. My sister, my kindred.

The Summer of Light and Dark

When I dream of fire
You're still the one I'd save
Though I've come to think of myself
As the flames, the splintering rafters

—Lucy Grealy

I don't trust my daughters to want to be on a solo vacation with me—much less a "service trip" in a gritty Guatemalan city, where we will need to make use of our shabby Spanish and my profoundly introverted daughters will have to engage with scads of strangers—so before diving in deep at my friend Julie's educational foundation in Quetzaltenango (called Xela by everyone here), I aim to bombard Mags and Kaya with a few days of beauty in Antigua. It is July, and I have been separated for three months. This trip feels like some kind of Hail Mary to help me assess where I stand.

Our Antiguan hotel, Casa Santo Domingo, is magnificent, built on an old convent and containing ancient tombs within, aglow nightly with hundreds of candles to illuminate walkways and ruin sites. Even though Julie got us a discount and our luxurious three-room suite costs less than many chain motel rooms in the United States, the hotel's decadent vibe makes me nervous, makes me imagine my ex's irritation at the money I am spending on a trip that doesn't include him, even if he no longer wishes to be included in anything that involves my presence anyway.

Kaya and Mags promptly unload the minibar, snapping selfies while holding up unopened cans of Guatemalan beer and tiny bottles of booze. My daughters are freshly fifteen, with shimmering hair nearly to their waists and the kinds of coltish, long legs I envied on other girls in my teenhood. Kaya can ace every standardized test that crosses her path and attends the top-ranked high school in Illinois; Mags is a visual art major at another selective-enrollment school and has gotten exactly one B in her straight (and Type) A career. She can also spell any word backward, at lightning speed, as though reading the letters off a chalkboard in reverse. Give her a lengthy sentence, even, and watch her roll. Kaya, by contrast, can take that same sentence and alphabetize the letters in it: a feat I can't even track to see if she's right until she repeats it over again for me more slowly. I used to cajole the girls to take their twinly act to their elementary school's talent show when they were younger, but both despise being the center of attention, and scoffed. Now I watch them hamming it up with their liquor, even pose with them for a few shots, holding the closed bottles up to my own mouth theatrically. At this, too, I'm imagining my ex's reaction should he see these shots on social media—his disapproval that I am "condoning underage drinking," perhaps—but I don't have the energy or even the desire to pretend that two fifteen-year-old inner-city teens have never had access to alcohol on their own. By their age, I had friends who'd already gotten pregnant, raped, addicted, and murdered; my daughters' lives, despite a traumatic start, are comparatively sheltered compared to what I understood of fifteen. Still, half of me is watching myself from a distance through his eyes—*Is this something only a bad mother would do?*—while the other half of me just wants my daughters to enjoy our trip, to have fun, to like me again.

To be clear: Mags and Kaya, with the exception of those rare *I hate you!* teen-girl fights, have never done anything to lead me to conclude that they do *not* like me. They cheerfully run banal errands with me to grocery-shop or pick up prescriptions at Walgreens or go to the post office, even when their presence is not required. They have never—ever—turned down an offer to go out to eat. Mags, whose bedroom is off the kitchen in our family home, at which I now spend four days per week to my ex's three, usually keeps up a running stream of conversation about her friends—all of whom I know—whenever I'm cooking or doing dishes, and sometimes, when we're watching TV, Kaya even "does my feet," wherein she whips out buffers and lotions and scours my heels until they are smooth: a practice I'm not sure whether she engages in because she enjoys it, or because my forty-something heels are offensive to her and she is trying to save me from being disgusting.

But the thing is, Mags and Kaya are sphinxes. Declarations of emotion are repulsive to them: I have not heard either girl say *I love you*—to me or anyone else—since they were nine or ten years old. At first (as this was years before my affair and my constant guilt), this annoyed me and I nagged them about it, especially Kaya, the even-more-reserved within their dyad. "Would it kill you to say 'I love you'?" I would pester her, feeling entitled to such declarations, which had never been in short supply between my mother and me, and on one occasion Kaya even caved, hurled herself into my arms with a force that nearly knocked me off my feet, shouting "I love you!" with some mixture of catharsis and defiance. After that, I let it go—released the expectation that their vocalized feelings were a thing they owed anybody—and took them on their own terms, which, to be blunt, was not only due to my desire to respect their innate natures but also a survival tactic. My daughters—less than one hundred pounds apiece—are mountains: unmovable, stubborn, and strong as rocks embedded in the ground. They suffer no bull-shit, which is precisely why I'm so worried that I have exceeded their patience and good graces—that I have become a thing they may tolerate rather than enjoy.

I counted on a couple of days alone before we headed off to Xela to volunteer at Julie's foundation, but it turned out that Julie picked us up at the airport in Guatemala City and transported us to Antigua herself, and that she has a room in our hotel, overseeing our time like a cruise director. I'm not sure how to feel about this, exactly. I don't know Julie all that well, and Kaya and Mags's aversion to strangers borders on intense. But I'm also grateful for the buffer. On most every trip our family has taken, local or far-flung, some sort of explosion has taken place, and although it was easy, the first handful of times, to blame my husband's temper, controlling nature, or taciturn silences, for the past three years I haven't been able to pretend to myself that I'm not a major contributor to the tension. Away from their father and Enzo, from school and friends and errands, who knows what kind of baggage might come up between my daughters and me after all my years of dishonesty? More: I've not sorted out yet whether my daughters are even glad I finally came clean (that I feel lighter is not a fact about which they necessarily have any shits to give), or whether they may think that part of the contract of our three-year lie of omission was that I was to take this secret to my grave and not "bother anybody" with some big, messy confession. If it's the latter, then this trip certainly puts an easy target on my back.

And so I find myself grateful at the sight of Julie—always smiling widely so that her eyes crinkle; always seeming relaxed and at ease given she is fluent in Spanish and Guatemala is her home—waiting for us in the swanky on-site restaurant for dinner. My daughters are already world travelers, but its splendor is enough to make us all giddy. Cheerily, Julie leads our mealtime conversations, asking my daughters personal questions with no fear of being invasive, being stonewalled, being judged. Together, we devour every dessert the restaurant has on offer, and Mags and Kaya take tiny sips of our red wine and make faces of distaste. Note to self: whatever they may be experimenting with in Chicago with their friends, it's not red wine.

This is not my first time in Guatemala. My ex and I came together in 2005, when Mags and Kaya were not even in kindergarten yet, before I became pregnant with Enzo. It was the last solo trip we would ever make where we were indisputably "happy"—before his mother was diagnosed with cancer the same month my mother had a heart attack and stroke, and things began to quiver like a chain of dominos that took a decade to fall. A decade later, Antigua feels haunted by our former happiness. Everywhere my daughters and I go, it seems my ex-husband and I once stood holding hands. Every crumbly, magnificent street threatens to lead to our old, charming hotel with its brightly tiled patio, where he photographed me in a pink pashmina, smiling wide; to the colonial square where I ate the best cheese sandwich on earth (something about the grain of the bread, the avocados). If we wander far enough in that direction there, we might find ourselves at the strange Indian restaurant that operated out of someone's house, and I might glimpse the thirty-something version of my then-husband drinking beer from a bottle in its courtyard, slightly tanned despite his pale skin, loving me and believing his good feelings about me are a permanent condition.

I drag Kaya and Mags around to ruins, to markets, and we snap photos, beaming like our smiles might be a reassuring proof of something, every day together a delicately sown new ground. But for me, behind my smile, despite my beautiful daughters, despite my amazing fortune at being here at all, the streets of Antigua are paved with broken glass.

It is a relief, then, to cloister in at the small Casa Santo Domingo pool, Julie and I lounging side-by-side on plastic chaise lounges, drinking gin and tonics on empty stomachs, our middle-aged bodies unabashed in bikinis, books discarded on the damp pavement. My daughters in the water, out of earshot or pretending to be, I fill Julie in about my impending divorce, which for a couple of months teetered on the great hope of amicability but has been rapidly deteriorating for about a month. I suck on my ice cubes, marveling aloud at the *civility* of infidelity in James Salter's *Light Years*, which I'm reading on a recommendation from a friend who knows my situation. "Everyone is so urbane," I tell Julie like a plea, tipsy enough to drop my cloak of 24/7 repentance. "It's all so Noel Coward, like infidelity and divorce are no big deal. I mean, I know it's a big deal—I know what I did was huge, but Jesus. Can't I get a little of that laissez-faire sophistication over here? Why does my ex have to act like I'm the only one in the history of the world who's ever fucked up? He talks about me to the kids like I'm a war criminal."

"Don't bite the hook," Julie advises in more even tones, though clearly the hook is so far down my throat that I'm choking. "He's trying to bait you, to prove himself right about you. You need to allow him his anger. He'll come around. And if he doesn't, doesn't that confirm that you did the right thing?"

Does it, though? At home, too, my friends keep telling me that I have the right to pursue happiness, but I have never been less happy in my life. I've never felt worse about myself . . . except of course *before* confessing. Now I'm a home-wrecker, but at least no longer a liar.

On the pages of *Light Years*, long after their cheating and cleaving, the ex-husband and his new wife nurse his former wife through cancer and death. That kind of scenario makes a certain emotional sense to me: its resistance to the idea of easy victims and perpetrators; an acceptance of moral ambiguities; a history that transcends sexual bonds and outlives lies. But maybe that is only easy to believe because *I* was the liar. More and more, such concepts seem the pretty possibilities of fiction. The splendor of Casa Santo Domingo may be distracting my fifteen-year-old daughters from the mess of our lives at home, but I still feel stuck on a hamster's wheel of playing the villain, like it or not.

Is not living a lie the best I have any right to hope for, going forward?

In the doorway of Education and Hope, Julie doles out hugs and kisses. It's the kind of scene—a white, vaguely bohemian middle-aged woman embracing one school-uniformed Guatemalan child after another—that would look contrived in a Hollywood film, but in person, the mutual joy of both Julie and the children at being reunited is a visceral force. Before her few days in Antigua with us, Julie was in Connecticut, where she was raised and where her husband lives and works—she spends approximately half the year in Xela overseeing Education and Hope, the nonprofit she launched in 1994 when she was barely out of college. Back then, she only intended to study Spanish in Xela, but she ended up spearheading a campaign to raise the money to send a small handful of her Guatemalan neighbors' kids to school—families who otherwise couldn't afford the costs. Of course it turned out that just sending the kids was insufficient: their parents were in many cases illiterate and working multiple jobs to support the family, so there was no structure at home to support the children's educational endeavors. Many were going hungry or had no one to assist them with homework. Instead of deciding that her efforts were in vain, as many people would have—as I likely would have—Julie doubled down.

Twenty-one years later, Education and Hope's after-school program serves hot, home-cooked meals and provides tutoring to more than one hundred kids daily, and has cumulatively provided scholarships, textbooks, uniforms, shoes, supplies, and even medical care to thousands of children in Xela.

My daughters and I stand by as child after child greets Julie in rapid-fire Spanish ("Julia," they call her, like *Julio*) while clinging to her neck. Five years ago, when we were in Kenya and went to a children's home to donate supplies, our family was subjected to a series of cringeworthy White Savior performances, such as the orphanage director dragging every child out to the courtyard—even one in a wheelchair—to take photos with us and our stacked-up donated goods, and in the end, even though we had brought a month's worth of rice and toiletries and school supplies, we all left feeling slightly dirty. By contrast, Julie makes no effort to make this reunion moment about us—she doesn't even introduce us, much less prompt the children to thank us, hug us, introduce themselves, or speak English on cue—slowly, my anxiety about being here begins to soften, even if I'm not sure what to do with myself yet.

Though Education and Hope provides a shit-ton of practical services, Julie—a practicing Catholic, like most of those she serves—refers to its core mission as "love." Hundreds of kids from the past keep in close touch with her, and a smattering, now grown, work for the foundation. Still, when I say I'd like to write about her foundation for a magazine, to raise awareness, even money, she grimaces a little. "I hate being thought of as saintly," she explains. "Most people portray me as something I'm not."

From where I'm standing, being thought of as saintly seems a high-class problem to have. I also know that being thought of as something I wasn't—as more altruistic, more selfless, more tirelessly giving than I was—was one root of most of my current troubles. And Julie is . . . well, complicated. There's a slightly New Age, social justice Christianity about her that admittedly isn't in line with my usual taste in friends. She's also married to a significantly younger, long-haired man; she swears a lot; she has a penchant for bourbon— and she suffers from a pervasively acute case of interstitial cystitis, as well as chronic fatigue, like some mash-up of my lover's wife's medical issues and my own. Both conditions have been historically dismissed by mainstream medicine as vague somatoform afflictions of neurotic women, and indeed Julie has had little success in finding help for either her pain or her exhaustion. Her constant travel does her health no favors, and she admits she has an easier time caring for others than for herself—that if avoiding stress is any key to managing her illnesses, she's failing miserably. This summer, one of her siblings is in such perpetual crisis from addiction that Julie is anxious about the safety of her niece and nephew, feeling guilty for focusing on children in another country when her own house is in disrepair.

It surprises me not even a little that being a woman can result in feeling like you are a bad person for literally dedicating your life to helping others.

The history of the United States in Guatemala is even more complicated than our hostess. In 1954, a CIA-led coup ended—and ultimately reversed—the Guatemalan Revolution, overthrowing the progressive, democratically elected government and installing a dictatorship. Political parties were banned, and widespread torture, repression, and murder followed. United States–backed authoritarian governments didn't stop running Guatemala until 1996, essentially causing many of the very problems a young Julie happed upon when she first came to Xela. "Sainthood" for any American in Guatemala—as in many places around the globe—is hardly an option.

I'm familiar with this conundrum myself. My ex-husband and

I brought Kaya and Mags home from China in April 2001, five months before September 11 changed the landscape of America, setting off waves of knee-jerk patriotism and nationalism that gave birth to "freedom fries," the Patriot Act, the Tea Party, the birther movement, and now its chief instigator—Donald Trump—having just announced his candidacy for president. Before my daughters were U.S. citizens for a year, their newfound country embarked on a path of war that has persisted throughout their lifetime. Though my motives for adopting were simple—I wanted children; I believed myself infertile—I never questioned, going in, that the United States would offer better opportunities for my daughters than they would find in their country of origin. In China, abandoned girls who have been left behind (amid the massive female diaspora that has resulted in China being a leading exporter of daughters around North America and Europe) are generally turned out of their orphanages by the age of fifteen to—instead of going to highly ranked high schools to study painting and photography, or going on family service trips—support themselves in an economy they are ill-prepared to face, lacking any support system. Still, in the ensuing years postadoption, as the United States grew increasingly divided and militaristic, I had to at the very least challenge my own assumptions about what America offered my children, and to what extent the United States was complicit in the problems China faced, too. When they were babies, people—mostly white people, but not exclusively—often came up to me at playgrounds, in food courts of shopping malls, even in public restrooms—to praise me for "saving" my daughters, as though they were a philanthropic pet project; as though I were a missionary rather than a mom. Always, this had rankled me, but even then, for years, that rankling had never included a questioning as to whether the United States was a good place to raise a child, much less children of color. Lately, in addition to other epiphanies about my shortcomings as a parent, I've wondered, too, how much of my becoming a mother was bound up in American imperialism—in my own unexamined beliefs around what was "best"?

What have my daughters lost by American isolation and individualism serving as their national role model? What have they lost, caught between two superpower nations, neither of which seem capable of telling the truth about their pasts or valuing the lives of young girls? What have they lost by looking every day at my face, the faces around Chicago's north side, that made whiteness seem somehow "natural" throughout their childhoods: a norm from which they deviate?

What are the children at Education and Hope losing, too, by seeing a white American woman as capable of bestowing upon them a future that their own parents cannot?

Xela serves as a sharp contrast to Antigua and Casa Santo Domingo. Here, my daughters and I stay in one room for twenty-four dollars a night, where we have thus far found spiders in our beds, and in our shower the water that emerges from a pipe protruding from the wall is ice cold. The sink runs, rather than through a drain, directly into a bucket under the basin. My daughters are cranky and skittish from the bugs, and I keep assuring them that we don't have to be in the room much—that we are "here to volunteer"—but none of us understands what that even means yet, so my assurances calm nobody.

We are across the street from Education and Hope: two buildings that take up half a city block. Its rooftop play area is painted with murals from *Where the Wild Things Are*, and indoors, the individual classrooms are small and sparsely furnished, packed with tutors helping children grouped by age with their homework, or running computer classes. Across the street in a separate building is the sprawling cafeteria, with seven or eight traditionally dressed

Guatemalan women cooking at any given time. Whenever Kaya, Mags, and I enter, women hand us bowls of chicken stew or rice and beans. The teachers and administrators eat with the children, but as is the case everywhere, the cooks never seem to sit down.

A handful of the children have special needs. Many more are toddlers, too young really for tutoring and school, but already part of the Education and Hope family. Wandering around the periphery is an artsy twenty-something, sporting both a hipster scarf and a camera slung around his neck. He looks almost as out of place as my daughters and I do, though it turns out he is an alum of the program and that he painted the *Wild Things* murals. Now he has a French girlfriend, about which Julie and the other *señoras* seem skeptical and cluck their tongues. Education and Hope is clearly a family, and like every family, its younger generation may not be doing things the way the elders would prefer. The cooks, glanced at as a group, appear to be homogenously women of a certain age, but on closer individual inspection many are younger than Julie and me, even if their attire and bearing remind me more of my Italian grandmother than of a peer.

Many of these women take buses for two hours to get to work, to begin cooking for the kids at the crack of dawn. Some bring their children with them. I find myself wondering how many are divorced or have been abandoned by their men. I don't wonder how many *abandoned* their men, as I have jumped to the assumption that such a thing might be unfeasible here. But what do I know of their lives? Wrecked love and broken families and betrayal and its subsequent rage know no borders. Maybe the only difference is that my daughters and I can afford to temporarily get away from it all, our holiday landing us as tourists in other people's everyday lives, which, my daughters often quip, is the specialty of "white people."

My daughters spent their first nine months in an orphanage

that makes Education and Hope look like an elite Swiss boarding
school. Before the orphanage, the story goes, they were found in
a train station with umbilical hernias, weighing three and a half
pounds each . . . but over the past few years it's been uncovered that
many "origin stories" of how and where China's so-called orphans
were found were actually a sham. Certain commonalities among
the stories emerged as so prevalent that it felt almost as though an
internal memo had circulated, creating one swooping talking point
for how the baby girls of China had come to find themselves in the
arms of foreigners. In truth, though the one-child policy led many
birth families to abandon children they could not afford to pay
steep fines or face legal consequences for having—sometimes including forced sterilization—it's also true that sometimes "forbidden" second babies were sold to orphanages for money, even though
this technically reduced China's overall population not at all, and
that some wanted children were even kidnapped by local merce-
naries seeking a slice of the Chinese government's profit from international adoptions. There are few things about Mags's and Kaya's
lives Before that I "know" for sure anymore . . . though one is that
the doctor at their orphanage proudly reported feeding them with
a dropper at first because they were so premature, yet survived.
When we first met our daughters, Kaya's legs didn't seem to work,
and remained perpetually in the fetal position from some combina-
tion of languishing too often in a crib and being born profoundly
early without adequate intervention—whenever we stretched her
legs out straight, they sprang back up, protectively curled. But of
course Kaya and Mags have no memory of that: both participated
in Girls on the Run, then track in elementary school. All of their
early physical delays evaporated within the first six months postadoption, like putting a rabbit back into a hat so that any vestiges
of their harrowing first year on earth became harder to pinpoint: a
Now you see it, now you don't portrait of early trauma. And isn't that

the quintessential American myth of reinvention? My daughters, though derisively, sometimes include themselves in the bad joke of white privilege these days. "Oh my god, we are so white," they groan.

When I was their age, I'd never left the United States—I'd been on an airplane only once, my family living on my father's disability checks while my mother, out of the workforce since my birth, scrounged for a low-wage, low-skill job. Though I spent my late teens and early twenties traveling relentlessly, "travel" at that time certainly didn't mean Kenyan safaris or even Casa Santo Domingo, but rather sleeping on train floors around Europe, squatting in the traveler's subculture of London surrounded mostly by men and working under-the-table jobs as a bartender or maid. Travel also meant the kinds of dangerous misadventures to which solo women are no doubt just as subjected today as in the late 1980s . . . such as the time Tori and I were essentially kidnapped in Greece by a couple of asshole vacationing pilots and were rescued only when our would-be abductors took us out in public (no doubt confident that we couldn't extricate ourselves without speaking the language) and we randomly happened upon a group of American college guys at an otherwise untouristed restaurant and threw ourselves at them, dancing as sluttily as possible on the empty dance floor until they spoke to us. It seemed a given that in order to be saved from dangerous men, less dangerous men who wanted to rescue damsels in distress were required, and our young, female bodies were the commodity over which different types of men might be set against each other, to compete for who would have us that night. For me—for most women travelers (despite some level of privilege being an implicit component of travel: the price of plane tickets; the not needing to be home working three jobs to support a family)—danger was part of the deal if you wanted to see anything outside your backyard . . . which was fine since if you are young and female, chances are your backyard is dangerous too.

Unless you count camping, my children have never previously vacationed anywhere rougher than a Super 8 motel—a fact that fills me with shame and pride simultaneously.

I want my daughters to understand the world and its multitudes. But one week in a shabby hotel in Xela—one week volunteering at Education and Hope—isn't going to change the fact that I've spent my years as a mother trying to shelter my children from precisely the kind of life I led. One week of "service" in Guatemala isn't going to undo the fact that my ex-husband and I paid $23,000 to an American adoption agency and the Chinese government for our daughters, making international adoption largely a moneyed enterprise I could not have afforded without his auspices, or that the Hunan province, where our daughters were born, is one of those most heavily associated with financial corruption and dishonesty surrounding adoptions. Yes: I want Mags and Kaya to witness Julie's important work—to grow into women who will seek to help others—and I hope this short trip will leave an impression, spark a desire to return, to service if not to Education and Hope specifically. And maybe I half-want to *be* Julie too, as I'm sure many people who meet her do. But boiled down to the smallest possible essence: I am on this trip looking to give my daughters some window into *myself*—into what matters to me—no matter how politically tricky, no matter how loaded or paradoxical. I am looking to draft a template for our future relationship without their father's presence, protection, or greater income—I am trying to figure out what and who I offer them going forward, alone. I am looking for, if not exactly understanding, some shot at redemption.

What's clear already is that only the wildly privileged have the ability to traverse continents looking for things to begin with.

•

"Do you have children?" the little girls in the Education and Hope English classroom ask my daughters.

Our Spanish is crappy, their English not better, and for a moment we all stand gaping at one another and saying sentence fragments back and forth, trying to figure out what they mean. Only after some repetition does it become clear that of course that *is* what they mean: do my daughters, barely fifteen, have any children?

It is not such a preposterous question. My father was working full-time in a factory by thirteen; aunts on both sides of my family married at fourteen and sixteen, respectively. I was the first person on either side of my family to go away to college, at a time when my parents made $9,000 annually. I wanted nothing more than a different kind of life, and I found it: at age thirty-two, I was among the first in my friend groups to become a mother. How quickly, though, in less than one generation, what was once normative can begin to seem implausible.

"We *are* children," my daughters try to explain to the students, pointing at themselves. *Nosotros somos niños!* But they have been to Kenya, to Europe, to Belize, to Saint Lucia, to arts camp at Interlochen, and now they are here, teaching a class at Education and Hope. Soon enough, another teacher snags me away to my own classroom to help with math, leaving my daughters to teach (and take selfies with) their students alone. In a country where the average national income is $3,440 per year—about the price of this trip, give or take our donation to Education and Hope?—my daughters have lived dozens of lifetimes in experience.

Wife of twenty-two years. Chinese orphans. American traveler studying Spanish. We are always permeable, shifting. We are all only one strange leap away from becoming inconceivable to our former selves.

•

One of the cooks at Education and Hope, Marta Maria, invites my daughters and me to her home. Julie comes with us, of course. We drive about an hour away to a gravel road, an assortment of small, squat buildings lining it, one of which is an auto shop, the other an indoor/outdoor barn. Dispersed among these shanties are other rooms: the kitchen, a bedroom where the family sleeps. The smell of fire from the stove, of gasoline from the cars, of manure from the animals, intermixes; the ground is muddy and strewn with straw.

Marta Maria's husband materializes, and my daughters and I are friendly, but it soon becomes clear that no one else here likes him much. Marta Maria herself ignores him, launches into a monologue that my daughters and I can't quite follow though it is clear that she is praising Julie, whom she kisses and hugs while she talks. There is a half-taken-apart car in what would be the living room, and in the yard a giant hog they encourage us to photograph, smiling. The outdoor bathroom is in a whole separate area, and to get to it we pass through piles of used car parts. Julie is hugging Marta Maria back, grudgingly translating some of what she is saying so we aren't left out—her cheeks turn red with embarrassment as she repeats Marta Maria's claims that Julie saved the family's lives, is the most wonderful person they have ever known.

We have been invited here as a courtesy to Julie—but now that we are here there are no chairs to sit on and only one person speaks both English and Spanish, so we all stand around awkwardly, giving and receiving hugs, until we pile back into Julie's truck, leaving Marta Maria and her family behind. Julie explains to us how Marta Maria's husband was once chronically unfaithful, drank too much, was never around, but then he got cancer so now Marta Maria is stuck caring for him, and I am reminded of *Light Years*, of the strange universality of the human condition, nothing new under the sun. "I've tried to urge her that she needs to either forgive him or leave," Julie says. "But sometimes holding on to anger is important to people and is what keeps them going."

My daughters and I have been given an almost too-intimate glimpse into the lives of people we will probably never see again, who know nothing about ours. The sense of being a spectator and also of gratitude floods me, contradictory and intermingling. My daughters, mostly silent on the car ride back, are inscrutable—as they were during the years I was lying to them about my affair being over and they never confronted me, their resentment and mistrust palpable but unspoken as we went about our daily lives, our familial intimacy locking their tongues. My ex-husband and I both once believed we knew each other inside out, but in both cases we were proved dead wrong. Do I know who my daughters are—these babies I carried on my hips for three years straight, who screamed if I left the room even to use the toilet, who imprinted on me with such raw totality after the double trauma of abandonment and adoption to a new country that they began to seem extensions of my body, of myself? Or do I only *think* I know them, based on their childhood reliance on me that they are fast outgrowing?

But back in our shabby hotel room, they say things like "This place is actually pretty nice for only twenty-four dollars a night," and "Look how they decorated the dresser, they're really trying to make it look nice for us," and "Our shower really isn't that bad."

No one mentions the spiders.

If love were a thing that could split a body open, I would be flayed. My daughters watch *Friends* on Spanish-language TV from a small set protruding from the wall, content with the familiar, no words required. I would say that *perspective* is a thing you can't buy, except maybe you can if you're in the market and lucky enough to afford the fee. I find myself hoping, silently, that Marta Maria's husband understands what she is doing for him, as I understand what my daughters are doing for me in allowing an After beyond my transgressions. I have spent this entire trip constantly checking myself for one more thing I've done wrong, one more mistake that might take my remaining love away. Tonight, I dare try on the idea that maybe, just maybe, my children will love me through my imperfections just as I have loved my father through his—that I don't need to be perfect or even better to be worthy of our bond.

Once upon a time in Guatemala, my husband and I visited Lake Atitlán. We traveled by speedboat to a rented romantic cabin, but later that evening, after dinner, we either forgot our key or it didn't work, and we ended up stranded on the steps in a rainstorm, him venturing out to see if any of the neighbors had the landlord's number. Almost miraculously, he met with luck, so that instead of getting pneumonia we ended up laughing about our short-lived mishap from the comfort of our warm bed. The next day, the sun blaring again, the mountains stood sentry surrounding calm azure waters. My husband and I caught a cab back to town, and our cabbie was an American hippie chick a bit younger than ourselves, though we were still young enough to forge the instant connection of fellow travelers. She gave us a CD of her Guatemalan boyfriend's music, and we listened to it faithfully for a while, titillated by our strange connection to the talented singer. Later—maybe a year or two—the cab driver even called me when she was in Chicago, and I met her at a Latin American café that had a play area for my kids.

She seemed so . . . different on Chicago soil. Just another twenty-something white American girl from the suburbs, lamenting her moody boyfriend—and I just another mom fast approaching middle age, with baby food stains on my shirt, breasts swollen with milk, and three small beings hanging noisily off my body. The magic of that taxi ride in Guatemala had evaporated, so that we were merely two relative strangers, stuck with each other for the duration of our meal, with nothing on earth in common to join us anymore.

Do you have children?

We are children.

Maybe, to Kaya, I love you is *eiloouvy*; maybe to Mags it reads *uoyevoli*. Maybe I still don't fully understand their language, because I have been thinking of myself so much I haven't listened hard enough yet.

Where you are standing—your spot on the ground amid this vast world—and what you choose to look at from there means absolutely everything.

For our final stop in Guatemala, Julie takes us to Lake Atitlán, where alongside the ghost of my ex-husband's and my own former selves, we lounge in an infinity hot tub surrounded by lush gardens and misty mountain views. By now, my daughters are calling Julie and me their "lesbian moms," joking that our shared boho aesthetic and whiteness mixed with their Asian-adoptedness makes us look like a stereotypical "alternative" family. We four have found, though Julie was a near stranger at the onset of this trip, an easy rhythm with one another by the end, assaulted together by splendor and kindness and hardship and hot springs in bright contrast to the cold morning air.

In Chicago my mother has been hospitalized yet again, and my ex-husband has turned her care over to my friends. I need to get home—I am *needed* at home. Being a home-wrecker, it turns out, doesn't exempt me from my domestic responsibilities—doesn't prevent me from having a home in the people remaining, who love me somehow, regardless. I miss Enzo intensely and I need to tend to my ailing parents and I cannot, despite my fantasies, stay here and "be Julie" any more than I could remain on the streets of Antigua with the perfect cheese sandwich and a marriage not yet imploded. My daughters and I pose as Julie takes our photos in paradise, and I feel water and sun and confusion and love and pain, and I ask it all for guidance as I let it go.

I have no idea that all too soon, this trip will come to seem to me like an easy time in my life. I know only to hold fast to the hope that, as Hemingway said, I can come together stronger at my "broken places." I know only that divorce and loss and illness and anger exist in Guatemala just as they do everywhere on our messy planet. In the harrowing months to come, I will often think of Julie—somewhere drinking a bourbon or bickering with her husband or holding a child or passing through her own needle's head of illness and pain or being a normal fucking human being and nothing like a saint— while simultaneously, somewhere else, she changes one small corner of the world, blooming constantly outward.

In the spring of 2017, Donald Trump already the president and neither of my daughters, proud and furious young women of color, ever again making so much as a tongue in cheek joke about their being "white," Kaya will organize a Habitat for Humanity trip and fundraiser for a group of teens and spend a week demolishing and building houses in Colorado, her deceptively strong, wiry arms defying every assumption anyone might have made about her on the spring day in 2001 when her seemingly fragile body was first placed into my arms. I will pick her up at Midway Airport, her skin browned from working outdoors, her smile suddenly shy with the same incongruity I remember from my own youth upon returning home to my familiar after an adventurous solo voyage—this the first of Kaya's many. In the summer of 2017, Mags will win a scholarship to study education as a human right in South Africa after writing about Education and Hope in her application, and for three weeks will exist at the southernmost tip of a faraway continent, being hospitalized twice for unexpected health problems but refusing to be

flown home, persisting to volunteer in schools there, to make friendships that will change her life, to return with a woman's strength
forged by the fire of knowing what it is to face her fears and stand
resolute in a foreign land alone.

As for me, I didn't mean to, but I forgot my copy of James Salter's
Light Years at Casa Santo Domingo in Antigua, that summer of 2015,
in what were still our last unwitting days of innocence. And though
for the rest of the trip I thought of the novel frequently, planning to
buy it again as soon as I got home, somehow I never do. By the time
we land in Chicago, it has become abundantly clear that James Salter
has nothing more to teach me—about forgiveness, about grace—that
I haven't learned from the women in my life, especially my daughters. As it turns out, I left that story somewhere just past the middle,
knowing it is up to me, now, to write my own end.

A Short Dictionary of Mutually Understood Words

If I get the story right, desire is continuous,
equatorial. There is still so much
I want to know . . .
Tell me our story: are we impetuous,
are we kind to each other, do we surrender
to what the mind cannot think past?
Where is the evidence I will learn
to be good at loving?

—Stacie Cassarino

Affair Bubble

Metaphorical place, actual state of being / what everyone will tell us
we were in. Related terms: **The Era of Our Spectacular Rationalizations, Butte, Chicago, Best Friend, Infinity, Given**.

Best Friend
Historical usage: "We're just very strange best friends"; see also **The Era of Our Spectacular Rationalizations**. Contemporary usage: "I need you to still be my best friend" as in: *even though I still live with my wife / while I cry over her.*

Butte
Where you say you would be happy, so long as I were there too. Side note: Commonly regarded as a less interesting or desirable place than **Chicago**.

Calgary River
1) The banks along which you wildly shout "Gina loves me" on our shared birthday in 2012, while I am in London with my husband and children wondering whether to end our affair because it has escalated beyond our control, but instead my husband has an explosion at our hostess on a public street and I end up texting you, *I know you would leave your marriage if I would leave mine*, and everything escalates still further from there; 2) A shorthand symbol of the intensity of our emotions; 3) An aching memory after your two-year clinical depression sets in, sometimes leading me to say things like, "But you used to be so happy that I loved you that you screamed my name into a river—how can you be so miserable now that I'm actually yours?"

Caregiver Fatigue
The feeling of emotional numbness that sets in as a result of being a sick person's entire world. Fatigue may be directly proportionate to: a) the sick person's willingness to engage in proactive self-care physically and psychologically, b) any ongoing responsibility for the sick person's friendships, sexuality, self-esteem, driving, waking up,

changing, bathing, food intake, happiness, will to live, c) the age of the sick person, i.e., infants produce lower-level **Caregiver Fatigue** despite being utterly helpless; wives produce high levels of **Caregiver Fatigue** even when they earn more money than the caregiver; parents with colostomy bags and/or holes in parts of the body where holes do not organically occur produce levels of **Caregiver Fatigue** that may eventually produce an alarming numbness in the giver who used to care so deeply.

Chicago
Historical usage: "I can't wait to move there," as you told all of our **Confidants** for years during our affair, even going so far as once asking your wife for a separation and suggesting to me that you get your own apartment in **Chicago** so as to be near me more regularly, years before I left my husband. Contemporary usage: "**Chicago** is gun-in-your-mouth cold" and "I've been doing things to make women happy my entire life, and I'm afraid moving to **Chicago** would just be repeating that pattern" and "This just isn't my **Home**."

Codependent
1) When your wife says things to you like: *It would have been kinder to kill me in my sleep than to abandon me this way*; 2) When you cannot even get out of your car to go to an AA meeting because you are crying so violently in an overload of guilt, grief, and the fear of living without her even if an outside eye might think you had been without each other for years; 3) When you are living for the scant hours when your wife, who so rarely—so almost-never—leaves the house, finally visits her sister and you can breathe in your own apartment without being the salt rubbing her wounds; 4) When I, bearing witness to this dynamic between you, fail to extricate myself and instead text you things

like, *Even the best cellmate on earth cannot change the fact that you are in prison*; 5) An utter failure to recognize that, by treating any of this as though my problem is "her" rather than you, I have consented to draw myself as the smallest angle in your marital scalene triangle.

Confidants

1) People of whom it is possible to take advantage; 2) A handful of people—S, especially, the first person I told and the only friend in whom we mutually confided—who initially will seem excited and giddy at being in the know about our love. Later it will turn out we burdened S terribly with our secret, and whom I especially emotionally taxed via such agonized texts as *I broke up my children's family for this, what have I done?* when it begins to seem that you will never leave your wife's apartment; 3) A twenty-year friendship that is, for several years, not quite the same.

Cuba

Metaphorical final destination for, as our friend S would once have romantically called it, "our unstoppable train."

Denial

A form of delusional thinking leading to such later epiphanies as, *If I could not even hide a journal safely in my full house of watchful eyes, and had to shred it over a trash can miles from my home in the dark, exactly how the fuck did I think I would explain a vial of blood had it been found in my underwear drawer?*

Differently Lit/Dimmer Switch

Applicable in both your written or spoken sentences. Examples: "When I was walking toward baggage claim, you were the first person I saw because you're so **Differently Lit**." / "I love that you have no **Dimmer Switch**."

The Era of Our Spectacular Rationalizations

Stage 1: A period of magical thinking, from December 2011 until June 2012, in which we are having first an emotional then a physical affair but telling ourselves that we are just "very strange **Best Friends**," and it will not hurt our marriages. Stage 2: As that **Denial** increasingly exposes itself as not just false but cruel and grandiose, a period in which we believe we can successfully end our affair but remain friends or, when that repeatedly fails, that we can delay ending our marriages for another decade, until my children are grown.

Feminis(m/t)

Am I a worst **Feminist** if: a) I steal another woman's man, b) but men are not property and cannot be "stolen," c) yeah but the woman who thought she owned the man is sick, d) and I cannot deny having valued romantic and sexual connections with said man over any honor toward said woman, e) whom I barely knew, but I pretended to be friendly toward for reasons I still don't fully understand (*why couldn't I just have avoided her entirely—why, why?*), f) and what if they were sexually and socially estranged for years before I ever came around and everyone we knew in common noted that fact in my presence? g) come on, marriage is an oppressive patriarchal institution anyway; it's **Feminist** to refuse to play by patriarchal rules! h) are you listening to yourself? I mean, *really* listening to yourself? i) yes, I'm afraid I am, j) all of the above.

Fingernail

Where your fingerprint embedded in my nail polish even though I had painted my nails twenty-four hours ago, that's how hard you held my hand. Example: In the New York cab on the way to JFK, I held my **Fingernail** to my lips and traced the pattern of you with my tongue.

Getting Marked Up to Get Marked Up
The habit of making a pass at one's spouse a day or two prior to going to see one's lover, and instigating a sexual act that will leave marks, so as to eliminate any suspicion should one return home from a lover's tryst with evidence like bite marks or bruises.

Given
1) What we were supposed to be; 2) What our respective spouses no doubt assumed their marriages to be; 3) A romantic construct or fallacy; 4) Still, aren't we—*aren't* we?

Home
Colloquial usage during **Affair Bubble**: "Anywhere you are is my home." Except this does not translate, it turns out, to lived practice unless my kids can be there too. See also: *Why I cannot move to California*. Similar terms that do not translate from Then to Now: **Our Bed**, **Butte**.

Honesty
A thing that makes it necessary to inform you every time I have sex with my husband and exactly what constituted said sex. Alternately called "radical honesty" by Jean-Paul Sartre and Simone de Beauvoir, usually when he wanted her to introduce him to a very young woman to seduce. Synonym: emotional masochism.

Honor Among Thieves
1) Why not one single day goes by in 3.5 years without our mutually emailing and texting each other no matter what else is going on in

our respective lives; 2) Total **Honesty** inside the context of a dishonest situation; 3) What I violated by telling my husband about us without warning or a plan, without consulting you first as we always promised we would do if one of us needed to reveal the truth. [Sidebar: *Will you ever forgive me? Is this why you won't move here? I'm sorry.*]

Infinity
1) Cliché from a John Green novel; 2) Word used in some form in the sign-off of almost every email or text we send over a five-year period. Examples: *You are the expander of my infinities* or *I love you infinitely*; 3) Often symbolized by the signature **xxx**; 4) Did you know that if bamboo exist in a large enough quantity, the number is known simply as infinite?

Journals
(see **Self-erasure**; see Kate Zambreno's *Heroines*): 1) A thing to be shredded by twilight, across from the Drake Hotel, into a city-owned trash can, for fear of being discovered for who and what I actually am; 2) A thing forever lost, that I would do almost anything to have back.

More
(descriptive part of speech that defies description): Drug of choice of intensity junkies.

Our Bed
Noun, indiscriminate. Any bed in which we can intertwine our bodies tightly enough that no air can cool the space between us.

Partners in Crime
Exhibit A: The time we sat on a bench sharing a cigarette, and a friend strolled by and quipped, "Ah, so this is where the cool kids

hang out," and we, in our mid-forties, relished the sense of being young outlaws again more than we should have (see also **Affair Bubble**).

Exhibit B: The unspoken implication that any guilt or self-loathing either of us feels during the affair and ensuing breakup of our marriages is, by all logic, applicable to each other, too, as a partner in our mutual emotional crimes.

Safe Word

1) A thing I have no desire for when you straddle me on the bed of the Gershwin Hotel and slap my face repeatedly, knowing that all of my life I have barely been able to have my face touched, that I fantasize about your pushing me this far beyond my comfort zone. "Don't flinch," you command, locking your eyes on mine while we fuck, my hammering heart thrilling at my ability to obey, at the way my neck arches to bring me closer to your hand; 2) The tenderness of your voice saying into my slapped face, "It's okay to cry. You're beautiful, it's okay to cry"; 3) The simultaneous overload of peace and euphoria that makes me moan, "You can do anything to me, you can do anything you want to me"; 4) How can I prove to you that my words are safe for you to believe when they have previously been proven unsafe?

Self-erasure

1) See transcripts of Scott and Zelda Fitzgerald's sessions with doctors and psychiatrists who allied to convince Zelda that Scott "owned" the material of their lives and was the "serious writer" between them and therefore she should refrain from writing; 2) It was 2012, not 1898, and no one was threatening to institutionalize me if I didn't shred my journal to erase all traces of our affair; 3) Is it the ultimate hat-trick of patriarchy that I volitionally did this to *myself*?

Sentimentality

Synonyms: death of literature / emotional manipulation practiced by hacks and universally feared by "literary" writers / a thing glutted out by us ecstatically in emails and texts. Topics for further research: *Why is it so difficult to convey love and joy yet so easy to find language for everything that was foolish, grandiose, or selfish about our affair? Why can't I describe the quality of your eyes when we sat in the dark on the floor of the Gershwin Hotel bathroom, me on your lap, just kissing, for two hours? Why did it particularly undo me when your drawing "The Map of My United States" arrived coincidentally on Valentine's Day, when you probably didn't know what month it was?* Antonyms: all of postmodernism.

Sexual Preference

Sitting on the porch of your desert cabin, passing our habitual one cigarette back and forth, you saying, "You are my **Sexual Preference**. I used to think I might be more driven by my desire for specific sexual acts than by who I was doing the acts with—I used to wonder, even, whether I would rather be with a man who wanted to do the things I wanted done to me than with a woman who had no interest in those particular things, even though I always preferred women. This is the first time in my life that what I'm doing hardly matters and it's all about the person I'm doing them with." Later, when you covered my feet with a blanket while massaging me slowly, "so you won't get cold," I wept as though joy was making my skin porous and parts of me were spilling all over the bed—later still, when we kissed too soon, the Suboxone you were still prescribed then lingering on your tongue, and I spent the next hour vomiting, how could I explain to you or anyone that it was still the happiest I had ever been, and that you, mixing a fun-pack-size cereal with milk and bringing it to me in bed, were rewiring my entire body and brain. Synonym: You.

Sisterhood
(active verb): A thing, apparently, that a **Thieving Cunt Whore** does not understand.

Sunset Towers Loop
Where we happen to be the first time you start to ecstatically moan, *I love you I love you I love you,* unable to stop the words from bubbling out, your body wrapping around mine like a rhesus monkey, your I love yous flowing like a **Calgary River**.

Thieving Cunt Whore
(compound phrase best used in its entirety): What a wife will call the "other woman" when said woman once accepted her hand-beaded bracelet as a gift while secretly fucking the wife's husband / Find also under rhetorical questions such as: *What kind of person spends the night in her lover's wife's guest room, even letting her show off old photographs of the two of them together?* and *Why the fuck did I agree to drive to Michigan in the same car?* (Other relevant compound phrases: "What kind of hypocritical **Feminist** steals a sick woman's man?")

Twin
1) The surprise encountered when, after talking nonstop for some seventeen hours, you realize that we share a birthday; 2) *I feel like we are twinned,* you wrote to me, months before Kathy's death. *Like I have finally found someone who matches me emotionally and intellectually and in intensity;* 3) When "coincidence" is confused with causality or destiny.

Unconditional Love
(relevant only as a compound term): 1) Rendered meaningless, in retrospect, when things are easy; 2) A state of emotion I thought

applied only to my children; 3) Even though the moment I first fell a little in love with you was the first time you said to me, "I've got your back," the fact remains that even if in the end you haven't, it won't make you responsible for *my* choices or for anything I gave up to have my heart's desire; 4) Which is you.

Whore

(term of affection): 1) When you are staying in my basement guest suite, only days after we have kissed for the first time, and I sneak down after my husband has gone to work and get under the green duvet with you, you ask, "Did you have sex with him last night?" and I say "Of course," and you nuzzle your face into my neck, wrapping your entire body around mine and tenderly murmur, "You **Whore**," while kissing me; 2) I swear to you, I honestly didn't know for at least four more months that you were jealous when I fucked him—I didn't know that jealousy was a thing you understood; 3) What if you had *not* become jealous, would I still have come to dread his touch so intensely that the times I felt happiest and cleanest were those moments when sex was first over and I knew I could buy at least a few more days without his trying again; 4) Without your jealousy, would I still have become unable to orgasm consistently with my husband even while fantasizing about you, and started faking orgasms for the first time in my life; 5) To what extent was your jealousy the final nail in the coffin that had been slowly built for my marriage since 2007?

XXX

1) The city symbol of Amsterdam, where we have both lived at different times; 2) One more x than we would be likely to include in an email to a random acquaintance; 3) Shorthand for **Infinity**; 4) A tattoo you get impulsively on the inside of your right wrist and of which you text me photos while I am out for sushi with S, back

when she still thinks we are an exciting, hot idea; 5) Maybe this is my reciprocal tattoo, for you: all of it, even the painful parts; 6) Because even if **Infinity** is make-believe, an abstract concept designed to make lovers forget how easy it is to lose each other before we all lose ourselves too when we shift tenses, still, my **Sexual Preference**, my **Partner in Crime**, my **Best Friend**, my **Whore**, my infinite bamboo, my person, my **Given**, my **Unconditional Love**, my emotional **Home** (whether or not we ever forge a shared physical home on the ground), I can promise you this: I will never regret you.

Blood Moon

The desire to be loved is the last illusion. Give it up
and you will be free.

$\qquad$ —Margaret Atwood

M y world was burning when my father died, but he was not part
of the wreckage. After having been an enormous part of my
life, my father was barely present in the story of his own death.

In the days leading up to my father's memorial service, my
ex-husband and I debated about whether he should attend. First, he
asked if he could bring a date. We had split up less than half a year
prior and had only recently started a mediation process to get the
divorce off the ground—some of the people who would be in attendance didn't even know yet that we had parted ways. I was not
bringing my own lover to the memorial service, because I wanted to
honor my father and focus on his life (read: I was ashamed), rather
than turning the event into a gossipy cocktail party where the focus of conversation would be the demise of my long marriage. My
ex-husband, who had started our separation by often citing the way
a friend of his had divorced parents who were still close and often
had brunch together with their kids, had spent the past few months
becoming increasingly hostile to me: a state of events I could scarcely
protest on moral grounds, though sometimes I did anyway. He said

he needed to bring his new girlfriend to the service "as support," and I pointed out that he had known everyone who would be attending the service for his entire adult life and was the wronged party in our breakup—support would be dripping from the walls. I added that his own father would be there, although somehow that didn't turn out to be the case, as my ex-husband managed to fight with his father just before the service and uninvited him. He was in a state of spectacularly burning bridges, though the true range of the raging fire could only be seen later, from a distance. At that time, the earth was not yet scorched. At that time, we seemed to be suffering only, as many divorcing couples do, from an excess of drama and messy emotions. I told my almost-ex-husband that he was more than welcome to bring a friend, and he chose a nice musician from the men's group he had belonged to for nearly a decade—a group that played no minor role, for better or worse, in my having fallen out of love with the slightly aloof, fiercely independent young intellectual I'd married. Still, the "warrior brother" he brought with him was a good man, vaguely hippie with an artistic and gentle demeanor. He struck me as a true friend to my ex-husband, and was the sort of diplomatic person who hugged me hello and expressed his sympathy about my father despite the fact that I was, as my lover's wife had termed it, a "thieving cunt whore."

My ex did not speak to me, seeming to make a point to leave any room in the funeral parlor that I entered. This sounds more disruptive, perhaps, than I experienced it being at the time. I was happy to see him there, in his dark suit. I was grateful whenever I saw him talking to our three children or our formerly shared friends. My father had loved my ex-husband, though he also sometimes thought he was a chump for buying cars full-price and had issues with his temper—by which I mean he had loved my ex as *family*, wherein you can feel attached and beholden to a person with connections not based on interpersonal compatibility.

At one point in the service, I saw my ex kneeling beside my mother's chair, telling her that she was his mother too and that he would always love her, embracing her and weeping. Having never been divorced before, I was naïve enough to believe that these things would be true in an immutable way, and that some police-drawn chalk outline of Family remained, surrounding us all, despite my crime.

Later, I would discover that my extended paternal side of the family collectively believed the nice hippie musician my ex brought to the service was his new lover, and that a narrative was spreading like wildfire among them that the reason for our severing was my (very straight) husband's long-closeted homosexuality. I could cite here how long it took me to dispel this rumor, but on my Italian side of the family there are still legends intact about things like Death knocking on my grandmother's door by accident, instead of the next-door neighbor's, and erroneously knocking three times before getting the right apartment and the neighbor dropping dead. My grandmother knew it had been Death at the door, you see, because there were no footprints in the snow. This Thing That Never Happened allegedly occurred some one hundred years ago, yet is still repeated at many parties in the Frangello clan, so you can see how something as pedantic as whether or not my ex-husband and the delicate, gentle friend he brought to the memorial service were a couple would be a detail of little interest to my extended family once they had decreed among them that this had caused my divorce.

"I wish he were gay," I would sometimes say, when confronted with this rumor. "Then we would still be friends."

What I meant, of course, was: I wish he had been the liar.

When you are keeping a secret from someone, and that person dies, the secret becomes impossible to dislodge from inside you. You can come clean, shed the toxicity of leading a double life, run around trying to make amends to the various people your actions hurt and disrupted, but a part of you remains frozen forever in time, enacting the lie that slid away with the deceased. When somebody dies thinking you are someone you haven't been in years—someone you maybe never were to begin with—what parts of your identity, real and constructed, do the dead take with them?

My father died approximately four years after Kathy's unexpected death, and sometimes it seems that everything that marks and haunts me stems from the disappearance of one or the other. In their dying, a part of me became fossilized, too: the me who was perceived by them.

Of course, that's based on a romantic construction of Identity as somehow being one fixed thing, when in reality identity is as impossible to pin down and hold as an ocean. I was forty-three years old when Kathy died—it would be absurd to say that I somehow "began" at that moment. I had been in the same relationship for twenty-one years, had two master's degrees, three children, and had traveled all over the world. I was a middle-aged, economically and racially privileged white American woman, a feminist, a writer, a mother, a friend, *a wife a wife a wife*. And a daughter. Always a devoted daughter. I was a good Italian girl in that way.

Because my father had been ninety-three years old and "crazy," my mother, my ex-husband, and I had all hidden the demise of my marriage from him. He died believing in a fairy tale. His first words to my mother, upon my birth, were "I hope she doesn't marry a bum." My ex-husband had given them a free place to live for almost sixteen years: clearly he was not a bum. My father's greatest wish for me—perhaps any man of his generation's greatest wish for a daughter—had come true in that I had "married well"—married up.

He died unaware that, any time he saw my ex-husband coming through the front door and striding up the stairs to our apartment, it meant I was actually four blocks away in the "nesting pad" we time-shared. He died not having computed that it had probably been half a year since he had seen us at the same time. My mother, ex-husband, and I were all complicit in this collusion, though it was my big idea. We agreed that my father was "too far gone" by the time of the separation, and that the anxiety of knowing might annihilate what was left of his fragile peace of mind. My ex-husband, no doubt aware that my father would have been royally pissed off that I had engaged in a three-year affair and instigated this separation, was openly resentful of the collusion to keep my father in the dark, but even with the clarity of hindsight I don't recall him making any serious efforts to rectify the lie. We'd all been protecting my father from things for years.

Other than where my father was concerned, my ex-husband had become something of a town crier about our separation. My favorite move of his during this time, when we were still on good terms despite being broken up, was his telling his sob story to a mattress salesman so as to get a better deal on the bed we were setting up in the nesting pad, where we would each spend half the week so that our kids never had to move. My least favorite town-crier move was his insistence on talking to our nine-year-old son repeatedly about my affair. But although he told some neighbors, the old friend he ran into at a restaurant during his frenetic OkCupid period, and a fellow parent at our son's school all about my infidelity, he held his tongue with my father: an act of decency for which I am still grateful, despite my current knowledge that it was the wrong thing to do.

At the Pad, my daughters would come by on "my" nights and throw pebbles at the windows like suitors in a 1940s film. The doorbell worked but they rarely used it. Once they got my attention, sometimes they would come upstairs and watch *Game of Thrones* in marathon sessions on the uncomfortable sofa my ex and I had purchased in haste. Alicia and her two daughters, who lived downstairs, would often come up too, and we would order pizza or Thai or eat the leftovers Alicia and her husband had served for dinner that night. I never cooked at the Pad. My diet during the seven months I spent three nights per week there consisted of dry bagels, Greek yogurt, red wine, and green tea. At night, missing any usual "cues" that it was time to sleep, such as putting my son to bed or watching *The Daily Show* side by side in bed with my husband, I numbed my whirling mind with lorazepam or weed until I could convince myself to turn out the lights.

Sometimes my ex-husband would complain to me via text that I was not allowed to spend time with the kids on "his" nights, so I had to tell my daughters they could no longer come over and watch *Game of Thrones* on my shitty sofa for seven hours straight. Then they had to stay at our main house, where they reported that their father was often shut up in the master bedroom engaging in sometimes-heated four-hour phone conversations (with his warrior brothers, his new girlfriend, who knew?), even though I had never known my husband to speak much on the telephone. When we'd twice lived long-distance, we spoke only once a week, at his imperative, on Sundays.

In my ex-husband's defense, whenever he attempted to spend "quality time" with our daughters, they had a tendency to flee the room. If they were watching a show and he came down and sat on the couch, they would soon wander back to their bedrooms and close their doors. Our daughters were beautiful, formidably intelligent, and slightly terrifying in the way that only teenage girls can be. Their silent treatments were unparalleled. I didn't blame my ex-husband for not wanting two of his three children to spend all of his parenting time at my wine-and-weed pad, but I did complain that he virtually never organized any of his time around our children, still conducting himself like a man with a wife even in my absence, as though someone else would manage his domestic relationships even though he was now the only one there. I heard from the kids of his often popping frozen pizzas in the oven for them before rushing out for dinner dates, and felt frustrated that my painful separation from my children did not seem to be resulting in the bonding between my ex and them that I'd assumed was to be part of the nesting-pad bargain. Increasingly, the kids complained that even when their father did manage to engage them in conversation, his topics ranged from things like *I hope you grow up to make better moral choices than your mother made* to *Your mother shattered my heart and destroyed my life* to *Your mother did the worst thing to me that anyone can do to another person* to *I don't know why you even want to spend time with your mother given the things she's done*. These conversational tactics worked, especially on two teenage girls, about as well as you might imagine they would.

Now that they had been forbidden to hang out at the Pad on nights they were supposed to be with their father, my daughters invented excuses to walk to Walgreens or run other errands, and instead of coming upstairs would loiter out on the pavement in front of the Pad until I came down to talk to them. They rarely spoke of their father, or really of anything memorable; they mocked each other and made small talk or just sat on the steps with their long legs bent up to their chins, looking bored and aimless. My ex-husband and I had decided to nest in an attempt to preserve stability for our children, but it turned out that for at least two of them, "stability" wasn't located in a particular place, but rather in the act of physical proximity to their mother. Or do I flatter myself with that sentence? My daughters were simmering with a constant low-grade rage at me for the hideousness of my actions, yet they seemed to find comfort in my presence even amid their anger. The degree to which they were trying to avoid their father vs. trying to seek me out is not a quantifiable thing I can pin down even now.

The night before my father died, my daughters threw pebbles at the window but I didn't hear them. My lover was in town from

California and staying with me at the Pad. Alicia ended up calling my cell phone to tell me that she and her daughters were outside with mine, looking at the blood moon. I came down—alone, as both my lover and I understood him to be unwelcome—to hang out with them on the sidewalk. It was hard to see the sky from the front of the building, the way urban skies are glimpsed only in patches: between a tall school and crammed-together trees. Alicia's husband was an avid gardener and their house was conspicuously well maintained and lush by the otherwise lax standards of the block, the sprinklers spurting even in late September. We had to go to the southwest corner of the street to get away from the sprinklers and see the moon. I had never heard of a blood moon, but no one was surprised because these were the people who knew me best and I am somewhat famous for being oblivious to things everyone is supposed to know.

The blood moon hung to the east of us, giant and orange-tinted, and I tried to remember when, exactly, I'd stopped feeling anything but constantly sick to my stomach. By this point it was clear that whatever was wrong was not merely circumstantial, but also had to do with some frenetic core of me that wouldn't stop thrashing and analyzing and mercilessly wanting more. My lover was upstairs in the Pad doing whatever he did when alone in an apartment that wasn't his, which often seemed to be texting his wife about how much he loved and missed her, even though he had chosen to be here with me instead. He was at what turned out to be almost the halfway point of a two-and-a-half-year depression that had descended in August 2014, during one of our "breakups," and that would not lift until January 4, 2017. Depression had started to feel like a fifth party in our relationship, his wife and my ex-husband being the third and fourth parties. The more parties were added to our dyad, the lonelier I felt. The moon was hauntingly beautiful and I wanted to go home with my children and go back to some other, former life in which all of my grief had been buried under layers of busyness and convention and felt less naked. I wanted to be safely unhappily married to my ex-husband again, because it had been almost a decade since I'd been romantically in love with him, and consequently he'd possessed little emotional power over me in our daily lives for some years prior to our separation. I did not hang over his every mood, nuance, word, and sign the way I did my lover's, and there had been something genuinely liberating about that amid the constant sadness of it. It had been pleasant to live under the illusion that my emotions and moods were no longer tied to any man—to fancy that I had transcended all that early twenty-something romantic angst and melodrama and could now, in middle age, focus on my writing, children, and friendships. Life with my lover had blasted all such notions out of commission. I loved him with a ferocity that bordered on sickness, and his every word and gesture could become a complication or a cure. It was exhausting to love this much. I walked around wet all the time, my stomach lurching.

My lover had talked of his desire to move to Chicago all throughout our affair—he had told confidants how much he adored me, and that he would live "in Butte" if it meant being in my presence, and how I never bored him and he loved everything about me. Now I had been free for five months, but we were in a limbo of his spending his meager income on plane tickets to Chicago, to spend days or a week in this strange no-man's-land of the Pad and not be allowed in my family home, then to reboard a plane and go back to the apartment he still shared with his wife in California. The plan was for him to move out, but not one gesture had been made to instigate that unless we counted my lover occasionally browsing ads for studio rentals in Los Angeles—not Chicago—and lamenting how he could not afford them.

Miss you, love you, they wrote in texts I would see flash right on the screen of his phone.

Many mornings at the Pad, I woke to long strings of texts of my own from my ex-husband, sometimes just wanting to talk but increasingly focusing on all the reasons he was furious with me and all the ways I had done him wrong. I missed my son, who couldn't yet walk four blocks alone to the Pad in the dark to throw stones at my window. My daughters were clingy yet wrathful and I didn't know how to manage their emotions, and was only just learning that my attempts to manage the emotions of others was part of what had led me here, to what was supposed to be my emancipation from the shackles of a flatlined marriage, my emergence from a toxic lie into the truth, but didn't feel like any of those things after the first few heady weeks of confession. I hadn't written in months. I often told Alicia I thought I had a tumor consuming me from the inside. It seemed hard to believe I had ever been anything but This: this state of perpetual reaction, a ping-pong ball between the tidal emotions of two men. I wanted to be happy, but the desire felt flimsy, maybe even tangible proof of my lack of depth and substance compared to my lover's profound depression and my ex-husband's justified rage. I wanted to escape, but I had three kids and no paying job and my parents to care for and I couldn't imagine what escape even looked like. I'd thought it had looked like what I'd done—the falling passionately in love; the leaving a volatile yet boring, resentful marriage. Here on what was meant to be the other side, however, my daughters' judgments and anger still made me nervous; my ex-husband's wrath still made me nervous; my lover's depression and codependence with his sort-of-ex made me more nervous than when we'd been secret co-conspirators. Increasingly, the calm I had felt as a woman in a long-term marriage, who wasn't in love with her husband anymore and therefore had little to worry about emotionally, was like a siren song to the easiest days of my life.

We all stared at the blood moon hanging from the sky, but it was late and my daughters were not even supposed to be here, and my lover was upstairs alone, and any moment I might get a text from my ex chastising me for monopolizing the children, so after I had *oohed* and *ahhed* to the extent that I hoped to come off as a normal, positive person rather than one who couldn't eat and believed a tumor was devouring her slowly, I sent my daughters home.

It wasn't some "fiction" that my father might not have been able to handle the news of my divorce. He was confined to a wheelchair now, and had been for almost two years, since breaking a hip for the second time, at which point I'd become incapable of managing his needs alone. For the past two years my ex-husband had been paying for a private caregiver—Grace—who managed his toileting, dressing, and bathing. His legs were only a small fraction of my father's problems, however. His deafness, long an issue, had become complete, though he still wouldn't wear a hearing aid. With the onset of dementia and a host of other pills meant to keep his various physical ailments and pains at bay, his antidepressant and antipsychotic didn't work the way they once had and my father hallucinated on the regular, from floods in his closet to Grace stealing shirts and sweaters to "sell on the street." The fact that we always found the missing clothing did nothing to deter my father from the belief that he was being robbed, and he would shout at my mother and me, "I'm not fucking crazy—are you saying I'm fucking crazy!" My mother, who used a walker herself, would scuttle away and avoid him, while I would stand my ground and try to explain, "Yes, Dad, you are crazy. Stop making it worse by yelling at people."

Of course, if the definition of crazy is, as my lover likes to quote, doing the same thing over and over again and expecting a different result, then I was the crazy one. My father gave me pillowcases stuffed with collectible coins and pristine wool sweaters from Ireland and Italy and insisted I hide them in my apartment where Grace couldn't "get her hands on them." When he was in a rage, he shouted racial slurs at Grace, even though I had never in my life heard him say anything negative about people of color prior to this final deterioration, and even though he adored my Chinese daughters despite their comparative disinterest. The fact that Grace never yelled back made me doubly angry and frustrated: of course she didn't stand up for herself—she needed this job so that she could send money to her parents in the Philippines. Her mother was on dialysis in some small village and bedridden, in her fifties. Grace was periodically engaged to one U.S. citizen or another, but her engagements would always go awry and she would wake my mother up at four in the morning to cry about her problems with men. My mother loves nothing more than giving advice, so this bothered her much less than logic might indicate.

My father had wanted to be dead for at least two years. His list of collected maladies was epic. He'd had two thirds of his stomach removed before I was even born, then spent the bulk of my youth hemorrhaging from his ulcer, looking whiter than the sheets of every ICU. He had spinal stenosis, peripheral neuropathy that made him experience his feet as round, and a condition that would lead the arteries in his head to explode and blind—then kill—him if he didn't take steroids daily. This is not a comprehensive list by even half. He had taken to screaming at the ceiling, in the direction, I presumed, of the god in whom he claimed not to believe, begging, "Jesus Christ, enough already, just kill me!" But although he had enough Norco for his back and leg pain to suicide a small compound, he never took matters into his own hands, and then eventually, as tends to happen to everyone who waits too long, it was too late.

It might be fair to say, then, that my father's belief in my perfect family was all he had to cling to by the end. When your own life has gone so irrevocably to shit, only the concept of a legacy can offer comfort. He had not left anything lasting in the way of a career; he was financially dependent on his son-in-law; he and my mother hadn't had sex since the year I was born. He had outlived every last person from his youth. Maybe there is an argument to be made that allowing my father to die wondering what would become of me, now that I had thrown my respectable husband over for a recovering junkie with bipolar who was still living in an apartment with his wife half a country away, would have been cruel. I only know that when you have been lying long enough, you start to forget that the purpose of relationships is not to spoon-feed other people what you think they want or need to hear.

I would wake on my own in the Pad—back in those early months of my separation, before the constant nausea set in—and my first feeling would be one of gulping fresh air after a long time underground. I sent my ex cruel (at the time believing them to be friendly and honest) texts about how relieved I was to have broken out of the box of his expectations for me, and to be in my own space for literally the first time in my entire life, even during my childhood. Because my mother was a stay-at-home mom until I started high school, and my father was on disability, I was the only one with a schedule, for school. Therefore, I was given the bigger (though still tiny) bedroom in the back of the apartment, farthest from the noise of the TV, sleeping in the double bed intended for my parents, but which they hadn't shared since I was in preschool. When I left Chicago for college, I was always broke and had as many roommates as possible, culminating in a period spent squatting in London, where I shared living quarters and one bathroom with eleven men and one woman from all over the world. I had gone from that circumstance to living with my husband, and slowly adding three kids and my parents to the mix. Consequently, the Pad felt wild, raw, heady: like a first apartment. I was forty-seven years old, but I had dropped fifteen pounds from the stress of my divorce or the tumor I believed was devouring me, and I looked like some youthful, borderline anorexic version of myself. I listened to Florence and the Machine or

Jason Isbell as loudly as I wanted at any hour of the day. I could call my lover on the phone without getting in my car and driving to some isolated street to park and talk without being heard. I didn't have to grocery shop or cook for a family of five—seven if it included my parents. More than anything, I didn't have to lie anymore, which I had been doing in increments to my husband for so long that it felt slippery to pinpoint the start. I didn't have to walk on eggshells around his temper, waiting for him to explode at me in public, at the Art Institute, at a restaurant with my mother and the kids. I woke with my heart pounding in my throat like a person who has waded through a filthy river and thrown off the dogs trailing their scent and can no longer see the prison walls in the distance. I felt so gloriously free that every morning seemed to shimmer.

It would only be later that I would realize my "freedom" was one more lie. I was texting my ex these epiphanies from a bed we time-shared, in an apartment we co-owned with our oldest friends. We still shared a bank account. I didn't have a paying job. I was writing my longtime husband, who I loved like a difficult brother even though hearing that enraged him, and with whom I was as enmeshed in my own way as my lover was with his wife in California. I was spending my time processing my so-called freedom with the person from whom I was allegedly trying to break free, trying to sell him on my own logic and make him not only understand but agree with me. What is clear now is that yes, I had broken free from certain societal roles that women are both pushed into and unthinkingly corral ourselves into, and from the constant hamster's wheel of responsibilities and emotional labor that come with those roles, but I was only playing at real freedom. It was freedom with an emotional net. My ex and I lay in our respective beds and texted each other all about our angers, our reliefs, our resentments like a morning ritual. We read the same books on divorce, which we passed between us and then dissected together. It was like I had all the benefits of marriage—and even some of the pitfalls, like his temper—without any of the obligations. We were still mirroring each other like twins, checking the other's reactions to find out who we were.

It was only once this mirroring was withdrawn that I began to understand that freedom is only ever a fall without a net.

The blood moon lasted another night. My mother called me to say my father's breathing had become labored. We had both known and not known that he was dying. It was the twilight of September, and since sometime in July, my father had been declining. He'd spent a brief stint at an assisted-living facility near our house, but had been so disruptive and abusive to the staff that they kicked him out— which of course was exactly what he was trying to achieve. When he returned home in August, I'd called a hospice, and they had been managing his situation for the past couple of months. He was on a morphine dropper for pain and liquid benzos for relaxation. He never left the hospital bed next to the living room window anymore, even to sit in his wheelchair. He also didn't have conversations. Prior to this last deterioration, he was still lucid most of the time, or if not most of the time then half of the time. Now he sometimes could say hello or goodbye but that was about it. He had started to moan and carry on if my mother left the room, so she had to sit next to him all the time, even though he couldn't converse. It would be fair to say that she was clinically depressed herself.

From April to July, it felt like some kind of French farce that my mother, husband, and I were all trying to hide the separation from my father when he lived in the same building. It seemed a clear recipe for failure. After July, however, all our earlier efforts proved obsolete. My father no longer took any interest in our comings and goings. I could have brought my lover over for dinner and my father would not have noticed. This had been going on for a couple of months; still doctors found nothing wrong with his heart, no cancer, no clear medical reason for his sudden and dramatic decay. He had some wounds that had failed to heal due to his peripheral neuropathy and poor circulation, but they were being tended to and didn't look like the kind of thing that caused sepsis and death. Though it seems foolish in retrospect, my mother and I assumed he could go on like this indefinitely. After all, he had been thirty-five when he met my mother and told her he would be dead by forty. My father had been crying death for so many years that we had all forgotten he was eventually going to die.

I left my lover at the Pad and walked to our family home in the dark, the blood moon hovering over me. There are so many things I see clearly now that I did not see on that walk: that I should have brought my lover with me; that cheating on my husband did not eradicate my right to support on the night my father died; that I should have already been sitting vigil with my mother for days by that point, instead of spending time getting tied to the bed by my lover, followed by talking about his depression on Alicia's front porch, passing a cigarette back and forth between us. There are so many ways I failed my father in his final months, even though up to that point I had been at least a passably good daughter. I am wary, too, of the ways that narratives focused on our own "failures" can be narcissistic ones that still posit us—*me*—as the piece of shit at the center of the universe and deprive other people of agency. There is so much more to my father's life and death than how it impacted, reflected on, or revealed me.

What I knew then was only that I had never heard of a blood moon the night prior, and now to some extent one would follow the rest of my days. I remembered a walk I'd made in 1998, when I had been called home from Amsterdam, where my husband was working, because my father was in the ICU and not expected to last another twenty-four hours. I'd flown to Chicago alone in a frenzy, taken a taxi to the apartment where I was raised. My mother was at the hospital when I arrived, so I walked the six blocks or so through my old neighborhood to the shithole hospital where my father was interred, alone in the August daylight saying aloud, *This is the day my father dies.*

I tried the sentence again, aloud. *This is the night my father dies.* But it had lost the urgency of 1998's fevered mantra. My mind was jumbled. I was "visiting" my parents in the home I co-owned and had lived in for sixteen years. My children were upstairs, but I couldn't sleep there because it was my ex-husband's night. He couldn't swap with me and go to the Pad, even if he had been so inclined (which he probably was not), because my lover was at the Pad waiting for me. My father's death was two years overdue and I hoped for his sake that it would finally be achieved, and this hope, too, seemed wrong and unsettling.

Nothing about the scene was right. Even Grace, who had fallen into a sweet and companionable relationship with my father now that he was immobile and mute, calling him Honey in a loud, boisterous voice, was off that day, and only the aide from Catholic Charities was on hand. She was a Black woman my own age, and she liked my parents because she had not been subjected to my father's brief, freakish months of racial expletives. My mother was sitting near my father but not near enough to touch him, and when I entered the apartment the aide said to me, "I think he's already dead." She and I began an experiment with a mirror to see whether he was exhaling, and both pronounced him still alive. I sat next to my father's head and kept my hand on his chest and stroked his bald head and kissed it and said things to him about how I was here and how I loved him and how he was going to be free and released and not in pain anymore and everything would be okay. I held his fragile, brittle body under the thick blue sweatshirt he often wore, and cried, though not as much as I felt I should. My mind was half on the apartment upstairs, my long-term home, my children. I wanted the children to come downstairs and be with us too, but it felt wrong to ask them to come and witness a death. We waited for hospice care to arrive. At some point, I said to the aide, "I think he really *may* already be dead," and we tested it again. Grace called on the phone. She indicated that in her opinion he had been dead for hours. This made no sense; he seemed to be breathing.

When I'd seen him the night before, my father had been moaning with discomfort. Now he was silent, still, his mouth frozen open. An hour or two passed, waiting for the hospice worker. I kept talking to my father. At one point my kids came downstairs to see him and say goodbye, but left quickly. My ex-husband arrived home from work or wherever he'd been, and came through the apartment taking in the scene, but did not linger. He did not hug my mother or speak to me. He headed up the stairs as though we had all betrayed him en masse, and maybe we had. My parents had benefited from his money for years, but of course they'd had no clue I was not what I seemed to be. His money had been my money too. We were raising three kids together. We were married. My parents had loved my husband like a son, had obviously not been trying to scam or take advantage of him, but I could imagine how it might seem that way to him now: a family of grifters; an absurdly long con.

The hospice worker arrived. She pronounced my father dead and said that in all likelihood he had been dead for a couple of hours. I had been talking to and stroking only his corpse. The Catholic Charities aide asked about the things we'd taken as signs of life and the hospice worker explained that these things were common in the immediate aftermath of death; the body continues to exhale gasses or to tremor slightly. I held my father's dead body and cried some more, but I wasn't sure whether I was crying because he was dead or because he hadn't heard the things I'd said.

What I never said, even when I believed him still alive and possibly cognizant: *I'm not who you think I am.*

Maybe that is all I can say in my own defense: that I didn't attempt some deathbed confession—that I didn't try to wrangle the spotlight of his death onto myself and let him slide away while screaming *Me Me Me.*

The result, however, was that he died without knowing my house of cards had already fallen. He died not knowing that four blocks away from me, a man who reminded me much more of him than my ex-husband ever did was waiting to cook me dinner. He died not realizing I had in some manner of speaking returned to my roots, to my familiar. My father would never have the chance to laugh at my lover's jokes or talk jazz with him or even engage in the gallows humor that only those who rely on a cocktail of pills to keep the noonday demon at bay understand. I had a brief window—April to July—in which my lover and my father could have approached each other, even if in both cases they would only be meeting a darker, more shadowy version of the other—in which I could have watched them shake hands, and try, each, to convey to the other the urgency and joy of their love for me, and perhaps their mutual helpless grief that love was all they could offer, and that it alone could not protect me as my husband, with all his respectability and successes, had. April to July, in which I could somehow have conveyed to them and to myself that protection was not what I was after—that all I wanted was to be seen, to be known, to feel alive even if it was my undoing. Then Time's window snapped shut in a sharp wind, and I had caused that: had ignored the obvious forecast, taken careless shelter from the gale in the wrong company, ringleader in a coven of liars. I had squandered those months and now it was that worst of all things: too late.

When they took my father's corpse away, I didn't know what to do with my own body, made of his. My father had come from a generation in which widows dressed in black threw themselves into open graves after the casket, but I was of a different world and stood by politely, watching him disappear into a zipped bag, knowing the next time I saw him, he would be ash and bone. We had bought this building originally so that I could take care of him, and in his irrevocable absence I felt orphaned and unmoored. Unable to get myself to leave the house, as though leaving would make him more gone, I eventually drifted up the stairs on a kind of autopilot and told my kids that Papa was dead. None of them cried. In my memory, my son was there, but in reality he may have already been asleep and heard it the next day. My father had been dying for so long that his relationship with the children had ended years ago, really. He was a phantom at the bottom of the stairs: the crazy neighbor who believed his caregiver was peddling his shirts on the street for cash.

Finally, I wandered up the flight of stairs to the master bedroom, and told my ex-husband that my father was dead. He had known my father since 1990, a time so long ago that my husband and I both seemed rosy and unformed in my memories, like babies in nightclub attire. My husband had, for twenty years, been closer both geographically and emotionally to my family than to his own. But I had taken that away from him now. I had taken everything: our beautiful and formidable daughters who threw pebbles at my window; our friend group who had mainly known me since grade school, high school, and college and predated him; even this city, where he had moved for me to be near my parents. I sat on the carpet of our bedroom and cried, talking about my father, mistaking what had transpired for a shared experience, a shared grief, but my husband/ex-husband cut me off, stating simply that it was not his job to comfort me anymore, so I gathered what was left of myself to go.

Maybe I have never grieved for my father properly, or even at all. He died during a period in which it felt like the bells were ringing every morning, voices booming, *Bring out your dead!* I was still habitually reaching for my cell phone to call Kathy. Only once she was gone did I realize how much she had occupied me emotionally for decades, serving as balm and distraction whenever my husband withdrew. She had been my date to foreign films, Chuck E. Cheese, thrift stores, old man bars, and yoga classes—was the one who still made me "mixtapes" (though she had graduated to CDs). Her phone calls numerous times per day to tell me stories or ask my advice had made it somehow easier to accept that my husband rarely remembered to call even if he would be two hours late. From high school physics to chemotherapy rooms, she had needed me, in ways my husband—a self-contained orbit of one—never quite seemed to need me. But more, she had *wanted* my company, always. She and I had loved each other in sickness and in health, and without her I felt reckless, mad to reinvent my life—a widow in need of a new spouse. The fact that I'd already had a husband did little to mend whatever was leaking in me.

Without Kathy, everything rearranged itself unrecognizably. Without my father, by contrast, nothing was particularly different in my daily life. He had spent two years in a chair, saying nonsensical things. Even my mother said his death was a relief—she no longer had anyone crying for her company if she tried to walk into the kitchen; she no longer had to watch him suffer. Still, she quietly went on antidepressants for the first time. They had been married for fifty-four years. Their marriage had seemed sad to me, but the volume and history of it was more than I had been able to manage.

"Neither of our parents got divorced," my ex-husband often said in the early days of our separation, trying to counter my desire to cleave. But in my logic, that was a *counter*argument to staying together. His mother had been an alcoholic who hurt everyone in her wake; my parents had been as sexless and simmering in mutual regret as conjoined twins. I didn't want to go quietly into the night of a companionable old age. I didn't want who I was now to be the most I'd ever be. My ex-husband and I were looking at the same templates, the same precedents, but he read the fine print as saying *Stay put* and I read it as *Run*.

At my father's memorial service, we played his old jazz albums on Kaya's vintage turntable, which we brought to the funeral parlor ourselves. At first the records played reliably, but sometime mid-event the music stopped.

"Ask your father if he can take a look at it and see what's wrong," I told my daughters, and soon I saw my ex-husband, handsome and cold and wounded in his suit, bent over the turntable, examining it. After a while, I looked back and he was gone, so I went to put on a Stan Getz album, but it still wasn't working. Several friends stood by, making suggestions, wondering if the funeral director could help, but I waved them off. If my ex-husband couldn't fix the turntable, I explained, then it could not be fixed.

Maybe that, then, is the definition of freedom: to be neither protected by nor tethered to a man who can fix anything. I put the turntable away and did not play music for the remainder of the memorial.

On the night my father died, I walked back to the Pad alone under the same blood moon, but this time I didn't watch it in the sky. I didn't think about my father on the walk to what was now, in some sense, my home. I wanted, more than I had ever wanted anything in my life, to turn back the clock and climb into the bed in which my ex-husband would be sleeping tonight: to undo the revelation of my affair, to go back to being a woman with a double life, lying to everyone in my midst. Or maybe I wanted to wind the clock back even further: to have never met my lover at all; to have never stood close enough in his proximity to understand that everything that had ever passed as intimacy or desire in me in all the decades of my adulthood had been only a facsimile of something, the polite version, the academic signifier rather than the hurricane signified. Maybe I wanted to undo everything I now knew, that meant I would never be safe inside a box again. Were I asked, on that lonely walk home to a deeply depressed man I knew loved me—who had been my most intimate confidant for years; who understood me better than anyone ever had; who was still living in limbo with his childless wife after I had broken down my children's family over a refusal to give him up—whether I really wanted to continue lying in this bed I'd made, I am both proud and ashamed to say I would unquestionably have reversed courses and run back to the stagnant marriage I knew. I am proud because I understand that there are times when self-preservation is more important than sentiment, especially when one is a mother, and I could not afford to be perpetually devoured from the inside out, surrendering my hours and days and weeks and months to this turbulent anxiety over whether some man would ever fully "choose me." Yet I am also ashamed, because the moment I opened the door to the Pad and saw my lover's face, heard his voice, I understood anew that he was more than some spectacular electrical storm that could ruin me by daring not to want the identical thing I wanted—that he was more than my ticket out of some other existence, now responsible for filling in all the roughly hewn lines of my new life. He was *himself*, and although in these five months I had proven myself quite capable of living without a man next to me every day, my lover still changed the air in every room, and I saw him cooking dinner for me and wondered why I had gone upstairs to my longtime bedroom looking for my ex to give me something he had struggled to give me even in our marriage, instead of coming straight here, where I was known, where I was home.

Within a few weeks, my ex-husband would offer me the chance I didn't have the night my father died—would promise to forgive my affair and go to therapy with me and even help me grieve the loss of my lover, to whom of course in this scenario I could never speak again. And although I would consider this offer for two days— longer than I should have, longer than was kind—in the end I would decline it, opting for life without our net. I didn't want to be my parents, or my ex's parents. I didn't want to love my husband like a difficult sibling, and although I was jealous of whatever codependency my lover and his wife were still holding on to, I didn't want that either. I wanted precisely a love with the power to annihilate me in its intensity, but that would expand and nourish me instead because we would choose creative over destructive power. Maybe my lover would give me that, and maybe he wouldn't. Maybe he would move to Chicago the way he'd longed to during our affair, or maybe that would never happen and he would languish at his wife's apartment until I had no choice but to leave him. Maybe he would rent himself a tiny studio in L.A. and find a new life with someone local, someone who came without the baggage of angry children, sick parents, the frigid Midwest; maybe someday we would both look back on this time and refer to each other as "transitional objects" we had both needed on our way to some other, more final destination.

This, I came to understand, was what freedom tasted like. It wasn't a heady illusion in the safety of a time-shared bed, seeking the approval of the person whose heart you are breaking. It is being willing to have your own heart broken and not blaming the outcome on anyone. It is being an orphan, and love not being an obligation or prescription, but always a risky, transformative choice.

My secret died with my father. I have made too many mistakes in my life to even call that lie of omission my biggest. But he died without knowing who I was because I wanted it that way—I chose it to be that way—for reasons that seemed urgent at the time but now usually feel like mist I can't grab. I used to lean into him when I was two or three years old and whisper, "Let me tell you a cigarette," and I wish I could do that now. I wish he could see me: working full-time, paying the bills, managing maintenance, head of our former household. I wish I could throw pebbles at my father's window, and this time there would really be someone on the porch, someone he might recognize but barely. *It's me*, I would say to him as the windowpane reflected our faces back at each other and we had to look closely not to mistake one for the other, *this is what I really look like*. Sometimes I still talk to the sky, but although I am my father's daughter, the sky never talks back; the sky absorbs, but doesn't listen; the moon is only a plain white orb now, drained of blood.

Affliction

Two Ophelias

In becoming forcibly and essentially aware of my mortality, and of what I wished and wanted for my life, however short it might be, priorities and omissions became strongly etched in a merciless light, and what I regretted most were my silences. Of what had I ever been afraid?

—Audre Lorde

My lover first notices you, Lump, while casually stroking my breast at the Pad. At your sudden insertion into the space between us, we mutter sentences back and forth at each other: *I'm sure it's nothing* and *this happened to me once before—they even biopsied it and nothing was wrong* and *these kinds of scares are common and it's almost never cancer,* until we sound like we are reading aloud from WebMD. *Dense breasts, calcium deposits!* We are in the preliminary stages of fucking when you announce yourself under his fingers, and now we are supposed to be assuaged—supposed to charge ahead full-throttle, sex especially important these last six months as every other aspect of our respective lives unravels. Our fucking reassures us that we are still Us, my lover frequently stating that in previous depressions he's never been capable of arousal, never had a libido, *Everything is different with you,* he tells me.

Now sex is the only time he feels better, feels good, reminds me of himself. Otherwise, we have become a string of silences stretched across restaurant tables, a circular loop of texts in which he berates himself, reports on his (unchangingly) morose moods. Recently, at a conference we were both set to attend—the kind of thing he would have scaled mountains barefoot to get to during our affair— he could not bring himself to leave the apartment for the airport and stood up not just me but the conference organizer, who had to scramble to fill my lover's gap. His wife had gone to stay with her sister for a few days, and he said that between living with her agoraphobia and flying around at every opportunity to see me, he could scarcely remember the last time he'd been alone for a night, and that he couldn't stand the idea of being among people at an airport or performing for audiences at the conference. "I'll miss seeing you," he told me over and over again, but it was becoming harder to know whether he meant this, simply thought he meant it, or knew he was supposed to mean it. Still, here he is again in Chicago, at that pad, stroking your thickening mass in my left breast that I am pretending to believe is nothing so as not to spook or depress him further. Maybe you, Lump, are indeed a false alarm. But the fact that I left one man I spent some eight years walking on eggshells around only to find myself with another is real, even if my lover is prone to lying inert on beds instead of screaming at me and stalking off in huffs.

My lover's phone starts pinging staccato: five times, ten times, sometimes twenty times consecutively in the space of a few minutes, which always means his wife. I roll over on my side, murmur that I'm not in the mood anymore—the first time that's ever been true with him, the first time I've ever rebuffed his touch—and close my eyes, leaving him to her. Instead he curls up behind my body, tries again, "You're going to be okay—I promise." But who is either of us to promise anything? That night after he falls asleep, I retreat to the living room and sob in a ball on the couch. Somehow, my lover and I have fast-forwarded through two decades of coupledom and here we are, just where we both left off: a woman crying in another room and a stone-silent man pretending not to hear her.

By the time I can get in for a mammogram, he's back in California. He can never stay long, given that he doesn't sleep in the apartment with me and my children (a couple of times he's stayed in the basement for a night or two, but that feels awkward and depressing—hiding him in the bowels of the house, unacceptable for familial viewing), so usually after my three days in the Pad are up, he flies back "home," and in another few weeks plunks down the airfare to do it again. He doesn't have the money to come in at a moment's notice—to pay up for a hotel for a longer stay—and so my mammogram becomes the first in a series of solitary doctor appointments, solitary ultrasounds and tests, of sitting in waiting rooms drinking large bottles of radioactive liquid that will highlight the inside parts of me, of crying in my car on my way to hospitals to retrieve medical records to transfer to some other specialist. But none of that has happened yet, of course. Now it is the Tuesday before Thanksgiving and my father has been dead less than two months and I am sitting upright while a nurse and doctor give each other meaningful glances over my head. The speed with which we move from an ultrasound to a needle biopsy, there in my same exam chair with no additional scheduling, with no wait when there is always a wait, combined with the solicitous tone of the nurse's voice, tells me everything I need to know. I am a knower of things, but it would not take a knower of things to know this, Lump, about you.

My cousin Martin brings his three children to his brother's house for Thanksgiving, without the ex-wife he's spent several years hemorrhaging money on divorcing. She is a beautiful train wreck of a woman, a former model (or so her saying goes) of my age, who married my significantly older cousin at the height of her beauty and dazzled everyone in my mother's family with her moneyed inflections, her evident breeding. That was before their children came, each having some manner of affliction that tilted their narrative away from Glamorous Coupledom and toward the beleaguered and almost tragic. Kawasaki disease for their firstborn son together, and then Martin's daughter from his first marriage (to the Seventh Day Adventist who once served us a Special K casserole for Easter dinner) had a car accident that left her brain swollen so that no one thought she would speak again and for a time death seemed more merciful. But she did not die; somehow the brain damage that had been called irreparable ended up dissipating so that she is a wife of a military man now, living in Nevada and posting photos of their children on Facebook. Or maybe that accident was after Martin's youngest child—his third with his beautiful, well-bred young wife—was born with a hole in her heart? *Don't let her cry*, the doctors said, instructing them to keep the baby calm at all times until she was old enough to withstand the surgery to correct the hole. And so Martin's Beautiful Young Wife became a dragon mother, a bedraggled thing who shuffled her feet in a perpetual white nightgown, a receptacle who, to the extent that such a thing is possible, did not put the baby down for a year, until something seemed to crack and she became sleepless, fear-addled, manic, off.

We can't let her cry, Martin's beautiful no-longer-young wife kept saying, baby close to her breast while she aged a decade that year, and eventually the hole was repaired but nothing else seemed ever quite the same.

By which I mean a million little things. By which I mean alcohol was involved, privately at first and then so gaudily that Martin's

wife stole the family car, into which she put their youngest daughter
and disappeared. The baby—no longer a baby: maybe five, maybe
six?—was returned but the car not found. Where had they been? By
which I mean the way that Martin finally broke the news to us at
his sister's house in Indiana, in his sister's garage where the middle
generation, those sandwiched between our mothers and our children, gathered to drink beer and smoke early medicinal weed that
laid us flat on our asses, and Martin said things like, *While I was
at work she would bring home strangers.* There had been incidents,
aside from the car-and-daughter-stealing, apparently. Police had
been called. The police knew their house well, the beautiful dragon
mother turned Medea, calling her middle daughter names and
drinking until lines blurred. Until she became a Stanley Kowalski,
messy and screaming; a Blanche DuBois in her white gown too; an
every broken thing, ensemble. The hand that strikes, the bone that
breaks. *We have to get a divorce*, Martin told us in the garage, *not
because I don't love her anymore but because I have to protect the
children.* And we stood nodding, shocked, me leaning into my (not
yet ex-) husband's solid body, handing him my half-sipped beer in
the easy symbiosis of marriage, like our twins as babies had unthinkingly passed plastic toys back and forth between them, *Your
hand, my hand* ("Ne-ne," they called it—their twin word for "us";
"We-ness," my husband and I called it, Our love word for "us.") *My
god, my god, oh how terrible this is!* we all exclaimed to Martin,
while inside my mother and her sister talked heart attacks, macular
degeneration, gout.

But that was years ago now. Years before you, Lump. Years before I woke with my mother's breath in my mouth, her pulse ticking
under my eggshell skin, suddenly closer to the blood than the birth.
(*Liar, liar: the blood is the birth.*) That was back when I honestly believed my parents' collected list of maladies might conceivably be
the worst thing that ever happened to me. That was back when, as

Martin's divorce raged on, racking up hundreds of thousands of dollars in lawyer fees, I said to my husband, *Oh my god, if we ever get a divorce let's never behave that way*, and he looked at me like I was crazy and said, *We would never act like that*, and then, *Besides, we're not getting a divorce*, and I, having ended things with my lover for the first and therefore only even vaguely convincing time, looked down at my husband's forearm encircling my waist and remembered when the beauty of his forearms had been the poetry of my life. That was back when I believed I had dodged a speeding tram catapulted toward me, the way I once jumped back just in time in Amsterdam, feeling the wind from the tram graze against my hip bone like a lover, and I said to my husband, believing my every word correct, *You're right, we're not.*

Yet here we are: Thanksgiving 2015: Martin with his children but without his no-longer-young but still beautiful ex-wife, and me without my ex-husband, who just a month ago blocked me on his phone and seems stridently intent on our becoming strangers and enemies, and also without my father, who had not been to a family gathering in a couple of years anyway because he would not get in a wheelchair. *Three down*, I think, though it is really six because my children are not here either; they are with my ex-husband, who "gets Thanksgiving," while I, the primary caregiver, have been gifted with Christmas, the superior, nongenocidal holiday, pagan in its origins, which suits me and my atheist children just fine. Two days prior, the needle biopsy. *So maybe seven down, then.*

After the children get home from my ex-husband's, Thanksgiving returns to its usual, hypocritically celebratory state. One day late, I host a house full of guests, a turkey in the oven as I steal away upstairs to my bedroom to call the lab that did my biopsy. I am compelled to call despite not expecting to catch anyone the day after Thanksgiving, and to my surprise a technician answers on the second ring, informing me that all the doctors are out until Tuesday, which makes me wonder if he was supposed to answer the phone at all. *Because of the holiday*, he explains, and though I expected as much, the sound of his voice gives me dangerous hope and I can no longer withstand another moment of uncertainty, of being Sick and Not Sick at once. I ask this technician if he would like to wait until Tuesday to find out whether he has cancer, and he admits that no, he would not, and so he peeks in my medical file illicitly and tells me that the biopsied mass in my left breast is malignant. I thank him and hang up the phone. Then I go back downstairs and serve dinner.

I already had so much to make up for, you see. Lump now gone, Lump cut out, I am talking to you, my companion in those dark days. I already had so much to make up to my children and—I still believed back then—to their father, whom it hadn't yet occurred to me would never come back around to some manner of amicability or at least its pretense. I did not know how to make it up to them, Lump, with my joblessness, with my inappropriate-for-my-family's-social-milieu lover whom Mags and Kaya did not want setting foot in our house, and now with you, now you too, Lump, conspiring to make me incapable of undoing the damage I had wrought.

Incapable of grander gestures, I take the children to Chinatown, one place all three adore, and it is there we get the call from my mother telling us that Martin's ex-wife is missing—has been missing, it seems, since sometime Thanksgiving Day, when we were all gathered around Martin's brother's dining room table dishing her like the stuffing. *What do you mean missing?* I keep asking my mother, but my mother does not know any more. Has she run away again by choice, like the time she lost the family car? But that makes little sense. She is sober now, unlike in those days—she attends AA regularly, and despite all her antics and Martin's hundreds of thousands of dollars in legal fees, she has been granted not only joint custody of their children but "permanent maintenance," which I've learned from my own divorce is what alimony is called these days and to which I, too, am legally entitled, having married my ex-husband one month before Martin wed his then-young and beautiful bride, my ex-husband and I missing their more-extravagant wedding because we were on our honeymoon in Europe. I am waiving permanent maintenance in my own divorce, though my attorney keeps saying, *Divorce law is not about atonement*, first in a fatherly tone and then—when I fail to change my mind despite being unemployed—with increasing anxiety.

Why would Martin's ex-wife run away now, where no one could find her to send those alimony checks she worked so hard to secure?

My children and I drive home in the car, Kaya in the front seat with me with her feet up on the dashboard, her wiry body restless with anxiety. "What if she's in somebody's basement chained to the wall and being tortured," Mags or Kaya says aloud, voicing what I already believe as reality. It is dangerous to be a beautiful woman, even when you are sober and relatively sane. It is dangerous to be a woman, even if you are not beautiful at all. *She's been seeing some man*, my mother tells me on the phone, getting the stream of updates from Martin's mother. Does anyone know who he is? Did she attempt to break up with him, perhaps, and he is not having it? Will she be discovered raped and dismembered, another dead woman for the nightly news, another faceless body on the set of some TV crime documentary, another statistic? Is she even now in the trunk of some jilted man's car? I think of the way she carried her youngest around for a year straight, her love a ferocious beast, and I wonder, even though I would gladly give my children my kidneys or jump in front of buses for them, whether I would have had the stamina to sustain her year-long vigil. How easy would it have been to crack, to fall asleep sitting up and accidentally drop the child? How easy would it have been to take to her bed, rending her garments and gnashing her teeth in grief and fear, and pass the buck to someone who would promise to take a shift of vigilance but then set the baby down in her crib?

"Oh my god, I hope she's dead," one of my daughters says, and Enzo seems astonished and alarmed, but I understand completely. I am hoping for her death too, far less unthinkable than its alternative. That my daughters, only fifteen, suspect this too is, for the moment, Lump, a fact worse than you.

The news in Martin's small, incestuous town runs amok. It isn't every day a daughter of one of its oldest and largest families disappears off the face of the earth. Alicia calls me to say she heard about the disappearance on the nightly news. I think of how long it's been since I've seen Martin's ex. We've known each other since were both in our early twenties, and in those days of her Being Missing I think of three things:

1) That I should have called her, for fuck's sake, at some point over these past two years while their divorce raged and finally ended—that I should have honored our history enough to at the very least say I was sorry for what she was going through and that if she ever needed any help with the kids to call me . . . but I never did that because I was preoccupied with my sick parents and my young children and my writing and editing and my clandestine affair, and lately the shit of my own life has been flying into every imaginable fan and she has been the last thing on my mind.

2) That the last time I saw her, at a surprise birthday party I threw my mother, she seemed markedly less stable than ever in the past,

which was saying something—she talked incessantly, telling my mother's old lady friends that she was "put on this earth to help the plight of the Black man," even though to the best of my knowledge she never engaged in any kind of activism or, in fact, worked at all in the entire time I knew her other than part-time retail at a friend's clothing store, so the things she was saying were not only condescendingly racist but clearly delusional. Between my father and my lover, I understood enough about mental illness to know that she was in a manic state that had veered into grandiosity, but when I took her aside and tried to talk to her about bipolar disorder, she told me that she left a therapist for accusing her of having the condition and claimed he clearly was afraid of powerful women.

3) How once, long ago when she and Martin were still living in their ramshackle-but-enviable suburban home together, she told me that she understood the behavior of Mamah Cheney in Nancy Horan's novel *Loving Frank*—that loving a great man (she said that: "great man") was an extraordinary thing and that if it happened, you had to sacrifice everything to follow such a love, such a man, including custody of or even contact with your children if need be. And I thought again of how she never put her baby down, and how if some allegedly Great Man had come up to her and told her to chuck that baby onto the floor and run away with him, the woman I once knew would have kicked him in the balls, and yet here she was, not seeming manic or delusional in the moment, serving a civilized meal from Whole Foods at our family gathering because she wasn't much of a cook, and saying that to love a great man was everything. Of course I sanctimoniously disagreed with her—said that obligation to one's children surpassed the importance of romantic love—and these years later I stand by my belief, yet I know, too, the price my children have paid and are still paying for my romantic love, even though I am still here.

•

They find her body inside her car, on December 2, after her November 28 disappearance. She had, Martin tells us, called him several times on Thanksgiving morning to make sure he was really coming (he has a reputation for lateness) to get their two daughters, their son already living in a college dorm by then. *It seemed very important to her*, Martin keeps telling us, *that I was getting the girls out of the house*, though her dead body is not found particularly near her apartment, but rather in an industrial area where one of her regular AA meetings takes place. She took a bunch of pills and then—in a detail I will never be able to shake from my head—put a plastic bag over her head and died there in the front seat of her car, her body decomposing for days before she is found. A newspaper in their town prints all the grisly details of the suicide, though it will later remove the story from the Internet after being called out by many residents for its irresponsible reportage, leading to additional pain for her grieving family. Later, her youngest daughter, still troubled by heart issues into her teens, will tell Kaya and Mags that she is sometimes bullied at school not only because of her ill health but because her mother killed herself, and I want to scream into the void where compassion should be, *Why the fuck did you carry that little girl around for an entire year against your breast like something you would gladly sacrifice your own health and sanity for, only to do this to her now—* to do this thing that, like Kathy's father shooting himself in the head in their family home because Kathy's mother was cheating on him and had asked for a divorce, will become the kind of hole in her children's hearts that surgery can never fix.

It has been four days since I was diagnosed with breast cancer, though I've told neither my children nor my ex-husband, who isn't speaking to me anyway, and the day I learn of Martin's ex-wife's death I don't tell my ex about that either, despite that he knew her as long as I did. Maybe, I wonder, he would think she did the right thing: after all, if he is this angry at me for falling in love with a man I've been friendly with since 1998, how harshly might he judge her actions? Or maybe he reserves such judgments only for me, and might wish I'd follow suit, which makes me afraid to tell him about my cancer, afraid he will be glad.

I am not going quietly into the fucking night, I resolve to myself then and there, though already I understand that such decisions have little to do with my outcome—that the language of cancer (*battles, survivors, warriors*) is just a trick to make people feel they can control the uncontrollable, and that all it is possible to do is comply with doctors, to endure, to hope for the best. Still, no matter what my ex-husband or anyone may think I deserve, there remains hope for me—divorce and cancer and all—while there is no longer hope for Martin's ex-wife, no longer hope for Kathy, no longer hope for my father. I am still standing and this—this crucible year—is when I need to never put my children down.

Many nights I still wonder about the bag. Why, if she'd already taken so many pills, did she put that bag over her head? Why cause herself unnecessary suffering, make her death more grisly? For a time, I believed maybe this was an indication that she was murdered after all, and the killer made it look like a suicide—it seemed the gratuitous touch of a man who wanted a woman to suffer for what she did to him. But my lover explained that it is not uncommon for suicides to put a bag over their head for extra measure, to hasten death and make it less likely they will be found or rescued. That this is what people do, sometimes, when they mean business, when they are no longer crying out for help and no outcome but death is acceptable. *Maybe she'd relapsed,* my lover suggests, trying to find a reason for the unreasonable. *The shame of relapsing can be intense.* But I keep thinking about her children—about her children and my children— about how many times Kathy cried because she and her siblings had not been enough to make her father choose to live. How could she do this to them? *It doesn't work like that,* my lover, who came hip-grazingly close to killing himself too during a long-ago relapse, says gently. *By the time you get to that place, you're in a tunnel, you've lost empathy, you think you're doing everybody a favor. You truly believe you're so low that everyone would be better off without you.*

Is that what my lover was thinking even before your arrival, Lump: unable to get on a plane for a conference, convinced he can "never be happy again" after what he has done—after what we did together? If he is only a razor's edge away from the precipice, how will your presence tilt our delicate balancing act?

When I told my lover about my malignancy, he said all the right things—promised that whether or not I had breasts had no bearing on his love for me; promised that he would be here for my surgery and would take care of me, whether Mags and Kaya wanted him in the house or not; reiterated that despite his ongoing depression and guilt and self-loathing he, as Jeff Tweedy once wrote, had "reservations about so many things, but not about you." But if I expected the urgency of a cancer diagnosis to result in his saying he was packing his bag and would be on the next plane for Chicago, and that he is not leaving until my treatments are over and not then either because this life or death scare has made him realize there are things worse than upsetting his wife, or for that matter than moving to a cold climate . . . well, Lump, he does not say those things, does not show up that very night at my door.

And so it is going to be on me to keep the faith that I am not so low that everybody is better off without me, including my children. It is going to be on me to find the faith that Martin's ex-wife could not find—the faith that I still matter, even if I am no longer any man's Most Important Priority, even if I am not the mother I thought I'd be. Even if the only reason I can find to justify my continued existence is that the trauma of me alive is far lesser than the trauma of me dead; even if only for the sake of my children because I have lost any sense of myself as deserving of anything, this becomes the moment—alone in what was once my marital bed while my children sleep downstairs—that I refuse to join the endless body count of women lost to History. This dark night, I resolve to believe, irrevocably and whatever the cost, that I deserve to live.

The Cartographers

FIFTY MEDITATIONS

I want to describe myself
like a painting that I looked at
closely for a long time,
like a saying that I finally understood,
like the pitcher I use every day,
like the face of my mother,
like a ship
that carried me
through the wildest storm of all.

—Rainer Maria Rilke

1.

Pain and I have met before. We are old lovers whose relationship was full of tumult and abuse, yet we somehow parted amicably in the end, my drifting away unnoticed without his coming to stalk me as I had expected. I made my hasty retreat in August 1998, three years, two months, and roughly twenty days from our first meeting in May 1995, and ran for my life, not looking back.

It is strange that in this metaphor, I've labeled Pain as male. In

studies, women suffer from chronic pain—in particular those related to autoimmune conditions, from interstitial cystitis to chronic
fatigue to fibromyalgia to severe arthritis—three to four times more
frequently than men. This use of the term "autoimmune conditions"
as a catch-all is particularly significant because arthritis is easy to
see on an X-ray or MRI, unlike some of the more mysterious forms
of pain from which women suffer, which have historically been cast
as "all in our minds." In other words, women suffer from more pain
conditions that are poorly understood and may have psychosomatic
links, as well as those pain conditions that are easily spotted on the
most basic of medical tests and are empirically easy to "prove"—a
thing the medical profession often demands that you do when complaining of pain, especially if you are a woman.

After leaving my first Bad Relationship with pain behind in 1998,
I began using my other passport again, Sontag's infamous passport
to the country of the well. I could not, however, turn in my passport
to that other nation, in which I'd dwelt for more than three years. It
is easier to denounce and move on from an actual country in which
we reside than to leave behind our passport to Sickness, which, of
course, lives inside us. Sontag, who passionately argues against the
attribution of metaphorical characteristics to illnesses, begins her
classic *Illness as Metaphor* with, ironically, a metaphor, if a flawed
one. Sickness—in this case pain—is not a place to which one can
hold a passport. The image this calls to mind is that of Teresa in
The Unbearable Lightness of Being, returning to Communist Prague
and surrendering her passport so that she will forever be unable to
leave again. Yet pain offers no such loopholes, no options that you
just "play along" or even join in gleefully with the dominant power
group; pain offers no hope that you can somehow defect from it
forever.

It can be difficult to speak of pain without the use of metaphors
because of the essential gap between language and experience, and

if the reader has not felt the kind of pain of which I am speaking, all I can hope to do is spin conceptual webs: *it is like this; it is not like that.* No matter what words I choose to use to describe a migraine, I cannot give you the migraine. We are confined to allusions, analogies, to a futile if essential faith that language can be twisted to mean.

Pain is not like having an abusive boyfriend you're afraid to leave, because there isn't choice involved, even though that may be the best metaphor I've come up with simply because of how hopeless it feels, and also because having an abusive boyfriend hurts on a literal level.

Pain is not like watching your children starve or seeing them killed in a genocide, because it is not possible to care about your own body to the extent that you would care about these things happening to your children, so if you are in chronic, blinding pain, you will spend a lot of time thinking things like *At least my children aren't starving*, and *At least my children aren't abducted*, and *At least my children aren't sick*, and tell yourself you are counting your blessings, when what you are really doing is making yourself feel guilty for daring to be upset about the fact that your body is torturing you.

Of course in my interstitial cystitis years, from 1995 to 1998, I did not have children. I had: a husband, many interesting friends, travel, my parents, my writing, my work, and even money. I had all the external signs of a highly successful life, despite going for weekly IV infusions of taurine or plugging my nose to drink bizarre-smelling herbs my husband boiled down to a muddy Chinese tea for me nightly in our attempts to stop my battery-acid bladder pain. Complaining constantly about your pain makes you a depressing and stressful person to be around, which causes you to lose friends, and friends are ever more imperative when trapped inside your own skin in a kind of constantly fresh, unrelenting physical hell. As a result, I rarely complained except to my husband, though I had many strange habits of the sick that my friends probably thought were either eccentric or flat-out crazy. Still, I had learned not to be a downer.

As my lover once wrote, "The arc of mental illness does not conform to a redemption narrative." This is true, as well, of the arc of chronic pain. Unlike having a shitty boyfriend, there is no way to change your identity and go on the lam. There is no way to be a plucky heroine who triumphs over adversity. People in pain have three options: keep on living as normally as you can; make your pain so central to your identity that you will eventually become isolated; or, of course, kill yourself, as some people in chronic pain do.

During those IC years, the thought of suicide was a comfort. I had no imminent desire to die, and certainly no plan to take my life, but the knowledge that I *could* if it got bad enough may have paradoxically enabled me to keep going.

In August 1998, while living in Amsterdam, I went into a remission from my IC. My remission was most likely caused by high dosages of pau d'arco (a herb that at even higher doses apparently can also cure cancer, but not without killing you from its toxicity). Another metaphor: at first, when released from pain, which is more a prison than a country, more a prison than a bad relationship, all you can do is stand there blinking at the sun in disbelief and wanting to fall to your knees and kiss the ground. You think you will never get accustomed to feeling "normal" again, even though of course you will, and you do.

2.

"What would happen if one woman told the truth about her life?" Muriel Rukeyser wrote in 1968, the year of my birth. "The world would split open." But I have been waiting fifty years—I have devoured and memorized and heeded Hélène Cixous's call in "The Laugh of the Medusa" that women write our bodies, write our sexualities, write of our desire, our motherhood, our secrets "in white ink," and although it is now possible to have an entirely more kick-ass syllabus in any literary seminar than it was in Cixous's heyday, the fabric of the patriarchal world seems not only still woven tightly, but, one might even postulate, reinforced with duct tape.

3.

When I was finally able to talk to my doctor about my breast cancer diagnosis, I was told that I had cancer not only in the palpable lump my lover had found, but also in another location in my left breast, too, closer to the nipple. I was also told that the pathology report showed my Ki-67 proliferation to be strong, which is widely considered an indication of more aggressive cancer, with a higher chance of relapse, and that my results regarding a genetic marker, P53, also indicated a more aggressive cancer that is often associated with premenopausal onset, as was true in my case. Study after study on the Internet, which my doctor told me not to look at, indicated the high correlation of P53 with shorter periods of disease-free survival. When I told my primary care physician—the same primary care physician Kathy referred me to before her diagnosis and death—that I had chosen a radical bilateral mastectomy rather than removal of only one breast or a complex lumpectomy in more than one location, she said she would make the same decision.

Even prior to my revelation of cancer, my lover's depression had escalated into what his psychiatrist was calling a "red zone," the end result of which increasingly seemed likely to be hospitalization, an addiction relapse, suicide, or all of the above. Though he had repeatedly promised not to kill himself and said he would never do that to me or the other people who loved him, he often expressed the deep wish that he had died eight years prior, during a brief opiate relapse, so that he would not have been alive to "ruin everyone's lives" as he was doing now. By "everyone" he still meant primarily his sick, dependent wife, whom he seemed to think leaving akin to abandoning an infant in the dirt with no means of survival, even though his wife had a tenured job teaching online from home, an inheritance from her parents, good health insurance, and a PhD. In addition to his wife, he also meant my three children, whose family he had "blown apart," and of course me, whom he had "bait and switched" due to having started our affair when he was in a long-term hypomanic state, whereas now he was what he described as "a shell of the man you thought you were getting," "broken," and "incapable of ever being happy again."

Meanwhile, my ex-husband had become engaged to and moved in with another woman. Our daughters were on increasingly fraught terms with him, which included a series of dramas in his new household to which I was privy only secondhand. Though our son had fared better during the transition, my ex-husband had severed contact with every mutual friend he and I had ever had for a quarter century, so when Enzo went to his father's new home, he was cut off from everyone and everything he had known for nine years.

I sat stewing in my Ki-67 and P53. I was the one who had "bait and switched" the man I loved, as clinical depressions can end, but I could not regrow breasts or rewire my genes. Far worse, it seemed entirely plausible that before my children came of age, I would be dead. My daughters would be left with a man they had fled rooms to avoid since they were nine; I worried Enzo might feasibly lose access to anyone who would reassure him how profoundly I had loved him, instead of telling him how selfish I was and how my bad karma had gotten me in the end.

For better or worse, I have always had a strong impulse to "fix" things. Clearly, I should return to my ex and concentrate on helping my children and their father forge stronger relationships together and reconnect with our larger community, so that when I died, my children would have a parent they trusted and could lean on and grieve with, before he someday found another wife, one who could feel benevolent toward me from a distance given that I would be dead.

I thought little of what it might actually be like to die of cancer. I only wanted to be sure that once I was gone, my children could go on smoothly without me.

If you are smarter than I was, you have already noticed that, perhaps even more so than my cancer, my real problem was my ongoing belief that I could control the outcome of every situation—could maneuver other people's lives until the pattern was one I found suitable, in which my ex-husband—though I genuinely believed this plan of mine would benefit his relationship with our children—was again a pawn.

If you are smarter than I was, you will recognize that in this equation of my crawling back to a man I had chosen to leave (twice), I, for all my desire to live, was writing myself off as already dead.

4.

For about six weeks after my cancer diagnosis, my lover couldn't touch me without crying. Although verbally he insisted that he "didn't care" whether or not I had breasts, and although I understood him to be a man highly capable of finding beauty in the damage, in the scars, in the difference, something about my being sick had eradicated his desire, which had always been unquenchable between us even through his depression. On a literal level, he was a man suffering from caregiver fatigue, having already seen his marriage destroyed over the course of a decade by his wife's self-imposed isolation in response to her illness and his inability to either "save" her or to somehow find a way to live within the new morose confines of their lives, so the idea that he had jumped out of the frying pan into an even graver caregiver fire was no doubt hardly an aphrodisiac. But the truth was perhaps more complex than that.

After all, I didn't, in those six weeks, feel sick. Though we couldn't be positive of my cancer's staging until after my mastectomy, everyone agreed that my lover and I had "caught it early." I had no symptoms other than possibly the weight loss I had repeatedly told Alicia I thought was a tumor (back when such a thing seemed a joke and we believed I was really just stressed over my divorce). For New Year's, I flew to California to spend time at my lover's cabin near Joshua Tree National Park, and while there I went to a casino; I went out with other friends nearby; I drove to the laundromat and washed all the cabin's dusty sheets . . . I was hardly an invalid. I also, very much, perhaps more than ever in my entire life, wanted to fuck. I wanted to experience my breasts to the hilt while I still had them; I wanted my body to feel good while it still could. My lover and I lay holding each other, listening to Jonathan Richman, to Jay Bennett, in front of his quaint potbellied stove, but if we so much as attempted to make out, he would begin to weep. I had seen him cry a couple of times, before long partings during our affair, and then it had seemed sad but romantic. Then, I had licked his tears, and we had walked arm in arm to see the sea lions under a pier, the world crackling with beauty. This was nothing like that. His weeping now was an isolated thing I could neither share in nor comfort. I feared I had become a "duty," an obligation, within the blink of my diagnosis. Whatever had made me previously irresistible to him was gone, even though he was still here.

Was this what had happened when his wife got ill?

Maybe the things he was incapable of giving me were the same things he had been incapable of giving her. Maybe, though his wife's and my subjective responses to our bodies' maladies were entirely different, the outcome of losing this man's desire would be the same. And if that was actually true, then was his desire even a thing worth having, after all?

5.

According to a 2009 study, the pattern of divorce among couples where one member is sick changes radically when the researchers consider the breakdown by sex. When the man becomes ill, only 3 percent of marriages will end. But when the woman is the one who is sick, about 21 percent will end up separated or divorced.

6.

I am a woman of plans and schemes. In the end, it was my body that finally cut me off.

When I at last revealed to my ex-husband over the phone that I had cancer—when I told him blatantly that perhaps we should get back together for the sake of the children—he surprised me by, rather than gloating at my misfortune, agreeing. He seemed genuinely distraught that I was ill, and before we hung up asked me to commit, then and there, to reuniting: to not get on a plane the next day for a work trip where I would see my lover, but rather do what he had been asking of me all along and cut off all contact so as to rededicate myself to my marriage.

This was exactly, Ladies and Gentlemen of the Jury, what I had hoped he would say.

And yet I could not do as he asked. My body flew into a panic, my throat closing, my stomach roiling. "I need a day or two to make the decision firmly," I begged him, unable to get my unruly body to relax itself into the acquiescence I had sought. "I need to at least go out there to California and tell him in person."

Yet when I got to California, I found the man I wanted more than I had ever wanted anyone in the world still could not touch me and seemed so viscerally depressed that he did not even have the energy to cry anymore. "I am thinking," I said to him, because we had always been completely honest with each other, no matter what other bullshit we may have been guilty of, "that maybe I should go back to my marriage for the sake of the kids. I'm thinking that if I die, I can't leave them in this state with their relationships to their father so damaged. I'm thinking that maybe what I want doesn't matter anymore and that all I have to focus on is what's best for them, if they're going to lose their mother."

My lover was lying on his back with his arm over his face in a pose of utter despondency. "I understand," he said. "You have to do what's best for your children. They're more important than I am."

Was he relieved? Was he glad to be rid of me and my suddenly faulty cells? It was impossible to know.

"But will you be okay?" I asked, even though he had not been okay in some time. "What will you do? Will you be all right if we can't talk anymore—if we can't see each other while I'm sick and going through treatments, and no matter what the outcome is?"

"Well," he said, "if you die I'll probably kill myself anyway, no matter whether we're together or apart."

I don't know what kind of answer I had been expecting, but this was not it.

I didn't want to be responsible for whether he lived or died. I didn't want this man I adored, this person who had exploded into my life with such intimate intellectual and emotional connection, with so much laughter and attraction, to disappear from the world. But in that moment, I understood as perhaps I never had before that it was not my job to keep him here, and that he had presented me with a no-win riddle. That according to him, my dying—a situation beyond my control and that I did not in any way desire—would "result" in his killing himself, no matter which man I chose, if any man at all. That I needed, here in my Ki-67ed, P53ed, imminently breast-amputated skin, to feel guilty about my cancer and its outcomes, because the outcome had become responsible for his will to live.

Finding a private conference room in the hotel in which to talk, I called my ex-husband and, every nerve in my body more on edge with a fight-or-flight response than anything like passion or relief, I told him that yes, we could reunite. I told him, even, that all I wanted was to be back in bed with him, back in his arms, and as I said the words they felt true, even as I also felt like throwing up in confused grief over my lover. I told my ex-husband that I had made a terrible mistake, and that if he gave me the chance to correct it, I would spend whatever time I had left on this earth making sure he never regretted the decision. And even now, from this great a distance—even understanding the gut-churning ambivalence of my pleading in that moment—I still believe that I would have made good on that promise.

But you see, it was already too late.

In the time it had taken me to fly to California and behold the condition of my lover, my ex-husband had, simultaneously, spent a tearful and agonized dark night of the soul due to my refusal to commit to him the night before—my telling refusal to not get on the plane. And over the course of that time he had concluded—rightly, fucking rightly—that he should no way in hell come back to me.

"You had your chance," he told me when, still, I tried to convince him in vain. "You had so many chances. You don't really want me, you just want me to swoop in and save you."

This was partially true—true-adjacent at the least—but it did not assuage my desperation. And so I blurted frantic things about the children—about the fact that having a mother with cancer, much less a dead mother, was more than enough to withstand and that they could not deal with having two stepfamilies on top of it, neither of which they wanted nor were turning out particularly well for them thus far. I cited that Kaya and Mags had already lost their biological family and that what was happening now was simply "too much." I cited the escalating difficulties he had been having with our daughters, and how terrified I was for the kids if that state of affairs became all they had left in the world.

To which my ex-husband said, in an impatient tone as though he perhaps found me grotesquely narcissistic to worry about how my death might impact our children, that the kids would be "fine."

Ever since leaving my marriage, I had felt a continued abiding familial love for my ex-husband, and guilt that I was hurting him so terribly, but abruptly for the first time I hated him. For not understanding the stakes; for seeming not to care that our children, already traumatized for years by both of our bullshit antics, needed him to rise above my treason and repair our family so that they would have the strength to withstand my loss as a strong unit of four. I understood in that moment a million different things about why I had always refused to recommit to my marriage—from the moment I began my affair, to the moment I confessed it, to his trying to win me back two months prior, to finally just nights before my suggesting we reunite and then getting on a plane anyway.

Once upon a time, in the late 1990s, I had written my husband a series of erotic letters describing my sexual fantasies—one for each day of his work week—and slipped them, with suggestive (and in one case flat-out pornographic) Polaroids of myself, into his messenger bag. Then I waited . . . and waited . . . my sexy anticipation fading slowly into anxiety, then utter humiliation, as he ignored my naked revelations entirely, never mentioning a thing. Had the letters somehow fallen out of his bag? Had someone stolen them? Had I, even, somehow misremembered the entire thing, and never had the courage to give him the letters, instead throwing them away at some last minute I had blocked out? Finally, a year or two later, I brought the letters up in couples counseling and he stated that he had ignored them because they had been "selfish" and all about my desires. I had tried to open myself up to him, to hand him my innermost secret wishes, but he had refused them, because while I dared to believe my desires would be . . . interesting to him, some kind of gift . . . in fact he had wanted no such thing. He only wanted me to act as he wished. Or no, that's too simple. He wanted, perhaps, for me to long for such letters from *him*, even though he was not a man who would ever write them—he wanted his desires to be the gift I was hungry for, and was furious that I was only thinking about myself, even though he was also only thinking about himself. Now, nearly two decades later, I understood the difference between loving a person and loving the idea of a person, and what you think that person reflects about you. My ex-husband and I had loved each other that way, mutually, both looking past the other's reality, projecting our own fantasies off the other's walls, not seeing what was right in front of us, or worse, seeing but not caring, both trying to wrest the focus back to ourselves.

How he had loved the *idea* of me: the writer, the free spirit, the wild girl he had "saved" and redeemed, the affectionate mother who, when he saw me interacting with our son, made him realize anew all he had missed from his own mother growing up. How he had loved to tell other people how intelligent and special I was, or to sit in the audience while I gave a reading, thinking of me as his. Now, however, the idea of me had changed overnight. Not only to my lover in California, but to my ex-husband as well. Now I was *sick*. And all the reasons he had ever begged me to take him back, all the reasons he had ever insisted that I was an impossible act to follow, had seemingly evaporated because I was *not that woman* anymore and I had nothing to offer him now but the memory of my mistakes and flaws. Our children lay on the table between us, three mangled bargaining chips our reunion stood the best chance of not cracking further, but if the value of these chips was not the same in our respective economies, then maybe my hand was empty.

"I'll be an ally in this," he said, and I clutched at the words like a lifeline, my iPhone hot in my hand inside the overly air-conditioned conference room. At this point I had been blocked on my ex's phone for about a month and a half. Still, he had unblocked me for this conversation—only nights prior he had wanted to be married to me again—and so when he promised he would help the children through my illness, that we would put our differences aside, both despite and absolutely because of everything else that had transpired between us, I believed him completely.

Only days later, he blocked me on his phone again.

Shortly after I started chemo, he turned off all the utilities in the home I lived in with our three children, drained our joint bank account to zero, fired our mediation team and his reasonable attorney, filed partition actions to sell our house and Alicia's house, and served me with motions to sue for the "significant decision-making responsibility and the majority of parenting time" for our three children.

7.

When you have lived with a certain level of unremitting chronic pain, as I did in the late 1990s, if you are a certain kind of person, you will get a lot of mileage on the "perspective" that the ultimate relief from such pain has given you. Various things will seem to you Not As Bad as those three years and two months and roughly twenty days in which your body felt like something you wanted to slice open down the middle to escape, like stepping out of a gorilla suit. Those things may include but not be limited to: infertility, losing literary agents and book contracts, miscarriage, an increasingly unhappy marriage, hating yourself, being a liar, your father's death, a diagnosis of breast cancer, a mastectomy, chemotherapy, losing your hair.

The one thing that will feel worse than three and a half years in a stew of battery acid held in by your own skin: an ugly divorce.

We are all in the end those rhesus monkeys who cling to the soft plush mother for comfort, ignoring the food on the wire monkey until we starve.

Other people can hurt us more than our bodies can.

8.

I would say that cancer reacquainted me with pain, but that would be misleading. The type and level of pain that I suffered during my seven months of cancer treatment in 2016 were entirely minor compared to my three years of my interstitial cystitis. While I had been warned by several friends that I would need to buy some kind of camisole that zipped or tied up the front because I wouldn't— postmastectomy—be able to raise my arms above my head for weeks, in reality I was raising my arms above my head in the hospital room an hour after surgery, saying, *Look, I thought I wasn't supposed to be able to do this!* The reality is that, when I got home from the hospital, I immediately started trying to clean my dirty kitchen floor until my lover (staying with me and my children in our family home for the first time in our relationship) chastised me and got me into bed. The truth is that by the next night, he and I were walking a mile round-trip to dinner in one of those perfect snowstorms where the flakes are so fat you feel you are inside a snow globe.

For a time, we did not think I was going to require chemotherapy. I was told, even—my original biopsy having been transferred to the hospital where I was now receiving care—that as it turned out my actual tumor pathology was not even characterized by the P53 that had originally terrorized me so, and that my pathology report was, by confusing contrast, as positive as one could hope for, if one had to have cancer. Then I was given the standard-of-care Oncotype DX test, as well as the Mammaprint test and genetic testing to assess my risk of long-term metastasis . . . and abruptly things shifted again. Suddenly, on a recommendation from Northwestern's Robert Lurie Cancer Center and a second opinion from one of the top oncologists in the country at Cedars-Sinai in L.A., chemo was not only back on the table but the chef's recommended special. Chemotherapy could be capable of reducing my recurrence risk, I was told, by roughly twelve percentage points, or—as Kaya put it—capable of raising my ten-year chance of disease-free survival from a grade of a C to a high B.

If having surgery to remove my breasts had been, given my circumstances, almost an "easy" decision, then the choice to go bald, feel like death, and possibly face long-term side effects and ramifications of chemo's toxicity, even though my cancer was Stage 1 and had not spread even locally to the lymph nodes, was grueling and, for a time, touch and go. (A "C," after all, is still a passing grade . . .) In the end, however, with three minor children I knew I had to take every precaution my doctors advised, if only so that should my cancer later metastasize, I would have the peace of mind of knowing I had done all I could to remain healthy for my kids—that, unlike other decisions I had made, I would be incapable of blaming myself for any recurrence.

Chemotherapy was the most difficult physical experience I have ever undergone aside from my IC, yet it was wholly different in the sense of my knowing it was a transient thing. Wait, let me rephrase that. I had chemo every three weeks, for only four sessions, and hence it was unequivocally a temporary situation. Yet simultaneously, because the very reason I was having chemo was my elevated risk of recurrence, I also went through chemotherapy believing it my *first* experience with chemo, and one likely to be repeated someday. It felt both entirely finite and yet like the beginning of a circular pattern that would not stop spinning until I was dead.

As IC, unlike cancer, is never a terminal condition, it may therefore sound strange that my chemotherapy was less distressing. But the reality is that my IC had afflicted me twenty-four hours a day for more than three years, and as such, until my surprise remission (or perhaps "cure," being as it was twenty years ago?), I believed fully that I would never feel "normal" for even five minutes again in my life. With my chemo, I expected to feel normal again, possibly even for many years, before someday the cancer recurred.

9.

"I imagine one of the reasons people cling to their hates so stubbornly," James Baldwin wrote in *The Fire Next Time*, "is because they sense, once hate is gone, they will be forced to deal with pain."

Or is it really that easy for some, when a once-beloved has disappointed him, lied to him, proven not to be the stalwart pillar of good Italian girl loyalty he believed her to be, to simply decide that the liar, the betrayer, is not quite human at all? That there is not one single good thing about her; that any shred of decency was only ever an act, and therefore nobody should be beholden to any honor himself when interacting with such an inhuman beast of a woman, even if she has just lost her breasts, spent a month stripping four drains hanging from her body leaking foul-colored fluids, and is currently being flooded with poisons that have caused her pubic hair to fall out all in one fell swoop, after wiping on the toilet one day? Even if her children are witnessing all of this, quietly terrified? If this irredeemable woman is no longer deserving of compassion, are her children? Or is anyone who loves her likewise contaminated?

I would like to say that if such certainty in one's moral judgments is a skill, then please let me learn it—that I want to master it so fully it can permanently stop up the dam of my grief—but that would just be another lie. When we stop drawing a line between moral failings and evil, between the very things that make us human and those that take away our humanity—when we lose sight of mercy and mistake it for weakness, all is lost. The fact that missing and empathy can coexist side by side with fear, with anger, with a complex and contradictory desire to both never lay eyes on someone again and, paradoxically, to hold him tight and say how sorry I am until my voice goes hoarse and I can somehow allay his pain (I know I cannot allay his pain) . . . that is the human condition.

10.

Physical pain will not make you a better or more noble person, but sometimes, if you are wired a certain way, it will make you tougher, even to the point of glibness. When I was hospitalized with neutropenia at the end of my chemotherapy, when I had no neutrophils or white blood cells left and my fever was mounting and I was being kept in a quarantine room with a self-circulating air system and everyone who entered had to wear a mask and gloves; when the doctors were saying to me, "We don't think you're going to die, but this is very, very serious," all I would do was talk about needing to be released so I could make it to my son's mother/son dance at school in two nights. Of course, the doctors resisted mightily. But ultimately I was given shots to boost my white blood cell count and neutrophils and IV antibiotics that they transitioned to oral in time for me to be released—feeling and looking like a corpse in a wig—to go to the dance, which my son mercifully declared "stupid" because the gym lights were too bright and, due to the Hawaiian theme, no one was dressed up. We spent the evening watching a movie on the couch.

About a week after the mother/son dance, I went on tour for a few days with my lover's punk band, despite frequently falling asleep with chemo- and neutropenia-induced exhaustion in public places and being unable to eat because of sores in my mouth and nausea. Those days—I'd already had my last chemo session, given to me over some objections due to my borderline white blood cell counts to begin with, hence inviting in the neutropenic fever—felt both horrifying and thrilling to me. On the one hand, I had never felt so physically close to the knowledge of how rapidly and totally a body can decay and break down, all systems failing simultaneously—to how quickly you can, in the blink of an eye, become an unrecognizable version of yourself, your body a locked box from which you cannot escape, capable of only pain, pleasure a distant taunting memory . . . and then, from there, the exhaustion, the numbness, the indifference, the fog of sleep as the only escape from pain and then not even that . . . slipping away entirely without even having the energy to care.

On the other hand, it would also be fair to say that—not knowing quite what to do with this revelation—I did my best to outrun it. My chemo was "done" and I was cancer free and pretty soon everything would be physically "back to normal." Hair grows back! The medications worked! Look, here I am in Detroit, on tour: a city ravaged with ruin, like me, and trying to regrow itself, trying to remember that out of apocalypse can come beauty.

On tour with the band, no one asked if I was sick or eyed me with pity. My bald head and pale skin were merely taken for retro punk fashion aesthetics. Girls at the merch table, young enough to be my daughters and in skirts cut up past their thighs, complimented my look. It felt good, after six months of cancer immersion, to be able to "pass."

11.

When you have had cancer, you no longer think very often in phrases like *When I am eighty*. Perhaps no one should think in such phrases, but that would belie the fact that many people do indeed live to be eighty, ninety, longer—that even my father, who spent nearly three quarters of his life "dying," lived to ninety-three. Now, still with a significantly higher long-term risk for recurrence than most women who have had Stage 1 breast cancer despite my chemo, I live harder; I don't put things off.

I have also come to understand pain as a constant companion in many stages of our lives, and that the existence of pain does not make our lives exceptional—does not make us either more tragic or more interesting or morally superior. We live in a culture that fetishizes wounds, and it would be easy to make the mistake of thinking that this means being in pain would draw people to you, because you come with an emotionally powerful narrative, but this is usually the opposite of true. Only people who also live with pain want to know anything about that narrative—most others are spending far too much energy pretending to themselves that it will never happen to them, and assigning value judgments to those who are sick to determine what that person may have done to "invite" the problem (if not outright deserve it).

What I figured out in the late 1990s about pain not being the right choice of dinner party conversation still applies. Everyone loves a redemption story, and chronic pain (not to mention terminal illness) fails to offer a fix for that craving.

12.

Chemotherapy ultimately served as the customs point to reenter the Country of Pain. Though it is rarely mentioned by doctors, both chemo and cancer itself can deeply aggravate arthritis, and in my case seemed to accelerate a process that might otherwise have (judging by the timescales on which my parents slowly became disabled in old age) taken decades to occur. Instead, over the course of a few months, the cartilage of my left hip more or less disintegrated, leaving me with nothing but bone on bone. By the time I realized these symptoms were not fading as the oncologist predicted they would, X-rays revealed bone spurs and cysts proliferating. My motion— gradually at first and then with terrifying speed—became highly restricted in my entire left leg. Pain radiated, throbbed, stabbed continuously. The afflicted area ran from my lower back across my left ass cheek into my left outer hip, inner groin, and all down my left leg including the knee, ankle, and foot. The more "wrongly" I walked to compensate for the pain and restricted movement, the more the pain spread to other areas of my body as a result of the compensation. I developed a prominent limp. Soon I could not walk from the parking garage to my office or the classrooms where I taught (about three blocks) without it taking twenty minutes, requiring frequent stops and resulting in so much dizziness and nausea that I would break out sweating and have to sit down before I could begin class. Often I would stand up after sitting and my leg would buckle with pain so shooting I saw flashes of light, so I took to holding on to the desk or wall to "test" my weight before limping with small steps out of the classroom.

During this period, before I could find any effective treatments for my newfound disability, two things transpired: my lover's wife was also diagnosed with breast cancer, and Donald Trump won the presidency.

13.

I am not an organically depressed person. It is possible to be an impulsive person, an overly intense person, a person who perhaps wants and expects too much, who makes extravagant mistakes, and still be an essential optimist. What I mean to say is that, in the wake of becoming disabled in the year 2016—eighteen years after I went into remission from my IC—I fell into the first state of utter despondency of my entire life on November 8, sobbing in a room full of mothers and daughters who had baked celebratory cakes and brought bottles of champagne, as we watched Hillary Rodham Clinton win the popular vote by nearly three million, and lose the presidency.

To put it simply: I was tired of being a woman.

I was tired of living inside my woman's body, with its missing breasts and its genetic time bombs and its history of autoimmune mysteries that (lo and behold!) the medical community now recognizes, finally realizing interstitial cystitis is not just a synonym for Crazy. I was tired of the medical industrial complex and my inability to extricate myself from it. I was tired of being passed from doctor to doctor, given injections that didn't lessen my pain, given tramadol that made me unable to have an orgasm, being refused Norco because of the "opiate epidemic" even though I was a middle-aged cancer survivor who needed to hold down a full-time job to support my three children, and I could not walk properly.

I eventually found myself in a pain clinic, where the cortisone shots resulted in some improvement, but where I was tox-screened at every visit and told that if I had any trace of THC in my system I would be kicked out. I had been trying to experiment with CBD tinctures for pain management, which had appeared to me perfectly legal, as anyone of age could walk into a CBD store in all fifty states and proceed without any kind of medical marijuana card or prescription from a doctor. However, I was told at my pain clinic that I was not allowed to do this or I would be ousted. A nurse took me aside and told me that if I wanted to make a case for using CBD or medical marijuana, I should "get a card" and come back and advocate for myself about it. But I was afraid to do that, because I was a woman alone.

14.

By which I mean: I had an ex-husband who'd spent most of the spring and summer of 2016 trying to destroy every single component of my life, including citing in legal motions the fact that I "smoked marijuana" and kept it "in the home where the children reside" as reasons that it was "in the best interest of the children that the majority of parenting time and significant decision-making authority" be allocated to him. To be clear, he had been married to me for twenty-three years and had no previous problem with said pot consumption (in fact, by his frequent economic logic, he even paid for it), usually in bed, usually watching *The Daily Show*, always after our children were asleep on the lower floor of the house. Occasionally he even joined in, and often he was happy to fuck when I was a little bit high. By which I mean: I was afraid that a medical marijuana card might be used against me by this man in an attempt to punish me by taking my children away, and so I was afraid to get one, stopped using even CBD, and meekly went to the pain clinic, where every time I set foot in the office some menacing man or other would be shouting at the petite female receptionist because he couldn't get his drugs or be seen, and it seemed like a place where someone might pull out a gun.

Of course, medical marijuana and CBD are not covered by insurance, and a tiny bottle of CBD oil costs about $100. Norco, covered by insurance, costs absolutely nothing. Despite an epidemic of abuse and overdose (the fatalities of which are actually highly linked to the prescription of fentanyl, a drug that should be illegal outside of hospice situations), my opiate painkiller was "on the house" of my medical insurance, whereas THC is a Class 1 substance that could not only potentially influence a custody case but put a serious dent in my family finances. Hence, my income on my 2016 tax return being only $29,000, my position as a visiting lecturer being year-to-year and uncertain, and having financial responsibility for three children and my elderly mother, now that I was divorced I could not reasonably afford medical marijuana or CBD anyway.

15.

I have a history of sickliness that at one time seemed excellent fodder for comedy between Kathy and me. She, at five feet eight to my five feet one, often referred to herself as being as "hearty as a Polish washerwoman," and "the friend you call to help move your couch." For many years, she joked that someday she would become my children's stepmother when I kicked the bucket young from one of my obscure eighteenth-century diseases, which included up to that point chilblains, pleurisy, double pneumonia during my ninth month of pregnancy, and later *E. coli* picked up from eating sushi and salad with the carelessness of a royal food taster while in Mexico. Usually, once hospitalized for some primary strange condition, my interment would last longer than expected because my heart murmur would go wild at the first sign of distress anywhere else in my body, such that anything from high-altitude sickness to preg-nancy could bring my heart rate up past 150 and keep it there for days or weeks on end, while doctors panicked and strapped me to Holter monitors or refused to release me. "She gets tachycardic if you blow on her," my no-nonsense ob-gyn announced at the onset of my C-section to deliver Enzo—"We are in and out of here fast, people." Even after Kathy's death, I once managed to pass out three consecutive times during the strobe lighting of a Beck performance at the Pitchfork Festival and had to be strapped to a chair and car-ried to the medical tent simply because I'd had two hard ciders on an empty stomach (though my lover claimed that Beck's music can induce a spontaneous loss of consciousness in many people).

For her part, Kathy had never been sick a day in her life prior to her cancer diagnosis, unless you count being in a body cast as a toddler. Even with Stage 3c ovarian cancer, she continued to go to the gym in her headscarf and to show up at work every day, and never expressed feeling ill despite her morose depression. It was abundantly clear that she was the one who was supposed to outlive me, not the other way around—that she had been, almost, waiting in the wings to step in and comfort my husband and children, who all loved her, once some absurd thing befell me. Sometimes I cannot help but imagine her there in my place, maybe even finally learning to drive so that she could chauffeur my children around, being the only woman on the planet who wouldn't have minded listening to my widower husband talk about me. And so it is that, while many of my friends did not quite understand my patience with my lover's allusions to wishing he had died during his relapse so as to spare ev-eryone the pain of his eventual marital treason, the truth is that I un-derstood. I, too, found myself counting backward to my last illness during Kathy's lifetime, engaging in magical thinking that somehow I could swap places with her and be the one to take the hit for the team. I have no doubt that she would have made a better wife to my husband than I turned out to be; that my daughters would never have found any evidence of transgressive behavior on her phone.

It has taken me a long time to accept that Kathy was not the rightful heir of my life—the life she believed so perfect—and that I am my own heir, here in this new life without her, without the marriage and affluence and selfless version of motherhood she might have held more sacred than I did. It has taken me a long time to stop imagining her and my ex-husband amid our longtime group of Usual Suspects, side by side and looking almost more like siblings than a couple, everyone holding up glasses (maybe it is New Year's Eve) and nostalgically toasting me, in a world where I had the good graces to exit while I was still who everyone believed me to be.

16.

My ex-husband would call me from work to fight about the terms of our divorce, and while he was at it would mansplain to me why he thought I had borderline personality disorder.

Q: What do you say to someone who decides this after having spent twenty-five years saying you were the most loving and insightful person he had ever known, and the best mother?

What a heroine in a feminist novel might do: set fire to things, stage an attack, fight like a revolutionary, have wild lesbian sex. What I did: pointlessly defended myself. Tried to make a man who had known me since I was twenty-two understand that people with BPD do not have harmonious, close relationships with their parents and live upstairs from them for sixteen years without conflict, or have the same best friends they have had since they were ten. That BPD is characterized by "unstable personal relationships": the complete antithesis of my childhood, my teens, my adult life. That the only "unstable personal relationship" I have ever had was . . . with him.

Like reading a checklist off a website, my ex-husband would then inform me that I was "a cutter," that I had an eating disorder, and that, like some bonus jackpot of mental illness, I was a masochist. And I would sit on the other end of the line, listening to his voice saying things I would never have believed a man I would consent to so much as have a conversation with—much less raise children with—would say to a woman.

You suffer from an epidemic called misogyny, I sometimes fantasized about replying, *and you use your shitty mother to justify it.* But in reality I said weak things, pitiful things, like "You know that's not true—you *know* me," and "I wouldn't say a cutter, exactly," and "Having an affair is not proof of a psychiatric condition!"

It is true that, several times during my IC years, I cut myself with the razor pried from my eyeliner sharpener, and further that I was stupid enough to tell him about it, no doubt looking for attention.

It is true that I nursed a low-grade eating disorder on and off from the ages of thirteen to twenty-two, when I went to therapy and it ceased to be an ongoing issue.

These behaviors—common among girls and women for reasons far more nuanced than any armchair "personality disorder" diagnosis—had all taken place at least twenty years prior, before I became a mother.

As to my "masochism," what is there to say except that from 1990 to 2015, I never once heard this man—the only man with whom I'd had sex for some twenty-two years—frame my sexual psychology as anything other than either hot or, at worst, too focused on my own tastes? What is there to say other than that in every encounter involving my so-called masochism, it had taken two to consensually tango and I never heard any complaints?

Apparently my history and traits were all just fine for twenty-five fucking years, as long as I was coupled with him. They only became associated with borderline personality disorder—only became problematic—once I was no longer his.

Who is a woman so easily permitted to be, under the auspices of a man, vs. who she is permitted to be alone? How can it be that the same characteristics a woman possessed when a man chose to have children with her and hoped to remain married to her for the rest of his life and allowed her to be the primary child-rearer of said children are suddenly characteristics of "pathology" and a danger to the minors in her care, once the man in question no longer sees her interests as synonymous with his own? In what ways does the "protection" of a man grant a woman the freedom to break societal rules, so long as the one rule she does not break is her dependence on said man for her safety and to sanctify her appropriateness as a parent, as a human being? To what extent is what is *artistic, bohemian, colorful, interesting, intellectually radical* . . . suddenly branded as psychopathology the moment that a man says it is?

17.

When I was twelve years old, I had a crush on Joyce Davenport from *Hill Street Blues*, played by Veronica Hamel. Davenport, an attorney, made feminism look hot, in my world where neither "feminism" nor adult female sexual desire was part of the landscape.

I don't mean that women didn't have openly sexual relationships in my old neighborhood: if anything, it being the early 1980s, many of my friends' mothers were divorced and had boyfriends. Some got dressed up in tight jeans and silky blouses they left unbuttoned enough to show off their gold chains and décolletage and went out to bars on the weekend to pick up men, leaving their latchkey kids home alone. These women were sexual, clearly, but their desire seemed to lack agency. Their men either made passes at their daughters or dealt drugs or hit them or had other women on the side, or they were the women on the side, fucking a married landlord in exchange for a reduction in the rent. They didn't lie in bed with their lover, drinking red wine and having substantial conversations about their day, like Joyce Davenport did with her lover (later, husband)

Frank Furillo. They didn't keep their last names after marriage and demand that men take them seriously or move in the world with authority, such that if they were fucking someone, it was clear that they really wanted him, rather than only wanting to be wanted by a man.

I wanted to be Joyce Davenport. I had been told repeatedly by my sixth-grade teacher, Mr. Tortorici, that I should be a lawyer, because of my "big mouth" and penchant for arguing the case of every underdog. Although she married an Italian man, Joyce Davenport was of some nebulous WASPy background, which made her somehow more "universal" than I felt. I felt stuck in, trapped by, my particular specificity: the Italianness of my name and nose and hair and voice. Freedom like Davenport's was not for girls like me.

Of course, later, I would discover that one of the great privileges of whiteness is reinvention; I would discover that education and culture can supplant origin in the American conception of identity. I would remake myself from a frizzy-haired, bucktoothed, overweight ghetto girl into something else: into the bohemian artist slightly on the edge of something, into the kind of girl who squats in London and reads Milan Kundera and Anaïs Nin and whose professors in graduate school come to her parties. I would world-hop so entirely that the adult version of me would have infinitely more in common with Joyce Davenport than with my girlhood self.

Yet still, what she represented to me as a girl would remain elusive as I was financially supported by my husband, as I adopted and birthed children and had playdates and devoted myself to unpaid labors of love. For a long time, I would mistake my mission for accomplished; I would lie in bed with my own boyfriend-turned-husband and our glasses of red wine and discuss our respective days and think I had arrived . . . somewhere.

I not only mistook a TV show version of feminism for reality but mistook myself for exemplifying and embodying it. I neglected, over and over again, for twenty years, the economic realities of my inequality with the husband in my bed, and how in one fell swoop, I could be reduced to Nothing again.

I had thought it was our money. I thought my education made me safe. I thought our shared liberal politics made me safe. I thought I had left where I came from—every unprosecuted rape and female classmate's blackened eye and the pile of dead girls heaped on the stage of my old neighborhood—behind. Yet here I was, reliant on an attorney I couldn't even come close to affording on my own, in order to be granted temporary monthly "maintenance" because I could no longer access marital funds that had been "mine" for well over two decades. I'd recently lost my dream job teaching in the same program as my lover, due to decreased enrollment, and had no prospects for health insurance other than COBRA on my ex's policy to the tune of $500 a month. I was teaching one class in Chicago as an adjunct for $5,000 per fifteen-week semester—at that rate, my annual income, after the IRS's cut, would not even cover our home's property taxes.

Had I made any progress at all? Had I gotten anywhere? Did I have anything of my own? Was I anyone?

18.

During my cancer-and-chemo months, it became abundantly clear that I'd been a caregiver for so long that nobody in my household, or maybe in my life, knew quite how to navigate our interactions in ways that didn't involve my doing things for them. Or maybe that was only the "unintended consequence," as my ex would have called it, of the fact that I did not know how to navigate my relationship to the world without being a chauffeur, a short-order cook, an errand runner, a therapist, a doctor on perpetual house call.

During the months of my chemotherapy, in addition to my normal parenting tasks, I also drove my daughters to the suburbs for regular sessions of therapy with their father, in an attempt to get their relationship on a more stable footing. Their father chose the therapist, and likewise made it clear that I should not be present even in the waiting room, as, our mediation having fallen apart, he would no longer be in a room with me. And so, during the months that I was bald and chemo-sick, I continued driving the girls—whom I had to cajole and sometimes threaten to get in the car—and dropping them off at the therapist's office, sometimes with Enzo, too, then driving to a nearby outdoor mall and either wandering aimlessly around the shops in the cold, places I could no longer afford, or if I was feeling too nauseated and exhausted to walk around, I would sit in my car with the heater running for an hour or take Enzo to some restaurant where I had no interest in the food because it hurt to eat and everything tasted of copper anyway. I parked a distance away from the therapist's door when picking up the children, so my ex would not have to see me, my heart pounding in fear of an accidental intersection he might accuse of being purposeful on my part.

On alternating weeks, I took my kids to this same therapist for sessions either individual, together among them, or with me. Kaya and Mags often cracked gallows humor jokes about how the therapist addressed me in the kind of overly solicitous tone usually reserved for toddlers and invalids—how things she said to them in sessions made it seem she suspected I was going to die soon and that she pitied them for their impending maternal orphaning. Whenever I spoke to the therapist alone, even for a few moments when paying a bill, I tried to slip in little facts about being cancer-free or the impressive survival stats for Stage 1 breast cancer. Finally, after my daughters apparently spent several sessions being coached by the therapist to gather their courage and ask their father to make his peace with me for their sake, to stop disparaging me to them and "accept their family," and he reportedly said he could not do that, my daughters refused to attend therapy anymore.

Still, my mother and Grace, who'd stopped working privately and taken a job with an accredited agency so as to have her services covered by my mother's insurance and remain living in our home, continued to treat me like their personal valet, often calling (my mother) or texting (Grace) to give me their grocery lists, prescription pickup requests, or a chronicling of new medical supplies they required that I would have to go to special stores to obtain. Grace didn't drive, which in addition to the fact that she had what seemed to me anorexia but was passing off as an ulcer, and was increasingly sick all the time, admittedly made her traveling around Chicago to buy things for my mother a challenge in these months blanketed by snow, breathing air that turned to smoke upon exhalation. Still, I grew so weary that finally I snapped—stormed downstairs and threw a near tantrum, pointing at my head and shouting, "I am not your errand bitch—I have fucking cancer, can't you see that I have cancer!"

This, even though I did not have cancer and had just spent considerable time trying to assure my children's therapist that I was just fine and not going anywhere anytime soon.

These were the facts of my life during those months of living between cancer and recovery: my friends all had full-time jobs; my mother was disabled; Kaya was increasingly depressed over our stressful familial circumstances and spent most of her nonschool time in bed with her door closed; Mags was usually accompanied by between three and thirty friends who seemed to go everywhere ensemble, shrieking and laughing and jumping and running around in our living room, on our balcony, in our basement; Enzo had just turned ten. When my lover was not in town, there was no one besides me to do the things that needed getting done. When my lover was in town, he cooked dinner, made runs to the corner store, accompanied me to doctor appointments, did dishes and litter, took out trash, and even made me come hard enough that I forgot for a few moments how horrible I felt . . . but when he was not doing any of those things, he often lay inert in bed, not dissimilarly to Kaya, talking about his depression or not talking at all.

When he was not in Chicago, all I wanted was to see him, to touch him, and for someone to just for god's sake bring me a fucking cup of tea rather than asking anything of me. But when he was with me, and I had to listen to him talk about his wife and his sadness over her while chemo toxins ravaged my body, I sometimes found myself wishing I could just be alone.

19.

Speaking of orgasms: during the very first month of chemotherapy, I was catapulted into menopause. Between my double mastectomy, my hairless and fragile body, and the end of my menstrual cycle, every message in the world around me seemed determine to erase my identity as a sexual being, or even a woman at all. Literature from my oncologist's office informed me that something like 35 percent of women (it may have been fewer—I threw the thick book into the trash in a fury, not even recycling it) who had been through mastectomy, chemo, and menopause would ever "regain" the ability to orgasm (this fear was among my reasons for nearly refusing chemo). Survivor friends with devoted husbands confided in me that they had been unable to be seen fully naked since their surgeries or that they still wept during every follow-up breast exam.

I had gone most of my life, as someone with polycystic ovarian syndrome and infertility, without much estrogen or regular menstrual cycles, but nobody had acted as though this was supposed to desexualize me or remove me from the male gaze at seventeen, at twenty-seven. By contrast, at forty-seven, I was supposed to become automatically neutered within the length of a season. (When I'd confided to my therapist that my lover and I had resumed having sex less than a week after my mastectomy, she audibly gasped.)

The medical literature placated me in reassuring jargon that nobody should blame me if I wasn't experiencing desire and urged me to consider "other forms of intimacy" like cuddling, kissing, and massage. Even on social media, menopausal friends who still had two good breasts crowed frequently about how relieved they were to be "over" being gawked at by men or being slaves to their biological desires, while others lamented feeling "invisible."

The war on menopausal sexuality is, of course, nothing new— no breast cancer required to enter. According to Elaine Showalter's *The Female Malady*, in Victorian England women who expressed an interest in sex after menopause were ridiculed and derided, and their husbands were advised to "withhold" any sexual stimulation. Some pioneering doctors "treated" oversexed (by which I mean sexed-at-all) middle-aged women's malady of desire with "a course of injections of ice water into the rectum, introduction of ice into the vagina, and leeching of the labia and the cervix." It's no doubt not unrelated that, when women tried to avail themselves of the Matrimonial Causes Act of 1857, one doctor began performing clitoridectomies after which, Showalter notes, the patients each "returned humbly" to their husbands. The squelching of women's desire has always been one of the main tentacles of patriarchy, and nothing squelches desire more effectively (well, sparing clitoridectomy) than sending a woman a clear message that she will never be desirable again.

My mother never had sex again after the age of thirty-five, and once confided in me that she had never in her life masturbated. I had spent my entire life trying to avoid her fate. What now?

Though I had never been the sort of feminist to participate in things like "Slut Walk" or to consider sex work synonymous with feminist activism, I began to understand, in my forty-seventh year, the power of sex as an act of rebellion against what the writer Lidia Yuknavitch would call "the story they made of you," even if only a private one: a necessary mutiny behind closed doors. Other than those dark six weeks when he had been unable to touch me without crying, desire ran between my lover and me like a circular current, an automatic and constant feedback loop.

And so the fact that my lover didn't desexualize me—far from it—became a whole new precious commodity. Was he, someone who had known me Before, capable of seeing me in ways the rest of the world no longer was? Was I, now, to be grateful to be the object of his hunger rather than our mutual wanting being an equal exchange? Without him, would I become Robert Hass's rebuffed Japanese painter, with her bowl of dead bees?

20.

How many dead, raped, maimed, and psychologically destroyed girls and women does it take to create secondary post-traumatic stress disorder?

At this point, Kathy had been dead for more than five years; Martin's wife for less than six months. But although these were the most recent female deaths in my life, they were far from the only ones.

Vicarious traumatization—which occurs among those intimate with PTSD survivors as well as among professional trauma workers—differs slightly from so-called secondary trauma, which can happen more suddenly, in a single session between, say, a therapist and a client who has been a victim of violence. According to most experts, the symptoms are virtually identical. Between my old neighborhood, my fledgling work as a therapist for domestic violence and sexual abuse survivors, and my relatives and friends, I had lost count of how many abuse stories to which I had somehow been party. Though I had stopped looking under my car for homemade bombs after I left New England and the battered women's agency where we sometimes received death threats for me by name (*I know what that bitch's car looks like and you can tell her I'm going to kill her!*), I was still—perpetually—waiting for the explosion.

For many years, I called this phenomenon "survivor guilt," even when it applied to women—like Angie—who were still among the living. Why had my father been a gentle man when so many other men in my old neighborhood were violent and brutal? Why had I been gifted with a particular academic intelligence that paved the way toward a selective-enrollment high school and grants and aid for college, while so many others I had grown up among were left behind? Why was I, at twenty-three years old, serving as a therapist for women in their thirties, their fifties, their seventies, who had lived through abuses one might expect in a POW camp rather than a quaint rural town? Why had so many girls I'd known in seventh or eighth grade blown adult men in exchange for cocaine, referred to their mother's boyfriends as "perverts," worn long sleeves to cover their bruises? Who had I been—barely twenty-five at the time—to merit witnessing a huddle of teenage foster girls clinging to one another, howling in pain as they gave testimony about the fathers and stepfathers and "family friends" who had raped them—about the mothers who turned blind eyes and stood next to their abusers when social services came to take their daughters away? Why had my lover's sister needed a new identity when she fled an abusive partner who threatened to kill her—why did we live in a world where my friend S had to make jokes about probably being in the trunk of her ex's car if none of her friends had heard from her for a few days? Why were my beloved daughters institutionalized as orphans, at 3.5 pounds apiece and with umbilical hernias, for the unpardonable "crime" of being female? Why were so many innocent girls and women dead, while I was still standing, facing a "good prognosis" for my cancer?

How high does the body count of women need to be before it becomes the only thing you know how to look for anymore—the obstruction beyond which you cannot see?

21.

What does it mean to "be anyone"? There are some thousand unsolved murders of prostitutes pending in the United States, primarily "lot lizards," or junkie prostitutes, who are picked up at truck stops and dropped off, dead, at the side of the interstate far from where they lived. It is understood that truckers are responsible for many of these, though unclear how many may be serial killings and how many may be, staggeringly, committed individually, on a whim. Many other presumably dead women are never found at all: they simply disappear off the face of the earth, and no one much goes looking for them. Sex workers don't rank serious inquiry or investigation. In Oklahoma alone, they once dubbed a serial killer "the I-40 Killer" because of thirty murders that have taken place where Interstate 40 meets Interstate 35. But there have been, at the time of this writing, more than three hundred murdered women within fifty miles of that interchange, and they now believe it's several serial killers, known as long-haul trucker killers. Authorities estimate it could be thirty to forty different men who have killed at least seven women each.

If more than a thousand white men had been murdered and probably another thousand missing, my lover texts me, *there would be a HUGE government task force.*

What does it mean to not be Anything?

Somewhere between 1,300 and 2,000 women are murdered annually in the United States. Of those, roughly 500 are Black women (and of approximately 28 trans women murdered each year, the majority are also Black), rendering Black women 8 percent of the general population of women but between 25 and 40 percent of the murdered. This body count of up to 2,000 women does not account for the missing/never found, which some estimates put at almost the same number.

More than half of the murders of women are committed by a

male partner, a former partner, or a family member, which are the murders most often solved. Your male partner has a high likelihood of killing you, apparently, but not a high chance of getting away with it, unless of course he is a celebrity.

I tell my lover that I believed this number was higher—that maybe 90 percent of murdered women had been killed by their significant other—that I did not realize there were so many stranger killings; I thought they were rare.

The solved murder rates in the 1960s and '70s were over 80 percent, he writes me back. *Now, in most places, it's down to 50 percent, which some people attribute to the increased number of murders of strangers . . . but I think it may have a lot to do with the DNA exoneration of a lot of Black men they used to just lock up with little evidence. Maybe a combo.*

There is more than one way not to be Anything. Women do not have a monopoly.

22.

That March I began chemotherapy, when the divorce was raging, when my ex-husband was canceling my utilities, when the lights and hot water and Internet and phones suddenly no longer worked, Chicago so menacingly cold that the gas company failed to comply with his termination of services and kept our heat on long enough for me to change the bill to my name—for a time, when my debit card stopped working and my checks bounced because he had moved the funds our original attorneys and mediator had told us to keep intact until the divorce was finalized, and legal motions kept arriving such that I had to rush to the courthouse with my newly bald head, my body full of toxins that required me to flush toilets twice to avoid passing contaminants to my children—for a time that spring, I began seriously contemplating that I might well end up as women with enraged men in their lives so often end up: dead.

The thought arrived first unbidden, easily dismissible. My ex-husband was not the type of man who got into physical fights—the macho man at the bar who swings a punch. Even when he received the news of my affair, he never threatened to kick my lover's ass or any similar escalated declarations of violent intent that might have seemed understandable in the moment. But how can I explain that it was, in the end, his very silence that began to chill me to the core—to make me lose my grasp on differentiating him from the dozens, maybe hundreds of men I'd encountered who had harmed women, children, people with different skin colors, enemies who'd done them wrong? I'd been blocked on his phone for five months, but since he'd fired our mediation team, I was too terrified to even email him. The barren expanse between us felt ominous. Was this how a man "turned"? How many women—my lover's sister among them; S among them; Kathy's mother among them—had married men they thought congenial, harmless, who ended up beating them, threatening their lives, stalking them, bringing a gun into the family home and leaving a bloodbath for his children to find? And these stories were, of course, all but "nothing" compared to the fates some of my old therapy clients had endured at the hands of male outrage, that age-old gendered battle for power. Word came to me that my ex had been put on leave from his job—a position I knew he loved, at a company where he'd risen meteorically. I was living full-time in our expensively renovated house; Mags and Kaya now refused to set foot in their father's new home; I had—even if by his own choosing—inherited all of our mutual friends. But if now his work, which I'd long accused him of confusing with his holistic identity, was in jeopardy . . . ?

Have there ever been any more dangerous creatures than men who believe they have nothing left to lose?

My dismissible thought gnawed its way into obsession. My ex-husband was a stranger to me that spring—but hadn't I always feared that true anyway? He'd never guessed the things of which I was capable. What if I, too, could not guess his?

In these imaginings, my death played in a violent and painful loop. I would be murdered before I could regrow my hair or have my breast reconstruction surgery—bludgeoned or stabbed or shot repeatedly and gratuitously the way only exes kill, long beyond the point when life slips out of a body. I imagined myself a corpse in disrepair, the state of my injured, broken body not provoking anything resembling pity. Rather, my wretched state might only enrage my ex further, make him feel I was somehow playing the world for sympathy: my mastectomy, my skin smoothed hairless by poison, all an affront to him, some "rehabilitation" for my crimes that he had not approved.

The last time he'd consented to speak to Alicia, he'd screamed about me, *I want her miserable and alone!* Clearly, cancer was not sufficient punishment for my transgressions.

What would be "enough," I wondered, for the likes of me?

23.

I kept saying to friends on the phone, "I'm not even pursuing permanent maintenance." I qualified this to everyone. Every conversation I ever had included the fact that I knew the divorce was "my fault" because I had cheated on my ex and left him, and that he should not have to support me for the rest of my life.

I wanted them all to understand, it seems, that if I turned up dead, I had not "deserved it" the way I might have if I took the alimony to which I was legally entitled in the state of Illinois, after twenty-three years of marriage. That was the subtext of my constant insistence that I was waiving my permanent maintenance: that perhaps alimony is a crime justly punishable by murder, if you are a cheating lying whore, as I was.

Permanent maintenance, which I had originally not sought

because it seemed a legal "golden handcuffs" system for women, discouraging divorcees from earning their own money or even marrying again out of fear of losing the alimony they are encouraged to rely on—money their exes are forced to fork over until death—now became more ominously synonymous in my mind with Motive. How many men throughout history had killed to avoid paying it?

Except given that I sometimes believed my impending murder already a foregone conclusion, with or without permanent alimony, I am no longer certain why I thought being twice-dead would be any worse than once.

24.

My lover, listening to me spin, developed even more severe insomnia than usual. I was afraid of sounding either delusional or vindictive— or both—and so I could not talk, of course, about my hysterical fears outside the sanctity of the bedroom my lover shared with me part-time. He woke from dreams of our door being broken down with axes, which no doubt did little to fuel his enthusiasm about living in a frozen Midwestern state with two teenage girls who did not particularly want him around. Back in California, too, he feared walking into his own home to find a dead woman, but in that case by her own hand.

I did not imagine that it would change the outcome much for me, but when a male friend who had once been close to my ex suggested that I have my locks changed, then, in order to assuage my lover's fear of axes—to at least divide his anxiety about the dead bodies of the women he loved into a conceptual half—I complied.

25.

In the late fall of 2016 and early winter of 2017, amid my postchemo disability in my left leg, Donald Trump kept strutting his abled orange body around the news circuit, gloating, and racists flew out of the woodwork to vandalize synagogues in Chicago, and I was one of the millions of American women who felt as though the patriarchy, and all it entailed, had won. Pure and simple. The goddamn patriarchy had won, and white women had helped it win, and after years and years of optimism, of gratitude, of pushing forward, of progress that had all come crashing down to this, it seemed completely fitting that I could no longer walk and was in pain every single moment of every single fucking day.

I had taught a class, for many years, called Women on the Verge. You know this class: *Lithium for Medea*, *The Bell Jar*, that kind of thing. The kind of class that asks the question: *Is insanity the only sane response to a woman-hating world?*

I was not, of course, "insane." Just as during my chemo months, I continued taking care of both My Things and Other People's Things out of necessity. I had procured a new full-time job as a visiting lecturer, and I went to campus three times a week to teach Comp and Technical Writing and other things I'd never imagined myself teaching but now was grateful to do; I cooked for my children while holding on to the countertops; I dutifully limped to the pain clinic for my tox screenings and to listen to men shout at the female receptionists; I explained to the male doctors that I really did need Norco because tramadol made me unable to orgasm and yes, even though I was nearly fifty and had no breasts and was in menopause, that was actually important. I edited. I did the grocery shopping and tried not to feel like a failure for making my children carry the heavier bags up the stairs because I could barely make the stairs even carrying nothing. I paid the bills on time. I even maintained an active social life, because the worst thing I could imagine was people thinking I was too broken to go out.

26.

My lover was still living in California more than half-time, caregiving his already sick wife through her cancer treatments ("You are the Typhoid Mary of breast cancer," a friend told him) and being the only one to sit with her in hospital rooms when she had surgery or appointments. I understood that they had unintentionally conspired for years to bring them to this lonely island, allowing her to neglect every prior friendship and even her own family members until he was all that was left in her world. Amid his twin albatrosses of Guilt and Depression, it often seemed to me that his vow to "take care of her" really meant the two of them languishing in mutual stasis, unable to meet their own basic needs, feeding off each other's sadness. Meanwhile, I was supporting my family for the first time in my life, which I took pride in even if such a thing should have been a given at forty-eight. I was a far cry from "needing" a man in order to live, and in fact it seemed blindingly clear to me that functioning without a man, when the man is not functioning well, was not only logistically and economically possible but, bluntly, easier.

I knew my lover and I had passed the point of decorum—that everyone we knew had started to anticipate my need to move on. I knew that by staying in this relationship while he lived, still married, in another state, my life had deteriorated to a humiliating condition of waiting to see whether some man would ever fully choose me above sunny California and his friends and band and recovery community, above his codependency and maybe most of all his fear of change. On the days I could see things clearly, I saw that I was a cancer survivor in chronic pain who was hoping to "win" a mate from another cancer survivor in chronic pain, and that this was not what feminism looked like, and I shared my lover's crushing, staggering guilt over what we had done to this person he had promised to take care of forever in her debilitation. More than anything, though, I worried that he would feel he was swapping "taking care of her forever" for "taking care of me forever," and that I had become just another suffocating obligation. I'd lost sight of why anyone would move two thousand miles cross-country for me, anyway, with my

limp and no breasts and scary divorce. His "bait and switch" proph-
ecy pounded in my head constantly like a racing heartbeat.

Instead of going to California, as I had the previous year, I spent
my New Year's Eve in Chicago with another recently divorced parent, a man who seemed to want to date me or at least fuck me and
in whom I had not the slightest interest. My lover was at home with
his wife, just as he had been on the day I was diagnosed with cancer
and on the eve of Trump's election, one of the worst nights of my
life. Shortly after midnight, as I was leaving the nice middle-class
home of this good and involved father I had no interest in sharing
the changing of the years with, I thought: *I can't wait around anymore.* I told myself, *I will love him forever, I may never want anyone
else again, but this has jumped the shark and something has to change
or I am done.*

27.
Yet there was also the fact—the uncontainable, naked matter—of
love.

Ladies and Gentlemen of the Jury . . . fuck, there was love.

"There was a crime," Ian McEwan wrote in *Atonement*. "But
there were also the lovers."

There is also the way that when my mastectomy was pending,
my lover's psychiatrist and his best friend in recovery both told
him that his psychological health was "too fragile" for him to fly
cross-country to nurse a cancer patient, but he said that unless he
was in a straitjacket, there was nothing that was going to stop him
from getting on the plane. There is the way that, as soon as I came
out of surgery, he was at my side, chair pulled up tight next to my
hospital bed, stroking my back, massaging my feet, talking to me
into the night until I fell asleep, never so much as glancing at his
phone or napping. There is the way I woke the next morning to
find him finally asleep on the tiny plastic couch, the weak sunlight

streaming in on his face, and to look at him was like the feeling I got my last night in Kenya, when I fell to my knees and kissed the dirt, so suffused with gratitude to have simply borne witness to its existence. There is the fact that, after six weeks of not being able to so much as kiss, when we finally went to my oncologist's office for the first time postmastectomy and got the pathology report indicating that my margins were clean and I was cancer-free, we went home, the kids still in school, and without so much as saying a word about it fucked madly and ecstatically with my stitched-up chest exposed and four postmastectomy drains hanging in tubes from my body, pinned up to an old lanyard around my neck. There is the way he came with me to get my head shaved and told me I looked like Kathy Acker with a thrilled opposite of pity, and we went out that night and I felt like the most beautiful woman in the room. There is the fact that, as I began to limp profoundly, as I began to suffer from chronic pain, he never once flinched, never once treated me differently, never once seemed to do anything other than vibrate at my touch. There is the way that even though dire clinical depression can make it Herculean to so much as brush your teeth or get out of bed, he never, not once since the night Kathy died and even when we were "broken up," went a single day without texting, emailing, or calling me, making me know that I was constantly on his mind, that he missed me, that he wanted to talk to me under any terms I would allow, his voice lifting at the sound of my voice, his arms opening to hold me every time I came to any bed we shared.

There is the fact that men, too, are more than one thing—that just as I ask you to hold this space for me, to acknowledge that despite every terrible error in judgment I have made, despite every selfishly cruel explosion I created, there is good in me, and I am capable of love, of loyalty, of honesty, of devotion, of change, so I ask you to believe this, too, of the man who rewired my heart, who made me understand that my unconditional love was not reserved for my children, who never stops trying to be better than he has been, and whose compassion for the woman he was leaving—slowly, god, so slowly—was a compassion I would want shown to me in my hour of loneliness and need. There is the truth that even as he struggled every single day not to hate himself, I never, not for one fucking infinitesimal second since we first touched, felt anything but love for him.

Ladies and Gentlemen of the Jury, maybe you—now or at some time of your life—have struggled not to hate yourself too—have had to trust, for a time, the love in someone else's eyes before you could find the strength to claw your way back from the ledge on your own steam? Or am I wrong in believing that if we are fully alive, if we are still growing and changing, it is hard, so unfathomably hard, to reach the age of fifty with hands that are clean?

28.

I was newly bald. Ninety percent of body heat escapes through the top of the head. Internet, landline, cable, electricity—all dead. My credit card had been denied filling my car up with gas. I stood with the frozen pump already in my hand, not understanding, the children in the car looking on. I would leave my old neighborhood like so much dust on my shoes; I would be Joyce Davenport; I was a published writer and adjunct professor and editor and mother of three inside my reinvented white skin; I was safe. Every last dime in the shared marital account that our civilized attorneys had advised us not to change until the divorce was final: gone. Our mediation team fired without my knowledge, a new lawyer representing my ex and serving me with litigation. I had sores on my tongue, bone pain, severe nausea, a foul taste in my mouth, broken-out skin, peripheral neuropathy. Where my breasts had once been was an "expander" under my skin: a kind of half-metallic tube top into which saline was pumped through a port, to prepare me for implants when chemo was finished. Often, the expander pinched nerves so badly I wanted to dig under my skin and straighten it out the way one might a tangled bra.

In less than two months I would be hospitalized with neutropenia, which I now understand as collateral damage from the relentless duress I was under throughout my chemotherapy and my inability to practice even a modicum of self-care while not only managing a complex family in crisis, but feeling under constant attack in my divorce proceedings. My fear of my ex-husband's malice toward me had escalated such that, on the eve of my neutropenia hospitalization, rather than informing him, I panicked and told the owner of Enzo's after-school day care center. You see, while I was making noise about that goddamn mother/son dance, I was still lucid enough to hear what the doctors were saying about the gravity of my condition. The owner of my son's day care center brought him to the hospital on the train, and outside my hospital room my son put on his gloves, his mask, before crawling into bed with me. I believed beyond a reasonable doubt that my ex-husband would not have brought my son to visit me, and I needed to see his face, in case it was the last time. In my hospital bed, my son and I giggled behind our masks and posed for absurd selfies. I promised I would do my best to be home to take him to the dance, and then the owner of the day care center took him home on the El and Alicia kept him for the night, waiting to see what transpired, and whether the shot of neutrophils worked. Soon I was home, and my ex-husband to the best of my knowledge never knew I had been hospitalized and that it was his "right" to come and claim our son until I was back, making decisions about my contact with our child as he wished, given that we were not yet divorced and there was no legal protocol in place.

Fear makes people lawless. If indifference is hate's opposite, then compassion is fear's. My ex-husband and I had come to fear each other to an extent that, for all my philosophizing to the contrary, for a time neither of us was capable of seeing the other as fully human.

Maybe fear is the most negative of all human emotions—the under-lying cause of every violence and envy.

It is also true that, without fear, there can be no revolution.

29.

When I was fifteen, a girl I had gone to school with from fifth through eighth grade was gang-raped, by a group of boys and men I also knew, before being beaten with coat hangers and thrown down a flight of stairs. When her family attempted to press charges, neighborhood women came out of the woodwork to provide alibis for the alleged rapists, and the case never moved forward. Eventually, the raped girl and her parents were driven from the neighborhood by harassment.

When I first heard the news from Angie, I agreed with her that of course the girl was a slut. Everyone knew she was fucking one of the rapists. Once, in my basement "clubhouse" when we were twelve or thirteen and drinking covertly during a block party, she had boasted that her "boyfriend" would fuck her even when she was on her period, because he knew she had been a virgin before him and was "clean." I want to say the man she was talking about was about twenty years old, but the truth is that I've forgotten who she was talking about, or if that man was one of the rapists. Angie's first boyfriend was one of those accused, but this seemed to faze her not at all. I remember, however, being more rankled by the incongruities of my memories of this boy from elementary school—his sweetness, and the way he often attached himself to my mother when she volunteered on field trips—than I was by the knowledge that my old friend had been raped. It was more troublesome to me to think of this boy as a rapist. Once, my mother had volunteered to be his personal chaperone on a school trip to Wrigley Field, from which he was being excluded for poor behavior, but the teacher did not accept my mother's offer, and the boy stayed home. He had been held back a year, maybe, but was at most sixteen at the time of the rape; it had been less than two years since we'd been in school together.

It was not our first neighborhood gang rape. It was not even our second.

The first in my recollection was of my close friend, Kim, who was in my class at Catholic school. She was developmentally disabled and often teased by the other kids, who did things like try to get her to pull down her pants in public. I had appointed myself her defender, despite being one of the smallest kids in my grade, and sometimes fought other kids when they teased her. We were all only six, only seven—she transferred schools, was no longer in a "mainstream" classroom when her rape occurred. The rapists were adult men; she was not a teenager yet. Her older brother, who had been her guardian for as long as I could remember, attacked one of the rapists and was sent to prison. Kim was in an institution the last I heard, which was probably thirty-five years ago. None of the rapists ever faced charges, so the others are presumably still out there, living their lives, unfettered by the rape of a prepubescent girl with a disability.

Do you see the way I qualified that, without even knowing I was going to do it?

As if she had reached puberty—as if she were neurotypical—it would somehow be better, sharing the streets with her rapists.

When I was fifteen, another girl with whom I'd graduated from eighth grade, who often came to school covered in bruises from her stepfather's beatings (we had no school counselor; no teacher, to my knowledge, ever asked her about the bruises), was beaten to death with a baseball bat by her downstairs neighbor.

When I was in my late teens, an old friend's younger sister was killed in her boyfriend's parked car, when the gang-motivated bullet meant for him went through his body and entered hers. She was pregnant.

When I was fourteen, a girl I loved confided to me that her father had been molesting her for years. Although she told her mother, her parents are still married. To the best of my knowledge, her molester is permitted unfettered access to his grandchildren.

I could go on, but I won't.

30.

When we were still married, my husband used to tell me it was an honor to provide for us so that I could write, so that I could run a press and champion other artists, so that I could be available for our children. He said all this helped him to find value in his work, to think of himself as a patron of the arts and a good provider.

Sometimes when we would fight, he would scream at me, *Who's making the money and supporting this family?*

31.

My lover is obsessed with music that "doesn't resolve," that ends in dissonance.

Four days after I hit bottom as the year changed over to 2017, after I resolved to begin extricating myself from my romantic and sexual relationship with my lover in order to save my own dignity and sanity, my lover hit bottom himself. On January 4, instead of going out to score heroin for the first time in decades, as he calmly informed me on the phone that he planned to do, he went to the apartment of his best friend in recovery and began an upward ascent out of his two-and-a-half-year depression. He did move out of his wife's apartment as soon as her cancer treatments ended, but although we remained a couple, he lived on his own out west for a year: for a while at a friend's music studio; for a while in a trailer on the Salton Sea in Bombay Beach; for a while couch surfing through the various friends he was reminded loved him, and understood him to be a worthwhile human being no matter with which woman—or any woman—he lived. He took ketamine treatments, went to therapy, began working on a new novel and writing songs again. Nearly one year to the day after he hit bottom, after a year of confronting and rediscovering himself, he relocated to Chicago, where we have been so blindingly happy that it feels like dancing at the end of the world.

And every day, we both live with the fact that there is now a lonely and frightened woman on her own "because" of us, sometimes not showing up to follow-up oncology appointments and saying it is because, without him, she doesn't really care if she lives or dies.

32.

I said I wouldn't go on, but . . .

My mother's mother divorced her father for refusing to let my mother have her tonsils removed because he was a Christian Scientist. Later, when my grandfather would come to visit my mother, he often ended their visits with a walk through the park, where he would take her into the bushes and finger her vagina and try to stimulate her clitoris while giving her "movie star kisses" with his tongue.

Alicia never saw her father again after he was sent to prison for stealing cars when she was three. Prior to his incarceration, he beat her mother and was addicted to heroin. Alicia's mother told him not to come back, and as some 40 percent of divorced fathers do even in this millennium (the term for it now is "ghost father"), he never did.

My other childhood best friend, Hector, recounts watching his father beat his mother in front of the neighbors in their garden in Venezuela. His father would disappear for weeks on end and the family would starve in his absence, awaiting his return so that they could be beaten again but have food. Eventually his father was shot and killed by the husband of one of his mistresses, and Hector's mother would move the family to Chicago, where she married a jovial Christian who often reprimanded her for letting Hector do the housework because it would "make him gay."

Kathy's father, upon learning she had shoplifted candy at the age of six, put her in his squad car and drove her to the police station, where he parked the car outside in the dark and began to calmly advise Kathy on how to avoid the rats when she was in prison, and to make sure to stay tightly wrapped in her blanket all night long. Only after she had cried sufficiently did he turn the car for home. Four years later, he put a bullet in his brain in their house, after learning that Kathy's mother planned to leave him for his partner. He was found by Kathy's younger sister; Kathy cut her wrists for the first time later that year.

33.

Of course my ex-husband didn't murder me (obviously). Not only did he never even threaten to do so—or in fact threaten me with any physical violence at all—but in retrospect, barring the fact that our children lived with me in the house at the time of his antics, most of the things he did during our hideous Jerry Springer of a divorce no longer seem strictly his fault. In our alternately frantic and stilted emails of that period, I can see my own hysteria rising off the computer screen like a tornado—my own desire to control how he interacted with the children, with me, as an invitation to the very kind of power struggling to which he was most vulnerable, and as a triggering force. How much wrong we did to each other, to our nearest and dearest of decades—how lesser than who we thought we were we both turned out to be.

Yet in the end, we went back to mediation and settled out of court and my ex-husband did not sell anyone's house and certainly did not stab me repeatedly in the heart. It turns out that punching a wall and murdering a cancer-ridden woman were never the same thing. That my internalized fear of men was extreme enough to make me conflate them for a time—to confuse a man whose heart I shattered with a killer of lot lizards, with O. J. Simpson, with the weekly predators on *Law & Order* or *Criminal Minds*, with the men of my old neighborhood. My hair has long since grown back, and I paid to change those locks and have new keys made for nothing.

He and I first grew up together, then grew apart, then undid each other nearly irreparably. In his continued silence—which I have every reason at this point to believe will last until one of us is dead—I have no space for atonement. It turned out that the one power he could exercise fully was to withhold any possibility of forgiveness or closure from me, and withhold it he does. This has extended to essentially everyone we ever knew in common, friends who loved him for a quarter century. On the day our divorce was finalized and we had to appear together before a judge—the last time I ever saw him in person—my friend Tori, fresh from the hospital for heart valve replacement surgery, accompanied me. At one time, she had designated my ex-husband and me as the guardians of her daughter in the event of her less-unlikely-than-would-be-ideal death. After our separation, briefly, Tori and my ex continued to socialize; my daughters even joked that maybe they would hook up, though I could imagine Kathy figuratively rolling around in her grave at that thought, and I don't believe either he or Tori ever entertained any such notions. Still, inside the courthouse, Tori stole away from me for a moment, the bandage on her chest visible above her shirt, and approached my ex-husband, her ex-friend, once one of the most important men in her life, to say that she missed him and loved him, but he would not speak to her and stalked away, leaving her there crying in the corridor.

Did he see the bandage? He knew her health history. Would he care, now, if she were to die?

He has built the fence around his fortress all the more tightly since then. He has chosen his self-imposed exile from his old life for so long now that perhaps it no longer even feels like a choice but like an inevitably fated thing, when it was never such. And so I can only forgive him in absentia, for everything both during and after our marriage, for everyone he has believed he needed to push away in order to move past me. I can only wish him every possible peace.

I would say that this is meant to be an excavation of why I was so afraid of him, a man I hurt more profoundly than he ever hurt me, but I already know why I was so afraid. I already understand that my ex-husband not in fact being a murderer, and my evidently suffering from PTSD from a lifelong proximity to male violence, does not mean that for many women with other ex-boyfriends, other ex-husbands, "false alarms" regarding their imminent murders only necessarily mean they have not been murdered *yet*.

Alas, just because we are fucking paranoid does not mean that a shit-ton of men are not out to kill us.

34.

How can I love my lover with every single thing I have, when the way women love men is so often a part of the problem?

How can I love myself when my broken body seems to be not only a physical manifestation of the wreckage I have wrought in the world, but of the endless brutality of the world itself?

35.

I had a hip replacement in May 2018, just about two years after I was hospitalized with neutropenia and insisted on going to the mother/son dance as though my appearance there could undo all the ways I had failed my son. A month after my hip replacement, I turned fifty years old.

I know enough to realize that any reprieve my body is granted is only ever temporary. The body has an expiration date, and for those of us who care enough to forge on, to race the clock, much of our life's work has to do with keeping that date at bay with maintenance, with spit and Band-Aids and all the laughter and intimacy and love we can cram into any twenty-four-hour day.

I used to become furious at my ex-husband when he implied that my IC was "stress induced" or even "in my mind." To say that it is one of the original reasons I began the gruelingly long process of falling out of love with him would not be untrue. It still rankles me, even now, despite my efforts to maintain a state of peace and forgiveness: those male assumptions about the female body in pain. "Hysteria" has simply morphed now into a slew of confusing auto-immune disorders, into the overdiagnosis of borderline personality disorder among women, into the collective national depression America's women feel at seeing a proud sexual predator in the White House, and all the ways in which this tells us that we don't count, and that many of us helped put him there.

36.

The ways in which women both love and support one another, and mistrust and betray and undermine one another, may be the most complex thing in the universe.

37.

I am too far removed to fully understand whether those years of blinding, all-consuming IC pain in the 1990s had anything to do with making sure I couldn't focus on other things—to promise that my bodily disease had nothing to do with my body trying to distract me from the dis-ease of living a life I didn't fully want. I am too far removed to know whether it could be that, in some slanted way, my ex-husband had a point. As the medical profession now acknowledges IC and has FDA-approved drugs to treat it, so recent studies, too, show that the chronic fatigue and fibromyalgia suffered by my lover's ex are not, in fact, best treated by cognitive behavioral therapy as long believed, dismantling the suspicion that these conditions too (which overwhelmingly afflict women) are in the mind. We know now that these conditions are "real."

What is the line, though, between living in a sick world and becoming sick? How many Real Fucking Diseases still may intersect with the mind?

What if, when you are female, everything is an environmental toxin?

38.

The heart wants what it wants. You have a right to be happy.

If he'll cheat with you, he'll cheat on you. Once a cheater always a cheater.

Brave.

Selfish.

Inspirational.

Badass.

Thieving cunt whore.

What is anyone entitled to? Is that answer different or identical for men vs. women?

What is the line between falling so madly in love that you didn't think such feelings or connections existed, and the fact that deep promises had already been made to other people, other people with their own baggage and illnesses and traumas?

What is the line between self-acceptance, self-love, and a refusal to take accountability?

What is the line between the living female body and the dysfunctional portrait that has been drawn of it in literature and psychology and medicine?

What is the line between the concrete X-ray of my bone-on-bone hip and how I personally perceived pain based on my individual and gendered history?

What does it mean to admit that a woman can be a perpetrator and a victim at once? That she can be legitimately biologically sick and in pain, and also manifesting what the culture has done to women since the beginning of time?

39.

We are all still just one accusation away from being witches.

40.

I thought this was about pain. What I was going to tell you is that the physical pain I went through in the late 1990s was both more intense—by the tenfold? the hundredfold?—than my chemo-induced arthritis pain, and that it has changed my perspective on everything to have known that kind of pain, that *death-would-be-a-mercy* kind of pain, as opposed to a more ordinary debilitation, and saying that would be true.

And yet there are ways that limping, that the inability to move with agility, my frozen leg and days of going up the stairs on my ass because my hip could not hold me up, were actually worse to me than living with a pain so severe that it obliterated any hope for the future. I am a woman to whom perception has meant too much, and the ability to keep my pain contained behind a smile in some ways was more bearable to me than manifesting that pain publicly.

Recent studies show that secrets actually make people sick. In some grotesque way, some might say that my keeping secrets "gave me cancer," even though my genetic testing, banked somewhere, likely holds the not-yet-understood mutations that did, in fact, give me cancer, no secrets required.

Still, what I mean to say is that maybe I preferred a secret pain to a visible one, no matter the degree. Maybe I preferred the option of suffering in silence to this business of hobbling around and not keeping up with the pace and having people ask me, *What's wrong?*

41.

Seven years passed without my speaking to my old friend Jun, who put my family up in London in 2012—who asked me if I was "safe" after my ex-husband shouted at us on the way to the Tate. When she calls me one night, then, having seen on Instagram that I had breast cancer, that I am now with a different man, she explains that the reason she never answered any of my emails after our trip was that she was horrified that I had not "defended" her from my ex-husband, as she would have expected a close friend and very vocal feminist to do. As she speaks, my mind searches back to that day, and I am ashamed to admit that my first thought is, *It isn't as though he physically threatened her!*

I am still unlearning the rules of the first forty-seven years of my life. I am still working on not making excuses for men's rage or feeling like they deserve medals for capping it before anyone is bleeding. "My daughter still talks about it," Jun tells me. "I thought you would yell at him and make him leave, but you just tried to appease him and brought him along to the Tate. I couldn't believe it. He verbally abused me in front of my child, and it didn't even occur to you that maybe you needed to get him out of my house and find a hotel."

Even as I hear myself apologize—even as I mean every apology and am thrilled and grateful to hear her voice again, I'm simultaneously doubting this narrative. *I am a woman who lost a close friendship because I failed to speak up against verbal abuse.* Despite all the emphasis on loyalty that my parents instilled in me, I still have an easier time digesting that I am an Adulterer, a liar, a breaker of bonds, than I do accepting that my ex-husband's behavior (even in 2012, a year after he had passed the worst of his emotional turbulence) was actually out of bounds, was something I was not only within my right to refuse but that I was *obligated*—on the part of other women, on the part of my daughters and hers, on the part of myself—to refuse. I remember my humiliation when she asked me

"Are you safe?" and how I tried to end that conversation as soon as humanly possible. It was the year Obama would win a second term; it was a year when most liberal Americans including my ex-husband and I believed Progress to be an unstoppable train. It did not match the picture of myself in my head, to say to her, *I'm pretty sure I'm physically safe but I've been walking on eggshells for five years, afraid of what will set him off.* It was so passé to sound that weak, to play the victim. He and I were "equals" in my mind. Even now, it is impossible for me to imagine, other than his punching her in the face, a scenario that would have made me feel entitled to tell him he could not come with us to the museum, and I am not sure there is anything on the planet he could have done that would have prompted me, in the absence of her saying it first, to tell him that he was no longer allowed in her house and that he had to find a hotel alone.

How much of that was about love? How much was about who earned the money? How much was about spending my childhood watching such gross abuses of women and children that relative micro-abuses such as "yelling" seemed to me a thing that a hard-ass former ghetto girl like myself wouldn't get her panties in a twist about, and that in fact my friend doing so was just evidence of her privileged life? (*Had no man ever yelled at her before? Imagine!*) Part of being fifty is, of course, realizing how much I just don't know.

Jun and I hang up, vowing to keep in better touch. She is divorced too, and living in California now, that land of perpetual reinvention; she is a yoga teacher and volunteers all summer at an orphanage for kids with special needs in China. She is also formidably intelligent, cosmopolitan, interesting, and I have missed her. I know I'm going to have to work my ass off to show her this, to keep the friendship going this time, and promise myself that I will, but the ugly truth is that I have not called her again, still out of shame.

Maybe today will be the day.

42.

A lover moves out of his wife's apartment and becomes a boyfriend. A boyfriend piles all his scant belongings into a U-Haul and relocates to Chicago full-time and becomes a life partner. A life partner files for divorce, proposing marriage on the final day I am fifty, and becomes a fiancé. A fiancé will utter vows he has written and can—unlike all the clandestine correspondence we once shared—say aloud before our family and friends and, presto, become a husband. And just like that, I will be a wife again.

There are too few words for who and what human beings are to each other.

Language is a territory still mostly uncharted.

We are the cartographers, every day, still mapping the human heart.

43.

I have a new hip. I have been cancer-free for more than two years. I am in love with a man who makes me laugh every morning and has changed the geography of his life to be with me. I have three beautiful and healthy children, two of whom got the kinds of scholarships to college that help remind me they will be all right—that they did not need affluence to be "safe" or to have good lives, any more than I did. My son and my partner love each other with a sweetness and acceptance that I could only once have dreamed of, believed ungraspable as smoke. What's more, here in what is supposed to be the postmenopausal Wasteland of Female Invisibility, I am having the best sex and orgasms of my life, am giddy like a teenager in her first love. And yet.

What's wrong?

It may be too late for me to escape the patriarchy, even though I left my traditional marriage. For women of my generation, perhaps fear still follows us everywhere. It is in the other mothers in our book clubs who secretly voted with their husbands for Trump, against their own beliefs. It is in generations of considering ourselves "worthless" without a man, of making these men territory over which to war, to win exclusive rights. It is about being shouted at on the street to "smile" so many times, for so many years, that maybe the body ultimately manifests all the Fuck Yous our lips could not, for fear that we could be attacked. It is #metoo feeling less like a triumph and more like an open wound constantly rubbed raw. It is all the tension in our stomachs as we walk down any dark or deserted street, and the self-deception it takes to lie spooned with a man who has terrified you and your children, telling yourself that he protects you. It is about every doctor who ever told you that it is all in your head, or prescribed you half the medication he would have prescribed a male patient, or asked you if your orgasms were "really that important?" It is about every male professor who told the class he was going to spank you for being late, about every man who put his knee between your legs to keep them open even when you were saying no. It is every single last way that women in every country on earth try to "protect" men from our difficult emotions, in order to keep them calm and content and therefore to protect ourselves.

Maybe, for you, it is about the men who repeatedly raped and beat you, who threatened to kill you, about the father who came into your room and told you to keep it a secret, about the way the color of your skin or your gender identity has exposed you to violence. I don't have stories that you may carry. Even in the worst of my days, the color of my skin, having been raised by a tender father, having the torrentially powerful love of my mother, rendered me lucky. But I know what it is to change the lock on my door because it seemed a man with whom I shared three children was unsatisfied by anything less than my total ruin, and everyone who has ever been female in any form understands that the logical response to male outrage, historically, has been fear.

44.

Why could I love one man unconditionally, and not the other? From this vantage point, half a century old, I am suspicious of my own "happy ending." I am suspicious of the legions of memoirs by women that end in these ways: with an affirmation of heterosexual monogamy, a soul mate, a shared bed as a place of salvation, a nuclear family launched or reformed. I vowed never to write such a story, believing this sort of ending poisoned some of my otherwise favorite radical narratives. I also think of my partner's obsession with music that does not resolve, and I know that I do not end here, on these pages, and that there is no such thing as a "happy ending" or an ending at all. The text simply stops, as Kathy stopped at forty-three while so much unfolded without her; as my mother "stopped" in so many ways by her own choice before she was even the age I am now. In their honor, I can only vow to continue unfolding for as long as I breathe.

There was a crime. But there were also the lovers.

How was my ex-husband, with his flaws and beauties, any less worthy of my loyalty, my empathy, during the years he was spiraling out of control during his mother's illness, than my current partner was worthy of those things during his depression, in which he at times seemed to be stringing two sick women along, yo-yoing between us out of the fear of anyone being angry at him? I could say that my compassion and unconditional love for my partner are related to the fact that he never displayed rage directed at me, and surely that plays a part in it, yes. I could say that my partner's behavior during his depression was at least somewhat dictated by diagnosed brain chemistry, by the tidal force of his rapid-rapid cycling bipolar disorder, but maybe that would be a cop-out. My ex-husband appeared no more "well" to me in those years he was singularly obsessed with imminent global apocalypse than my partner was when he could barely get out of bed and kept saying he wished he had already died—nor do I have many assumptions anymore about my own emotional stability during those years.

My ex-husband has claimed—to me, to our children—that he suffered PTSD due to the way I lied to him for more than three years of our marriage, leaving him uncertain whether anything in his own life had been real. I used to scoff at this claim as melodramatic and excessive—almost half of American marriages end in divorce; a full third involve the infidelity of one partner. "You weren't in a POW camp in Vietnam!" I shouted once when he made this accusation. Now I understand that the commonness of cheating and divorce does not mitigate the grief any more than we take the death of a loved one casually because, after all, "everyone dies."

The damage I did to my former spouse and our family was no lesser than any threat his rages posed. "Betrayal trauma," which is often associated with the discovery of a partner's infidelities, may not include a danger of physical violence, but it is now widely accepted in the field of psychology as producing the same symptoms as classic post-traumatic stress disorder, and many therapists include this syndrome under the same treatment umbrella. While often men are assumed to have power and women are assumed to have virtue, these assumptions are deeply complicated and tangled in our most intimate bonds. Sometimes I wish I had been able to love my ex-husband unconditionally, because I believe it is a thing we all deserve and need, but I was not able to love him that way. There is no line in the sand that makes him "better" or "worse" than the man I have been able to love through the kinds of losses, illnesses, grief, and indecisions that would have broken up many relationships and would, by all reason, have authorized either of us to run.

During the second half of my fiftieth year, though it would have seemed inconceivable at one time, my partner and I lived in a home with my daughters and son and our three cats. We cooked meals together and ran errands to Walgreens; my daughters made fun of how we never shut up in the kitchen and made lists of our most frequent topics of conversation (Aerosmith's "good" and "shit" periods weirdly making the list), and they bought shampoo for my partner after realizing he has spent fifty-two years washing his hair with soap. In the final weeks of my daughters' time at home, we drove to New Orleans and spent a night at the French Quarter hotel where Johnny Thunders died; we went to a cavernous warehouse gallery where I wrote my ex-husband's name on a scrap of paper at an interactive exhibit about forgiveness and threw it into artificial flames, thinking to honor his reverence for ritual with this action, though I felt no real solace.

Time heals, but healing isn't tidy. The scars on my breasts, my left thigh, are deep-rooted, gnarled in places, and will never fade completely. The August of my fiftieth year, my partner and I drove my daughters to start college in California. At one time, my daughters were shuddering preteen bodies under a blanket in July, crying with devastation at what they had discovered about us on my carelessly unprotected iPhone. Those scars, like the ones my ex-husband and I inflicted on each other and the ones on my body, go deep, even if my daughters may not recognize it now. Only time will tell if I have done enough to repair their trust in me. We are all judged by the courts of distance and hindsight.

My daughters are in California now, and my partner in Chicago. It took a long time—longer than may have been comfortable—for the two of us to understand whether we were capable of making something shimmering and joyful together out of the wreckage we had wrought, or whether even the intensity of our love and desire was going to amount to the perpetual rescraping of a wound. There is not language for how grateful I am, here in the midst of a middle age I may not live to see turn into old age, here in my mangled, no-dimmer-switch body, or for how I treasure every moment of combining our intersecting lives into something that is good for us both, that is good for my kids, that does no more harm. There is not a language for the miraculousness of how much I believe, even after all we have lost and proof of the transience of Everything, that we are each other's final acts—just as there is not a language for how I will love him even if someday we fail.

He reminds me of my father. His sense of humor, his tenderness, but also the time bomb that lives inside his brain. Over the eight years we have been close, his bipolar episodes have grown more frequent, as is often the course of the disease, and his memory, impacted both by increasing episodes and by seven or eight concussions during his early, hard-living years, has started showing signs of a hit. We live inside this tenuous and overwhelming joy, knowing that sooner or later, one of our bodies will be the first to fail, and that given both of our histories, it likely won't be in thirty or forty years, but sooner, *sooner, sooner.* Maybe this fuels the way he makes me laugh until my face hurts, and the fact that my body, even on hormone-suppressing aromatase inhibitors, still surges like a teenager's, wet and full of unbridled electrical storms, at his touch.

I don't want to apologize for loving a man this way.

Sometimes, knowing what the world is, I feel I should apologize for loving a man this way.

Ladies and Gentlemen of the Jury of My Mind, everyone I have wronged: add him to this list of so many things I am both sorry and not sorry about. Add him to the list of things I wish I had done differently, but god help me would do all over again.

45.

This was never about whether I had a "right" to leave my marriage. Of course I had a right. The fact that my husband never cheated on me or that he was a good provider or that he didn't abuse drugs or alcohol or didn't beat me has nothing to do with whether or not

I was obligated to stay. No one is obligated to stay. Despite recent setbacks in American culture, we live in a society in which women are no longer chattel, in which we are permitted to choose our relationships, in which divorce is painful, but common and legal. My residual guilt isn't about knowing that I was never going to love my husband the way I needed to again—the way I believe people should love each other if they are going to use up all the days of their fleeting lives on each other. I don't feel guilty anymore for the fact that I could already glimpse the picture on the other side of our intense parenting years—our children busy with their own lives, at college and out-of-state jobs, our retirement years alone together—and knew I could not stay inside that frame. My leaving was never about retribution for any fault of my husband's or any mistake he made, but rather that I believe with the core of my being that everyone has the right to choose what ships to go down with versus when to get into a lifeboat and save themselves. There is no one who doesn't have the right to leave a consensual relationship between adults: no marital atrocities required.

What I continue to regret is living, quite literally, inside the toxicity of a lie that had the power to knock down the walls of our home, even though it did not entirely knock down my body. How do we become so blind to ourselves that we come to believe we have the right to know more about the truth of someone else's life than they do, and *then* believe they actually owe us a friendship?

By "how do we," I mean of course "how did I?"

"[P]eople with self-respect have the courage of their mistakes," wrote Didion, whose impeccable coolness made people sometimes forget to discriminate against her for being a woman, even though she lost all the things a woman can lose. "If they choose to commit adultery, they do not then go running, in an access of bad conscience, to receive absolution from the wronged parties."

Okay, Joan. I finally believe you.

46.

In contrast to my loneliness when my father died, my partner and I found my mother's body together. In the March of my fiftieth year, when I was three years cancer-free, my mother's weekend caregiver rang our doorbell repeatedly past midnight instead of using the telephone or coming right up the stairs the way her regular caregiver would have done. As a result, we ignored the ringing for a time, thinking it some drunken teens pranking the house and then, finally—a vestige of old fear, the ringing so insistent—fearing it could be some man intent on doing harm. My partner took with him a paltry makeshift weapon and made his way down the stairs, but in the foyer it was only my mother's weekend substitute, whom we both suspected was not actually authorized to work in the United States despite her employment with an accredited agency that had been approved by my mother's long-term medical insurance. "I think," she told us, "something is wrong with Miss Alice." But by then I had entered my mother's apartment in my long white nightgown, and I had seen.

My mother was in her recliner, the remote control for the television still in her hand, a blanket still on her lap, like she might be sleeping. But there, the resemblance to somnolence ended. Though her apartment is small and she was seated in an area that would have been visible from anywhere except the recesses of my father's old bedroom, where her caregiver must have been sleeping or Skyping, my mother's body was already hours into decomposition. Bile leaked from her nose and mouth; her stomach was distended six or seven times its normal size. Later, the funeral director would tell us that he suspected she had been dead for a minimum of six hours but perhaps up to twelve. I had just seen her the day prior, delivering antibiotics for a recurring bladder infection. Her breathing, always labored from her COPD, had seemed more strained than usual and I asked if she wanted to go to the hospital, but my mother had been in and out of hospitals several times per year for thirteen years and she waved me away and said, "I'm not going to any more hospitals." I could hardly disagree.

These are the facts of my mother's death: that she died from a massive stroke, cardiac arrest, or a pulmonary embolism, all three of which she had been at constant risk of suffering for so many years now that her long-standing physician essentially just picked one at random for the death certificate. My mother had been through seventeen surgeries. She often ran into walls with her walker when having a seizure—later, wheelchair bound, she wet herself frequently because she had lost the strength to make the transfer to the toilet or the will to care about bodily dignity. She had endured heart attacks, strokes, a valve replacement, replacements of both hips and knees, and a pacemaker, and from 2015 to 2019 made so many ICU trips that resulted in a Bi-Pap machine strapped to her face that a hospice had all but started stalking me on the phone to sign her up. That she kept rallying, kept making it back home, kept breathing even without her nasal cannula. That, like my father, it seemed that she had ninety-nine lives and nothing could kill her. That my parents, who in many ways led lives of fabled "quiet desperation," were also the toughest, most resilient people I have ever known.

These are the facts of my mother's life: that she was molested by her biological father, teased relentlessly by her stepfather, and spent fifty-four years married to a man who would not fuck her or even make out a little bit or sleep in the same bed, due to his own demons. That after my father's death, a man from her past resurfaced who had loved her since high school, who had been a widower for many years, and that although he told her he had "always imagined they would end up married," he in fact developed dementia and died rapidly before they could so much as hold hands. That after her would-be-second-husband died and she told her best girlfriend that she wanted a boyfriend, her friend asked her what she had to offer and my mother said, "I'm nice," and her friend said, "Most women are nice." That she used to entertain her boss with stories of her dreams about our old dog running in circles, or about burning the pork chops—that she said, "I'm so repressed even my dreams aren't exciting." That the year my father died, my mother and I both began new lives of a sort, but hers too late, too far into her own decline, while I was busy buying new, non-underwire sexy bras and giving my father's sweaters and cufflinks to my partner. That I left her behind so many times—and that doing so was also her greatest hope for me.

That the last time I ever saw my mother and my ex-husband together, he was crouched over her chair promising she was his mother too and that he would always love her. That she called him her son until her death, even as she loved my partner with a childlike and joyful abandon, at times acting around him like a schoolgirl with a crush and at other times rejoicing to have an audience to whom to sing my praises, most of which were entirely less deserved than she imagined, but that her love for and belief in me were the lights of her life, and that I have learned the humility not to try to deny her them. That she was my first great love, and the person who taught me both how to love and how *not* to love, and that I can only hope with everything I am that the ways I mixed these things up will in the end fall short of the ways I got them right. That she was my most unbridled fan, my cheerleader, my first confidante, my caregiving burden, my one constant in the years in which I bled family members and body parts with the speed of light. That she and I had been talking casually about going to the new French restaurant in our neighborhood in her wheelchair and debating whether she could chew the food with her new set of false teeth, and had decided to go when the weather was warmer. That we never got the chance, and that I must content myself now with—unlike my father's regrets about *his* father—all the chances we did seize for half a century.

That at the memorial service celebrating her eighty-six years of life, I played a vinyl record she'd made before ever meeting my father, her girlish, spookily beautiful voice singing about wanting someone to love.

That love was the absolute center of her life. That she was the most loyal person I have ever known.

That when I saw her body, bloated and rotting in the same recliner by the window in which my father had died, I became animal. That I shouted *Mommy!* until my throat was raw, hurling myself on her gas-filled corpse so that her fluids leaked onto me with squeaking noises as I tried to crawl up her skin. That when the word "*Mommy*" could not form in my throat anymore I simply screamed, loudly and repeatedly, while my partner stood gingerly touching my back, crying quietly, and my mother's caregiver hid in my father's old bedroom until we finally had the presence of mind to send her home. That whatever grief I had never fully processed about my father, in the midst of my hellish divorce, flew into the room like a living force and knocked me to my mother's feet, where I held her swollen legs, keening with none of the self-conscious tentativeness of my tears over my father's body. That I sobbed, *They're both gone, they're both gone*, as though her death had made his real at last. That when the paramedics, the police, and finally the undertaker came, I did not know they were in the room until they repeatedly asked me questions while I sat howling in my sheer nightgown with nothing beneath it, a newly born orphan devoid of any sense of self or shame.

Between 2015 and 2019 I lost: a marriage, many useless luxuries and privileges, two breasts, my hair, my menstrual cycle, a hip, both parents, my sense of myself as inherently "deserving" of any of these things.

I gained a new life. A more complicated life, filled with more laughter, more joy, more fire, more accountability for my own future and survival, more confidence in my ability to endure.

I did not and will not regain my mother. I am the only mother now.

This time, there was no back-and-forth about whom my ex could or couldn't bring to the memorial. He told Enzo that he never read the email I sent telling him the woman he called his mother for twenty-five years was dead and inviting him to her service. He never texted or called any of our children to offer condolences. This time, my partner was the one to rush upstairs when Enzo heard my screaming and tried to come down, and the one who held Enzo and cried with him over their shared loss—who waited at home with our son while I picked my daughters up from the airport when they came home from California to see my mother off from our shared world. I specify this not because it is either an "improvement" or the way I wanted things to be, but merely because it is a fact. I say it because the time has come to relinquish at last, without apology, the grief over my ex-husband that has consumed and preoccupied me for four years, to make space for what will be the lifelong work of grieving my mother.

I am the oldest generation from here on out, the imperfect archetype whose successes and mistakes my children will strive to emulate or avoid. I am the one who will ultimately recede next, in order to make room for the splendor of them.

47.

The way things end changes how we interpret them. In E. L. Doctorow's *Book of Daniel*, he posits three possible endings to his fictional retelling of the Rosenberg execution, and it is here, near the close, that I am compelled to do the same, even though we are only supposed to be permitted one outcome, a unipolar Truth from which to derive meaning. But of course, as the French feminists pointed out long ago, singularity is never that simple, is even dangerous. My ex-husband, an avid reader of science journals, often spoke about the "dark matter" between things—the unexplained spaces in which he said, though he was an atheist, maybe God resides. Long preoccupied with the concept of parallel universes, quantum mechanics increasingly asserts that the "Many Worlds" theory is more plausible than previously believed.

If that is true, then in at least one reality my ex-husband is not my ex-husband at all. In any number of parallel universes that I will never be able to access, either Kathy died on a day I was in Chicago rather than California, or my lover reconsidered his attendance at a conference in my home city—as he in fact came very close to doing—and never kissed me in the arrivals lane of O'Hare. In still other worlds, I never told my husband about my lover, and despite my guilt carried this secret to the grave, the affair eventually collapsing under the weight of its long-distance constraints as my lover fell into a long depression that made it harder for him to dash around the country, or my breast cancer and hip disability brought me closer to the hearth, or his ex-wife's cancer diagnosis caused him to leave me and accept his role as her permanent caregiver. Somewhere out there, too, I have taken my husband back after his earnest play for a reunion following the death of my father, and although in that reality I suspect I would only betray him again in time, in still another—the one I've had the hardest time shaking—it is he who consents to take me back despite my repeated betrayals when I call from California fresh with P53 terror and malignancy, and promise to spend the rest of my life making sure he never regrets his choice to trust me again.

It is that final world that I visit sometimes, despite myself. In that Path Not Taken, I finally understand how much he loves me, and I am ready, after so many years of eroded empathy and angry disconnection and chilly distance, to accept him gratefully back into my heart. In that scenario, it is my lover who becomes the tram that grazed my hip many years ago, who—after waiting too long to come to Chicago, after making cracks about suicide in the face of my cancer—never has the chance to redeem himself, while my husband and I have now been married more than half our lives, and all of our crimes against one another seem paler each year against the backdrop of time.

In that Other World, I would be telling you another story altogether: a saga of two damaged people who married too young but found their way back to each other after inflicting much pain; who got individual and couples and family therapy and somehow made it through again to good times. In that book, my ex-husband is the hero who never lost faith in me, and I would be closing with a final scene of our family on that trip to Machu Picchu we used to talk about, Lorenzo squealing at the llamas, my postchemotherapy hair growing back in the tight curls my father once loved when I was five. In that Other Narrative, Mags and Kaya still see their father daily rather than once or twice a year, and there is all the time in the world for them to heal their divisions and find a place of peace.

In that Other World, I often remember my lover, of course— *My Long Lost Smutty Foster Wallace*—and the shimmering magic of what we shared sometimes flatlines me, makes me cry in secret, a Beautiful Thing Gone Wrong that I maybe talk about with Alicia over lunch when I've had some wine, before going home to my husband and this home we remodeled so long ago, where I hope, with everything I have, to live long enough to grow old by his side.

The veil that separates That Life from This Life is thin but impenetrable. And though it has been years now since I wished, even briefly, that I could step through the barrier and find myself there for real, still I ask you to understand, with me, that toxic male rage and lying, cheating women, and even the urgent wild love between two people born on the same day as though fated to belong to each other, are all subject to the particular filter of history's lens, and that with one sentence, one decision, this could be another story altogether: a reaffirmation of family, of till death do we part, of second and third and twentieth chances being worth it in the end.

I ask you to remember that, when you cheer for my new life or purse your lips at the Scarlet A I've worn too proudly for your tastes—I ask you to know this when you form your judgments of my ex-husband, whatever they may be.

This is who we are, yes.

And: there are so many paths we could have traveled—so many other people we could have been. Staying would not have rendered me weak—an inconsequential June Cleaver—just as cheating didn't make me a coldhearted monster. The clean reduction of a woman to any prime number is always a lie, even if some lies are prettier than others.

In Our World, though, the only one you or I can touch: I leave you seeing them—the family that was ours—laughing together again, marveling at the jagged mountaintops, breathing in the thin air carefully, still feeling things out—there on that trip to Machu Picchu that never was, somewhere on the Other Side.

48.

I am more than **A**. I am also more than a mother, than a daughter, than a cancer survivor, than any man's. To be a woman is to live in contradictions. We may be the new hysterics, but we are also the re-sistance, the phoenixes of history. We are sometimes treasonous and sometimes sisters. We are selfish and nurturing. We are in pain that sometimes shows on our X-rays, and sometimes would only show up if there were such a thing as a soul that could be photographed.

I am somebody. I am real. I am and am not the twenty-something young woman who hid my pain behind a smile and cuts on my arms; I both defy and exceed what my partner thought he was getting when he first fantasized about living in Chicago someday. I have made so many errors, held so many secrets, and if some of that lives inside the cells or genes or joint sockets of my body—if some of that lives in this text of my body—well, what of it?

49.

Today, three women in the United States have died at the hands of their intimate partners or ex-partners. I was not one of them. Still, I carry them inside me, as all women do: an archetypal knowledge that breeds both fear and compassion—a knowledge that both limits and expands us. Maybe someday, these facts will change and this cellular knowledge will evolve into something else, something like freedom. I hope my daughters and your daughters will be alive to see it.

50.

In the final days of my divorce proceedings, when the world seemed terrifying and sad and my hair was a fledgling duck-stubble grown back instantly gray, my ex-husband introduced an eleventh-hour gag order into our Marital Settlement Agreement. In it, I was to agree to never write about him, our children, our marriage, or our divorce, past, present, or future. I refused to sign. Although for more than a year all I had done was try to avoid a courtroom custody battle in which my character would be on trial, as women's characters have been on trial since litigation began, and although his lawyer made noise that without this nondisclosure clause the mediated deal would fall apart, I finally, *finally*, just said no.

In the face of my refusal, our legal teams verified that someone cannot be forced to sign a nondisclosure and have her freedom of speech curtailed: such an agreement must be entered into freely, in exchange for money or a job or something that is desired more than the right to free speech. I desired nothing more than my right to language. And so, in the end, our divorce went through without that caveat.

Reading this now, perhaps you empathize with my ex-husband's desire that I should be silenced. As do I.

But once there was a woman who stood over a public trash can in the dark cover of night, shredding her journal. Once there was a woman who was so afraid of who she was and what she wanted that she lived a double life for years, lying to everyone close to her and especially herself, perhaps making herself sick.

I am not that woman anymore.

For the girl I used to be, who quite literally wrote herself out of a dead-end violent neighborhood, and for every other girl on earth who refuses to relinquish her reality to the Father's Tongue, I write.

It is not my intention to hurt anyone with this story, even though I realize there are people who will be angry at me for telling it. I am fully aware of the subjective, one-sided nature of my experience—of the fact that dialogue is based on recollection; of the fact that I have no moral right to a monopoly on any narrative. But so help me, this story is mine, even if parts of it intersect with others' stories. This story is my history, my contradicting truth, my scratched-up lens, my sunlight rather than the dark end of the street. And no man alive can take it away from me.

The dirt is coming for us all as we free-fall. This much I know: that eventually, we all have to start screaming well before we hit the ground, so the women below us will understand when to scatter, when to take cover, when it is safe to come back outside and try again to change the world. So that future generations will know, from the echo of our voices, never to stop watching the sky.

Acknowledgments

I have never had so many people I've wanted to thank in the making of a book, because in this case before there could be any book at all there were so many of you who were my support team, my shelter, my tough love, the wind at my back, and my reminder that growth, laughter, gratitude, and beauty still existed throughout and beyond the events both depicted in this text and those left out.

Thank you as always to my Usual Suspects, who embraced my new life with flawless grace and stood by me in my every imperfection with chicken soup, songs and guitars, getaway homes, babysitting, medicinal scotch, ER and chemo ward trips, basement flood repairs, and especially with an extended family of love and support for my children. Special life-saving thanks to Alicia and Jason Schoenbeck, the truest and most stalwart makeshift family anyone has ever had, and to my brother in every way that counts, Tom Hernandez, and his amazing husband, Brad Suster, who have never failed to show up with boundless generosity whenever my kids and I needed them most.

To the best writing group on the planet—Rachel DeWoskin, Rebecca Makkai, Thea Goodman, Emily Gray Tedrowe, Dika Lam, and last but the antithesis of least my longtime lit comrade and dear friend Zoe Zolbrod. From outraged political text streams to Indochine cocktails to the best book recommendations, I love you all madly and count on your ferocious brilliance to ground me. "Hi, Moms!"

To all the writers who have given me a home outside the bounds of geography, especially Club 3012 (spouse-inclusive edition), Jennifer Banash, Martha Bayne, Stacy Bierlein, Laura Bogart, Eiren Caffall, Sarah Einstein, Angela Giles, Jillian Lauren, Billy Lombardo, Marina Lewis, Cris Mazza, Amy Monticello, Patrick O'Neil, Jen Pastiloff, Lisa Stolley, and so—my god—so many others who form this vibrant and nourishing community. Special thanks to the late Lois Hauselman who took a chance on me (over what I believe were some considerable reservations) when she handed over the editorial reins of *Other Voices* magazine to my twentysomething hands and set in motion far more than just professional opportunities but virtually every important friendship I've formed for the past 2+ decades.

To the other amazing mothers brought into my life by my children, with particularly acute gratitude to Sandy Hartman, Ellen Ryan, and Maria Loew for All The Things. Namaste and love to Deb Liu, for sharing small miracles that might have been with me and for offering healing in more ways than one.

To my business partner and one of the quickest and most shimmering minds I have ever encountered, Emily Rapp Black, who gets when to sit with me in the darkness versus when to get on a bullhorn and order me out, feeling in front of me for the sharp corners ahead. You *know*.

To the doctors, surgeons, lawyers, and therapists who sometimes took me apart, sometimes put me back together, and always did their very best, despite the limitations of various systems, to advocate for me and see me as a whole person rather than a statistic. Endless gratitude to the cancer survivors who offered wisdom, books, referrals, mushroom tinctures, testimonies, and the promise that I would learn life-changing things and connect with irreplaceable people as part of joining this club to which no one seeks membership. How impossible your words seemed at the time, and how right you turned out to be.

It was ironically when my chips were down that I became most acutely aware of my immense privilege in this world. And so to all the girls and women out there who did not and do not have access to the opportunities, exit signs, support systems, or financial and insurance resources to which I've had access, particularly those girls I've loved who add up to the composite character of "Angie," the memory of Judy Barbosa, and all my clients in rural New England circa 1991–1994. You made this book alongside me every step of the way.

As did Kathy. Always. Girl . . . always.

I want to thank the Ragdale Foundation for granting me two residencies in a single year, and in whose summer and winter haven I was able to get more done in a cumulative four weeks than I had in the previous four years. What you offer writers is priceless.

To everyone at *The Nervous Breakdown* (special shout-out to founder Brad Listi and the OGs), *The Rumpus,* and every other magazine editor who published earlier excerpts from this book and who helped me understand nonfiction writing as far more than individual catharsis but outreach, activism, a dialogue across generations, and a call to arms for changes both external and within.

To my irreplaceable agent, Alice Tasman, the whole team at Jean V. Naggar, and to the best editor on planet earth, Dan Smetanka . . . without you, all the words would be other words, and that would make me an Other Me. Beyond thanks, too, to the whole Counterpoint family—Andy Hunter, Megan Fishmann, Lena Moses-Schmitt, Rachel Fershleiser, Wah-Ming Chang, Dustin Kurtz, Alyson Forbes, Dan López, and Dana Li—for believing in and championing me and my work and for all you do for so many writers and readers who have been nourished by your vision.

I was blessed with the kindest, coolest, most eccentric and unconditionally loving parents in the history of the world, to whom not just this book but every good thing in me is dedicated.

"Thank you" is not enough for my three children—the strongest, most creative, resilient, ethical, and ferociously true-to-themselves people I know. A thousand books could not express my gratitude at getting to be your mother. You teach me and bring me wild joy every single day, and I am in your corners for as long as I draw breath. May this world someday rise to be equal to you.

Any book that includes issues like infidelity and secret-keeping should perhaps have not only an Acknowledgments section but an Amends section as well. To those who would fall into the latter rather than the former category—or who in some cases fall into both—that is written privately and etched inside me.

Finally, thank you to Rob Roberge: for existing, for being my twin, the love of my life, my Person, my final act, my husband, my safe haven, and always my best friend. You wrote to me once, "I wouldn't change a thing unless it was Everything." Now, it is.